Modern Languages in the Primary School

Philip Hood and Kristina Tobutt

Los Angeles | London | New Delhi
Singapore | Washington DC

First published 2009

SAGE Publications Ltd
1 Oliver's Yard
55 City Road
London EC1Y 1SP

SAGE Publications Inc.
2455 Teller Road
Thousand Oaks, California 91320

SAGE Publications India Pvt Ltd
B 1/I 1 Mohan Cooperative Industrial Area
Mathura Road
New Delhi 110 044

SAGE Publications Asia-Pacific Pte Ltd
33 Pekin Street #02-01
Far East Square
Singapore 048763

Library of Congress Control Number 2008940029

British Library Cataloguing in Publication data

A catalogue record for this book is available from the British Library

ISBN 978-1-84860-128-4
ISBN 978-1-84860-129-1 (pbk)

Typeset by C&M Digitals (P) Ltd, Chennai, India
Printed in Great Britain by TJ International Ltd, Padstow, Cornwall
Printed on paper from sustainable resources

Mixed Sources
Product group from well-managed
forests and other controlled sources
www.fsc.org Cert no. SGS-COC-2482
© 1996 Forest Stewardship Council
FSC

Modern Languages in
the Primary School

Contents

Preface – Who is this book for?

This book is written for a range of audiences. We aim to offer a full introduction to the planning, teaching and assessment of modern language (ML) teaching in the primary sector. But in addition to that we also intend to open up the wider theme of how languages can play a full part in the whole curriculum. Other writers have included this in discussion but have concluded that it is very difficult to attain (Driscoll and Frost 1999, Martin 2000, Muijs et al. 2005).

The book is certainly written for teachers in training (following PGCE or B Ed routes) and not just for those who are specialising in ML. An understanding of how to teach a language effectively will increasingly be part of a competent primary teacher's repertoire between 2010 and 2020. For you the book will contain references to the *Standards for QTS* and will provide links, where relevant, to DCSF, QCA and Teachernet webpages which give broader information both about ML teaching and how it links into the wider Primary Strategy agenda.

We also hope that the book will be used by teacher-educators as a support to their sessions with ML specialists and as a way of showing that ML shares many attributes with other subjects and can contribute to children's broader language development. We have attempted to link theory to practice and provide some authentic examples of different approaches. In addition, the more theoretical Chapter Nine draws together material about Communicative Teaching, Task-based Learning and Content and Language Integrated Learning (CLIL) written with primary languages in mind.

We also intend the book for experienced teachers who have an ML teaching or coordination role and who want to enter into what we regard as a dialogue about approaches, materials and objectives. This will include experienced primary teachers who know how to teach primary age children but who are perhaps less confident with language teaching approaches. It will also include secondary teachers with an outreach role who realise that secondary methodology does not transfer particularly well to primary schools. An important aspect of the book is that we outline language teaching approaches centred firmly on the needs of primary age children. As part of this aim we intend that the book can be used for whole-staff INSET, with suggestions for activities and reflection tasks offered to busy continuing professional development (CPD) coordinators.

We intend this book to be user-friendly at all points. It offers a range of different resources to a range of different audiences.

If you have come to it seeking an introduction to the background to primary languages – 'why and why now?' from both a policy and a child-centred perspective – you should start with Chapter One.

If you have come to it seeking a practical but also a global, more philosophical overview of what language learning can offer your school, then you should look at Chapter Two.

If you wish to gain an overview of how language learning might look in the Early Years Foundation Stage, then you should look at Chapter Three.

Chapter Four looks specifically at how you might launch language learning in a school, and considers Year One and Year Three starting points. You will find that Chapters Five and Six follow logically from that, dealing with progression in different ways.

If you have come to the book specifically to consider the role of the KS2 framework and assessment then Chapters Seven and Eight deal with those issues.

If you are interested in the theory that underpins communicative, task- and content-based, cross-curricular approaches, for example CLIL, then you should turn to Chapter Nine.

Chapter Ten supplies a list of resources and useful internet sites.

How the book is organised

To serve our various aims and purposes we have included in the book a range of features to increase its interactivity and to set up the dialogue we referred to earlier.

- Each chapter begins with an introductory vignette, drawn from policy or practice, which acts as an initial thinking point.
- Each chapter has clear objectives, again as an advance organiser for the reader. Relevant Q Standards are given at this point.
- Each chapter finishes with a summary of main messages and some key and further readings centred on references to websites or documents.
- Each chapter has embedded in it reflection points which are intended to support conceptualisation of the language teaching and learning process.
- Many chapters contain suggestions for pedagogical tasks to try in the classroom together with associated reflection points.

1

What is the background to primary language learning?

Introductory vignette

The European Year of Languages 2001 highlighted the many ways of promoting language learning and linguistic diversity. Heads of the State and Government in Barcelona in March 2002 recognised the need for European Union and Member State action to improve language learning; *they called for further action to improve the mastery of basic skills, in particular by teaching at least two foreign languages to all from a very early age.* (Commission of the European Communities 2003, emphasis added)

Chapter objectives

- To offer a philosophical view of the need for early language learning.
- To detail and interpret the rationale for the implementation of compulsory primary language learning in 2010–11.
- To explore aspects of motivation and self-esteem in younger learners.
- To explain the intentions of the different elements in the book.

Relevant Q Standards: Q3, Q15

Initial reflection point

How far do you consider that the UK, and specifically England, has responded to this call? Remember that the UK did sign the Barcelona Agreement in 2002.

Response

It is interesting to compare the statement above with one made by the Department for Education and Skills (DfES), who in *14–19 Opportunity and Excellence* (2003) ended the status of modern languages as a core subject to age 16. This paper also set out the government's intention to introduce languages from age seven.

> 3.2 We announced our conclusions on modern foreign languages in our Language Strategy in December. We are committed to supporting language learning, because of its vital contribution to cultural understanding and economic competitiveness. *However, we do not believe that requiring schools to teach languages to every young person beyond the age of 14 is the best way to achieve this objective, particularly where students struggle with a subject in which they have little interest or aptitude.* Every young person at this stage will be entitled to study a language if they wish, and we shall require schools to provide this entitlement to every young person that wants it. Our National Languages Strategy set out our plans to deliver an entitlement to language learning for pupils from the age of seven by 2010. Individual schools may continue to require pupils to study languages as part of their school policy.' (DfES 2003, emphasis added)

We will raise some of the implications of the removal of compulsory language learning post-14 in the next few pages. Clearly the commitment to primary language learning was made in 2003 and is being fulfilled. But an overt national priority for language learning was not evident in the decisions being made at that point. The UK, but especially England, stands apart from all other EU countries in this respect as we show over the next few pages. We should say at this point that both Wales and Scotland have their own policies with regard to language learning and that some of what we discuss here does not apply to those parts of the UK.

Language teaching in England: some current issues

 Reflection point

Do you know the status of modern languages at the different points from Foundation Stage to KS5? Do you know how this compares with other EU countries? How much do you know about why and how this pattern has emerged? (See Table 1.1 for a response.)

Before we turn to the recent initiatives and policy documents which have brought about the forthcoming introduction of compulsory primary languages in 2011, we will offer a statement of our philosophy on early language learning which will also offer a further view as to the nature of this book.

We believe passionately that the introduction of modern languages into the primary curriculum is a vital step towards restoring some credibility to England (as the other countries in the UK have their own policies with regard to language learning) in a very important area. As a developed nation that is itself pluricultural and plurilingual, the UK has a responsibility to play a role in a modern world that seeks to work towards global collaboration. Respect for other people's cultures is impossible without respect for their languages. Global English is a reality but not a substitute for communication that also uses other mother tongues. The recent dramatic drop in the numbers of students studying modern languages at 14–16 and at advanced level has yet to impact on our commercial, industrial and cultural competence internationally. There was in the decision to take ML out of the core 14–16 curriculum an admission that something was not right in the teaching methods being used. But this was not addressed with teachers and students in the sector itself, but a decision taken at government level that disenfranchised dedicated teachers and devalued the subject. When the European Union as an institution, as we showed at the beginning of the chapter, is working towards competence for its young people in two other languages, we removed the immediate need for even one at a level that went beyond basic survival.

The introduction of languages into primary schools was an attempt to 'start again' but without a skilled workforce in sufficient numbers. Paradoxically, at the time when fresh numbers of new primary teachers will be needed to expand the capability of the schools to deliver ML over the next ten years, the supply of those teachers with a language qualification will be dropping.

This makes it more vital that we offer our primary teachers language enhancement and that we discuss openly and fully what we need to do to ensure that children's undoubted interest and enjoyment of language learning is opened up, developed and nourished. We cannot afford to hand children over to secondary colleagues with any generalised disillusion or disaffection. As we will see later in this chapter, younger learners have certain advantages over later beginners in aspects of learning potential, motivation and the role that the subject can have in promoting their own self-esteem. We owe it to the children to demonstrate the relevance and value of using another language and to offer them active, engaging and challenging ways of learning, just as we do in all their other subjects. Some teachers will understandably find the wider agenda for language learning outlined in the book daunting as they feel their language competence is not high enough. We feel it important to outline visions of how primary language teaching could and should develop over the next ten years, so all involved are aware of possible directions for their work.

Table 1.1   The status of languages as a curriculum subject in four EU countries

| Age/(KS) | Country/ML status | | | |
	England	France	Germany	Spain
3–5 (EYFS)	Optional	Optional	Optional	Optional
5–7 (KS1)	Optional	Compulsory from age 6	Optional	Compulsory from age 8, soon to be from age 6
7–11 (KS2)	Compulsory from 2011	Compulsory	Compulsory from age 8	Compulsory from age 8
11–14 (KS3)	Compulsory one language, two languages sometimes offered	Compulsory, including two languages where possible	Compulsory, including two languages for the more able	Compulsory
14–16 (KS4)	Optional. 2007 take-up of 46% (reduced from a high of 78% in 2001). See http://www.cilt.org.uk/research/statistics/education/gcse_trends_dfesdata2007.doc for a full analysis Government policy is that 50–90% of students should be taking a language in KS4. Schools are required to set and implement targets. See http://www.teachernet.gov.uk/_doc/12233/letter_JimKnight.pdf for more detail	Compulsory, including two languages where possible	Compulsory, including two languages where possible	Compulsory
16–19 (KS5)	Optional and rarely studied	Compulsory to 18 in any education/training	Compulsory to 18 in any education/training	Optional but compulsory for academic study

Table 1.2   Summary of the important stages in primary languages

Date/Development	Main points/Web reference
1999 NACELL (National Centre for Early Language Learning) founded	The main official website for primary language teaching in England www.nacell.org.uk/index.htm
1999–2001 Good Practice Projects coordinated by NACELL	18 separate projects – see www.nacell.org.uk/official/ellreport_phase1.pdf
2000 Nuffield Enquiry into Language Learning – *Languages: The Next Generation*	A major independent enquiry into language learning: *Languages: The Next Generation* http://languages.nuffieldfoundation.org/filelibrary/pdf/languages_finalreport.pdf
2002 *Languages for All, Languages for Life* published	The government's action plan for language teaching www.dfes.gov.uk/languagesstrategy/pdf/DfESLanguagesStrategy.pdf
2003 Pathfinder Projects	The government funded 19 LAs to develop KS2 languages provision. The evaluation report summary can be accessed from www.dcsf.gov.uk/languages/DSP_whatson.cfm
2004 *Piece by Piece* published	An initial document for heads and governors about introducing languages to primary schools www.nacell.org.uk/cdrom/questions.pdf
2005 The KS2 Framework introduced	www.standards.dfes.gov.uk/primary/publications/languages/framework/
2007 The Dearing Review into Language Learning	The recommendations into an enquiry into language learning and teaching headed by Lord Dearing www.teachernet.gov.uk/_doc/11124/LanguageReview.pdf
2007 Primary Languages Training Zone website launched	The official training website for primary languages in England www.primarylanguages.org.uk/
2007 White Paper	The government announces that primary languages will have compulsory status by 2011

Primary languages – re-birth and transition: a summary

Let us turn to a brief summary of the important stages which have occurred since the mid-1990s. To make the development clearer we have summarised the major documents and initiatives in Table 1.2. Below this we will explore each item in a little more detail.

Recognising a need for coherence

From the mid-1990s there was a gradual development in awareness that the very disparate range of approaches to primary languages provision, often through clubs rather than on the curriculum should be given more coherence. Scotland had invested a great deal of money and time at the beginning of the decade in ensuring both language provision and training for primary teachers at the upper end of the schools. The House of Lords (Parliament 1990) had debated language learning at primary level in England but the government of the day was less inclined to act at that point.

During the 1990s there were some very good developments in certain areas. For example, one local authority (LA) (Kent) invested a great deal in linking with France and developing materials for learning French. This was fuelled by teachers who saw that they had a resource almost on the doorstep. They were anxious to use pupils' natural curiosity about and in many cases familiarity with an area of France which opened out from Calais and Boulogne, and which was minutes rather than hours away on fast ferries or the newly-opened channel tunnel. Materials (eventually published as *Pilote* (Rumney 1990)) produced by this group were in a fresh format which acknowledged the needs of younger learners and which raised the whole agenda for primary languages very successfully.

In an article in the *Curriculum Journal* (Hood 1994) we argued that the Burstall Report (Burstall *et al.* 1974) had been very partially interpreted when the decision was taken in the mid-1970s to end the primary French initiative that had run from the mid-1960s. It was now important to look forward and to avoid the earlier mistakes. These had centred on a lack of information and action at the point of transition to secondary education and a lack of differentiation built into teaching at all levels.

A very positive step was taken when the Centre for Information on Language Teaching and Research (CILT) formed the semi-autonomous branch NACELL (The National Centre for Early Language Learning) in 1999 and a website was launched which became for a while the focal point for Early Language Learning (ELL). A project was set up which investigated existing best practice provision and 18 schemes were drawn together under the banner of Good Practice Project and summarised on the website. Some teaching sequences were filmed and what became a series of three videos (now a DVD, see Chapter Nine) were begun. The regional network of Comenius Centres which CILT had instigated in 1990 began to address learning at primary level. Key books written at this time (for example, Driscoll and Frost 1999, Sharp 2001 and Cameron 2001) set out the agenda for early language learning in general.

After the Nuffield Languages Enquiry report, *Languages: The Next Generation* (2000), was published attention became much more widely fixed on primary languages. This was a positive move but the initial need was to highlight the problems. The report took a serious critical stance at a number of points, for example:

> The work of the enquiry has highlighted the serious mismatch between what the UK needs in languages capability and what the education system is providing ... The present system is incoherent, fragmented and increasingly ineffective in meeting national needs. (2003: 62)

The report gained much respect and the strong views were not ignored. The government also acknowledged the shortfall in our national provision in their own review published two years later:

> For too long we have failed to value language skills or recognise the contribution they make to society, to the economy and to raising standards in schools. This has led to a cycle of national underperformance in languages, a shortage of teachers, low take up of languages beyond schooling and a workforce unable to meet the demands of a globalised economy. We need to challenge these attitudes and inspire people of all ages to learn languages throughout life. (DfES 2002: 10)

Moving towards a solution

The Nuffield Enquiry was exhaustive. It produced 15 major recommendations, which themselves contained several smaller objectives. In total there were 121 separate points made. Clearly here is not the place to explore this in detail, but it is important to note that these recommendations covered all stages of language learning and all aspects from the organisation of the curriculum to the recruitment of teachers and the need for coherent organisation at government level, including the appointment of a National Languages Director. At the same time the Nuffield Foundation also made research and development grants available to people looking to innovate in the primary languages area. This made the government's task easier as they worked to produce the 2002 strategy and later ordered the Dearing Review. The decision to end the compulsory status of languages in KS4 seems ever more strange as time passes, and within three years of the decision being implemented, quotas and targets were being announced, with a figure of 50 per cent KS4 languages take-up demanded from schools by education ministers in communications given to heads in 2006 and 2007.

The government, in tune with the Nuffield Foundation, also noted the need for a change of approach:

> Transforming language competence in this country means first of all transforming language learning in schools – we depend on embedding language learning in primary schools to make our strategy work and then ensuring that opportunity to learn languages has a key place in the transformed secondary school of the future. (DfES 2002: 7)

In 2005 a new framework for primary language teaching in KS2 was published. This departed from previous ML curriculum specifications such as Qualifications and Curriculum Authority (QCA) Schemes and General Certificate of Secondary Education (GCSE) syllabuses in that it remained resolutely content free and instead highlighted strands of progression. The earlier KS3 Framework had focused quite heavily on knowledge about language in the way it was structured and through its objectives in an attempt to raise the cognitive nature of language learning at that stage. This framework took the view that teachers needed to link their objectives to the NLS (National Literacy Strategy) but in combining listening and speaking into oracy, reading and writing into literacy, and by adding intercultural understanding to create three major strands, it set out a new pathway for visualising language learning. Chapter Seven in this book looks in detail at how objectives and content might be linked to the framework.

The Dearing Review was conducted in 2006 and reported in 2007 (DfES 2007). This affirmed the need for primary languages to become an entitlement in 2010 and went a stage further, calling for it to be compulsory. This suggestion was accepted by the government in a White Paper, with 2011 set for this step to be implemented. Although this will be a ten-year span from Nuffield to entitlement, it represents the culmination of a very definite series of steps which have weighed up the needs at each stage and so decisions seem to have been made for good reasons and would seem to be permanent signs of progress. The primary modern languages training zone website, which went live in March 2007, is further evidence of a large-scale commitment.

As we write this book, a review of secondary education, including a revised national curriculum for KS3 and a new focus on the 14–19 sector is current. A parallel review of the primary national curriculum is planned to build on the newly established Early Years Foundation Stage Framework and the academic Primary Review programme, centred on the University of Cambridge is nearing its completion. This represents a root and branch re-evaluation of all stages of compulsory schooling, at least in England and Wales. Somewhere in all of this the role of modern languages teaching is being re-assessed along with the whole curriculum. As far as primary education is concerned, this in itself is a major change because for the first time ML will be considered as a part of a whole set of subjects rather than as an optional add-on, ungoverned by general regulation but also unnoticed by those who set policy.

Why has this movement for earlier language learning begun so strongly now? Can we be sure of the potential gains in comparison with the 11-year-old starting point which has persisted for so long?

 Reflection point

Look at the NACELL and Primary Languages Training Zone websites. (By the time you read this they may have been combined.) Is what you find there helpful? Are there areas you need information on which are not represented? Try to keep a list of questions you need answers to from this point on.

Is it true that younger learners are at an advantage in language learning?

In fact few L2 researchers now question the proposition that those learners whose exposure to the L2 begins early in life (and whose exposure is substantial) for the most part eventually attain higher levels of proficiency than those whose exposure begins in adolescence or adulthood. (Singleton 2003: 3)

There is a small amount of disagreement between different researchers about the advantages and disadvantages of different starting ages. Different aspects of language proficiency can reach higher levels from both early and later starting points, although all researchers seem to agree that pronunciation and intonation certainly develop generally better the younger the start age. Many claim that written grammatical accuracy and knowledge about language is likely to be no better amongst the early beginners, with some claiming that adolescent beginners achieve higher proficiency. The notion of a critical age for language learning (proposed by Lenneberg 1967) was discussed fully in Birdsong (1999), but was not resolved. Depending on the research focus, findings can be contradictory. But we can on the other hand be clear that stronger motivation is associated with younger learners and this seems to persist into adolescence and adulthood if learning continues consistently. In an environment such as a primary school where the general motivation for learning is often quite strong (and where, we should emphasise, there is high quality teaching), then the opportunities for faster progress are clearly greater. Much of this book will address the need to show children that they can progress in language learning, and that their competence in a variety of skills, both receptive and productive, will grow with each year. Much of it will address the need to engage them as learners with stimulating, challenging and enjoyable activities. Within this high-motivation environment teachers have an opportunity specifically in language learning (Hood 2006) to raise children's self-esteem and underpin their learning across the curriculum.

Why should we be concerned about self-esteem? School-life inevitably establishes a hierarchy of perceptions amongst children about who is and who is able to be successful, and, worryingly, who is neither. Dweck's (2000) notion of entity and incremental theories of intelligence which divide learners into those who believe they can alter and develop their ability to learn something and those who think they cannot, shows that for some pupils acceptance of a lack of progression in a subject is a potential danger. Anxiety is a potential problem in language learning (Horwitz 2001) and many of us may experience, even if only temporarily, that tension and accompanying feeling that we are 'tongue-tied' when in a situation where we have to use the target language. We know that we can say it, but it just seems not to want to come out. This was partly explained by Krashen's (1988) work on the 'affective filter' (a kind of barrier device) that related performance in foreign language production to levels of anxiety. Essentially writing about more permanent characteristics of learners (which is in harmony with Dweck's thinking), he maintained that low self-esteem and anxiety can combine to raise the affective filter and create a mental block. When the filter is 'up' it impedes language acquisition. Experience of success will develop self-esteem and it is likely that motivation will be higher as a result. But anxiety will lower the levels of both. Therefore we must avoid harming the good levels of motivation that we should find amongst our primary-age learners by avoiding creating those anxious circumstances when they experience the tongue-tied failure to communicate.

The now common practice of regular and carefully constructed target setting in primary schools has started in many cases to move pupils' own perceptions of themselves as learners. Still some will hold the view that they cannot improve their performance but very many schools have seen an increase in their percentages reaching Level Four and going further to gain Level Five in the core subjects at 11 years (KS2 SATS) over the last five years. Much of this is due to a culture where individual targets are set and groups of children receive special provision to boost their attainment. While some might argue that this is test- and performance-driven and not about 'caring for children', it seems logical that the more we can show children that they can improve, the more their own self-doubt can be modified.

When children first encounter a foreign language they will not have such fixed notions in place for this new subject. The oral base for learning often encourages children who lack confidence in reading and writing to participate much more fully and to enter into a cycle of confidence growth through success rather than confidence diminution through failure. So, for example in a Y3 context when languages start to be learned there is a levelling of established ability order perceptions. In the project reported in Hood (2006) this was stated most powerfully in a Y6 focus group who had developed strongly established 'pecking orders' particularly in the core subjects as they approached the end of primary education:

> Y6 Pupil 1 – I feel if you get a question wrong in French nobody laughs at you because they all know the same as you because we've all had the same amount of lessons but in maths and things you've got people who are good at it and people who are bad at it and they might laugh at you but in French everyone kind of knows the same thing. (2006: 7–8)

If we look briefly at more general issues of self-esteem in schools and classrooms we will find that language learning has the *potential* to augment levels of positivity amongst children and we hope that the rest of the book will give some examples of this in action. Both de Andres (1999) and Arnold (2007) mention a set of components of self-esteem listed by Reasoner (1982). These are: learners' security, identity, belonging, purpose and competence. Clearly we can use collaborative and active experiences to create a sense of belonging and purpose and, through planning carefully for enjoyable and meaningful outcomes by the whole group, we can emphasise competence rather than failure. By involving the learners in talking and eventually writing about themselves in another language we are giving them space to consider and express their identities in a positive framework. The involvement of children in a set of enjoyable activities and the availability of choice, for example in selecting songs and stories or roles, combine to create a secure feeling around language learning. Taking the positive sides of the 'difference' of French, German or Spanish lessons but still not sidelining them as not part of the normal curriculum gives modern languages the best of both worlds in some respects.

Similarly when writing about the more specific area of emotional literacy, Weare (2004: 90–1) gives examples of such potential contributions, noting several aspects commonly associated with language learning in her section on all subjects (for example, 'increasing emotional intensity through experiencing success, a sense of flow, laughter … celebrating learning' and 'emotional control, e.g. through waiting your turn … self-monitoring…').

Pollard and Triggs (2000) present a very full survey (PACE Project 1989–97) of pupil views gathered through longitudinal research. Extensive quotations from pupils show that issues of trust and ownership of practice, of independence and collaboration, of how they work and with whom are extremely important for their enjoyment of school and their avoidance of anxiety in some cases. They wish to be listened to and in language learning especially we should remember that the fine line between encouragement to participate and pressure, between challenge and barrier-erection is one to keep in focus. The particular mix of activity and experience held within good language teaching can build self-esteem very rapidly and very well, but can bring affective nightmares to some children if the balance is not right. We will reflect in a section on competition in Chapter Two that less secure children should not be individually exposed in lessons, and that collaboration is often the best mode of organisation for activities. Finding out what children enjoy and offering them it in a structured manner which combines fun with learning certainly seems to work. One eight-year-old boy summed up language learning as 'tingly and exciting' and that is clearly an effect we should all strive for.

Chapter summary

This chapter has attempted to set out the background to the growth of interest in primary languages and to the government's current position on the teaching of languages throughout young people's school experience. It has also looked at the role language learning and teaching (when planned and delivered successfully) can play in developing children's confidence and self-esteem.

Key and Further Reading

The most relevant reading which addresses the current position of primary languages is the DfES (2007) *Languages Review* 00212-2007DOM-EN. London: DfES. Accessible from www.teachernet.gov.uk/_doc/11124/LanguageReview.pdf.

To gain an overview of current practice through video material and associated text material you are advised to look at the Training Zone, which at the time of writing is at www.primarylanguages.org.uk/. The intention is to marry this with NACELL in the near future but the address given here is the likely overarching URL.

If you are teaching children in EYFS or KS1 we recommend that before you start to read about ML teaching and learning, you look at the document David, T. (2003) 'What Do We Know about Teaching Young Children' London: DfES. Accessible at: www.standards. dfes.gov.uk/eyfs/resources/downloads/eyyrsp1.pdf.

If you are interested in reading a recent summary about the theories around the critical period hypothesis then you should look at an article by David Singleton (2005) 'The Critical Period Hypothesis: A Coat of Many Colours'. *International Review of Applied Linguistics in Language Teaching.* 43(4): 269–85.

2

What does language learning offer a primary school?

Introductory vignette

I think for some children it's deeply motivating – they enjoy it because it's different. Whether it's because that's to do with the kind of lessons they are, because they're very oral and there's music and there's lots of games and so they see it as fun ... it's nice that the whole school does it and the whole school is doing it together. We played some French music in assembly recently and they all noticed that it was French and enjoyed that. (Headteacher, 2005 in Hood 2006: 6)

Comment

The headteacher quoted above introduced language learning into her school because when she interviewed for teachers to cover the new PPA arrangements in 2005, she found that a language teacher was one of the two best teachers she saw. She was primarily interested in appointing people who could add value to the school. Because this was her approach, she considered languages to be an integral part of the curriculum from that point on. She had a real sense that language learning could impact on the whole curriculum and the school experience of the children, and because the subject was given equal status with the rest of the curriculum and was well taught, it did.

Chapter objectives
- **To explore the nature of language learning at the primary stage.**
- **To suggest ways in which language learning can benefit children.**

(Continued)

(Continued)

- **To suggest ways in which teaching a language can benefit a school.**
- **To make links between Primary Strategy English and language learning.**
- **To make links between approaches to English as an Additional Language (EAL) and approaches to language teaching.**

Relevant Q Standards: Q1, Q2, Q4, Q5, Q6, Q7, Q8, Q14, Q18, Q19, Q32

 Initial reflection point

Consider the two brief lesson scenarios which follow; clearly there are differences, but what are they and do they matter?

Teacher A reads the class a simple story in another language about a boy who wants a pizza for tea. The boy finds the ingredients in the supermarket. There is a lot of repetition of the phrases for 'Here is …' and 'I like …'. Back at home his mother asks him to unpack the bag and she checks he has all the ingredients – 'Do you have …?'. He replies using 'Here is …' again. When the teacher reads it for the second time and pauses slightly at certain points the class gradually starts to join in with the names of the ingredients if they are not too hard and with the key phrases. By the end of the second reading the children are all able to say 'Yes, here it is!' and 'I like …'. The teacher then makes a three-ingredient pizza using a large card 'base' and chooses which three by asking the class to vote for their favourite ingredients. Individual pupils then create their own four- five- or six-ingredient toppings by adding other items. If they have forgotten the word for an item or if they want an extra item not in the story, they ask for it in the foreign language.

Teacher B has selected the key vocabulary for the pizza ingredients and teaches them to the class using flashcards and asking the children to repeat each of the words several times, using different tones or speeds or emotions to give variety. The teacher plays some flashcard games, for example using a noughts and crosses grid on the board with the flashcards turned away and pupils in teams competing to guess the right item and make a line of three. The teacher then adds the phrase for 'I would like' and plays pizza bingo with the class. Afterwards the class practices the word-set again in pairs, asking for certain items from each other.

Comment

You could see something like both of these approaches in primary language classrooms all over England. The point of comparing and contrasting them is not to decide which is better but to isolate what the children get from each 'lesson' and whether that meets your objectives as a languages teacher. In deciding what they get from each approach we need to think about the immediate learning and the more invisible acquisition that may be occurring. We also need to consider both immediate and longer-term motivation.

 Follow-up reflection

In which of those two lesson scenarios above would children be most motivated and in which would they remember more words? Would either approach lead to a greater longer-term motivation and would either embed language in their minds more strongly if used regularly?

Comment

There still are no 'right' answers to these questions, but you may have formed a strong view and this might reflect a personal standpoint (for example, a memory of successful language lessons when you were younger) or a deep knowledge of how primary children learn. This chapter, and indeed the whole book, seeks to offer a range of interpretations of how language learning might look, viewed from the standpoint of the children, the teachers and the school.

Some important ways of looking at the issue involve thinking about the purpose of language learning. What is language learning for? What type of language do we have in mind? Is the focus on learning the language, learning about the language or learning through the language? What about culture, and what is culture? Is it (to echo a previous series of course books) a matter of onions, sausages or castanets, or something deeper?

The teacher's objectives and how they shape what language learning can offer

We can start this dialogue by asking what appears to be a very basic question: When you as teacher walk into the classroom to start a language lesson, what are your objectives? We can paraphrase and widen this by asking: What do you intend to do? What do you intend that the children will know, understand and be able to do by the end of the lesson? Why are you doing this?

There are some very different possible answers to this set of questions that relate to the summary at the end of the Comment above. For example, you may see language learning as equipping children to survive in an authentic context such as a visit to a target language speaking country. Perhaps they will link with a class they have been writing to, and even stay a couple of nights with a family. If so, you may have an agenda which is about teaching and practising functional language around topics such as greeting, eating, exchanging essential personal information, expressing preferences and simple emotions. On the other hand, that may not be a likely scenario just yet and you may instead feel that to start the process of language learning you need to address some basic vocabulary areas such as numbers, colours, families, food/drink and favourite leisure time activities. In both of these cases you are very firmly in the language learning camp, with the 'doorstep intention' of presenting a specific set of vocabulary and phrases, mainly through aural/oral means and with the intention of equipping children to use them orally in structures such as dialogues. Your desired outcome is probably that they can use this body of language when they receive certain stimuli such as simple questions. You may decide to find out if you have been successful in this by 'testing' the class orally (or perhaps in writing with older children).

On the other hand, you may feel that it is still important even in the primary context that children start to build a grammatical awareness of the language they are learning. This might take the form either of some overt grammar or of another literacy-linked aspect such as strategy use. An example of the first could be awareness of parts of speech and their behaviour (agreement and position of adjectives in French or first/third person verb forms in German) and in this case it is possible that a lesson might be more expository with some rules being explained. The second might be accomplished more inductively through a 'language detectives' approach (as used by West Sussex LA materials, 2006 and 2008). In our earlier example with the 'pizza' lessons, a third scenario might involve the use of a menu in the target language with a task centred on children trying to work out what the items are and to give reasons for their choices. Clearly if you adopt such approaches you include learning *about* language as a major purpose.

A third scenario could have a completely different set of intentions at the threshold to the classroom. You may be using authentic texts (a story or song, for example) and think less about giving children a particular set of items for comprehension and re-use as about their overall experience of the sounds of the language. There would probably be some inherent repetition contained within the story or song, which they would begin to catch and rehearse more informally. It might be that you want to offer the children the chance to construct meaning through context (perhaps with the visuals associated with the text) and although they will not understand the literal meaning of every word, they might laugh or feel suspense or anticipate a particular ending. You might want to deal with non-fiction and link something in the foreign language with work they are doing in mathematics, science, geography or art. You might hope that through this they will experience some reinforcement (in a different way) of some of the concepts you have been dealing with at other points of the week or term. Later you might teach them in the foreign language something from one of those other areas that is completely new. If you have these intentions you are working within the approach that involves learning *in* or *through* the language.

We want to be clear that the options above are not described with a view to you choosing an approach. Of course a single teacher might have that range of intentions either with different classes or even with the same class over a period of time. It is probably healthy for any subject to be tackled from different directions and in different ways across a whole primary school, and even across the four years of KS2. The advocates of embedding the languages element into the whole curriculum (including ourselves as authors of this book) need to remember that there is a separate language curriculum based on authentic experience of life among mother-tongue speakers of that language, in other words 'survival' content, which children need to learn. We need to recognise that, just as the primary strategy English curriculum includes elements of grammar, so a foreign language curriculum lasting a minimum of four years needs that too. But all teachers of languages at primary level need to consider how children learn in general and how a focus on learning *through* the language can certainly offer other sorts of gains as research has shown (see Chapter 9). We will now look at the nature of that learning from the child's as well as the school's perspective.

What do children enjoy about language learning? What can language learning offer children?

One survey of a whole primary school where all children were learning languages from Nursery through to Y6 (and where they had all started the process at the same time), found that the most popular element of learning French was songs. This was noted by 75 per cent of the children in the school. In Hood (2006) we explored some early impressions of language learning from focus groups in the same school. In the plenary at the Primary Languages Show 2007 (Hood unpublished) we presented further data from that school which showed children able to identify the benefits of challenge, very willing to show what they knew in the form of singing authentic French songs and strongly involved in taking the language home.

So far this chapter has not mentioned the F-word. Many people associate learning languages with the fun-element and we need to address this now because fun *is* certainly something that language learning offers children and schools. Fun can emerge from a range of approaches: from lively active teaching and learning, from a real mixture of stimulating resources, from creative activities which use the language, from genuine contacts with speakers of the target language, and from games that involve problem-solving, collaboration and competition. It is vital to distinguish the fun that emerges from variety of stimuli and challenge from the fun which arises simply out of the games and simply out of the fact that for many children language learning, being so orally and game-based, is not 'real work.' That sort of fun seems to evaporate as repetition sets in, progression is more limited and challenge seems never to materialise. When children say that something is hard and then you ask them whether 'hard' is a good or a bad thing, very many will say that it is good, because 'hard' means you are learning. Similarly 'easy', implying a lack of challenge and a lack of thinking, is not often held up by learners as something positive. Above all they want work addressed to their own maturity level. This is illustrated by a Y10 boy on work experience in a primary school who at the end of a Year 3 lesson approached the teacher and said: 'I wish we had done languages in primary school, because then in Year 7 we could have done some real work.'

Language learning should be active and have a large proportion of orally-based activities and should relate to a range of aspects of children's lives, including their interests, their social life, their beliefs and their learning. This should guarantee that amongst different motivational qualities it contains genuine elements of fun. In fact fun should permeate the subject and not be a separate planning aim. Often in the early stages a combination of physical activity and rhythm and language can be stimulating and enjoyable; incorporating some thinking into this type of activity is always possible, giving both fun and challenge. A Y1 boy asked his French teacher who was teaching a supply morning which was not intended to include French: 'When are we going to do the fun thing, I mean French?' This teacher believed that challenge was vital in all her activities, and this is evidence that fun can be a broad phenomenon.

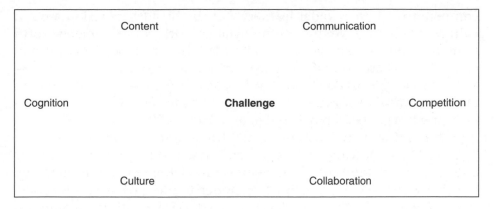

Figure 2.1 Qualities offered by language teaching

We will now consider the importance of some other qualities which language teaching, like all good teaching, can offer children. Conveniently these qualities can be expressed in a series of words that begin with C: these are culture, communication, content, challenge, cognition, collaboration and competition. We will look at each of these in turn, show how they link together and offer practical classroom examples through an activity or resource. We will also ask you to reflect on an aspect of each element.

Culture

Culture may seem to be an obvious component of learning a language. The Key Stage Two Framework (see Chapter 7) has intercultural understanding as one of its three equally important strands with a full set of objectives for each year group in the phase. Both French and Spanish, which are currently the major languages in primary schools, have the advantage of being global languages, spoken on three or more continents. France, Germany and Spain are themselves also multicultural societies. So 'culture' can include a fascinating range of aspects concerning daily lives in schools and in a multitude of different homes, cities and villages which have some resemblances to and some key differences from the experience our children will have here. And of course our own children will come at alternative cultures from a wide variety of different standpoints, many of which will not be British in origin.

The potential richness for the whole curriculum of encouraging interaction on a cultural level in language lessons is immense and some authors have approached this notion in detail (Kramsch 1996, Byram *et al.* 2001, Scarino *et al.* 2007). Such writers often deal with more advanced elements and discuss language learning and cultural competence amongst older learners. But the breadth of vision around culture that we will get by reading Byram's work, for example, is worth remembering, as an eventual aim. He has a model of cultural competences based on different types of 'knowledge': *savoir comprendre* – knowing how to understand, *savoir apprendre/faire* – knowing how to learn/do, *savoir s'engager* – knowing how to engage, *savoir être* – knowing how to be/behave (Byram and Zarate 1994, Byram 1997). This is useful in that it gives us a sense that true intercultural understanding leads to both knowing what to say and how to say it because we have a deeper understanding of the people with whom we are interacting. In other words it is eventually about understanding what makes people the way they are. At primary level we need to start with the realisation that many of our children will not have actually experienced different cultures and that we can unwittingly set up stereotypes if we dwell too much on stating over-simplistic differences and unintentionally inviting 'horror' (frogs' legs, snails and horse-meat come to mind!). This starts with the power of image that gives a stream of messages we are not even aware of. In *Reading Images: The Grammar of Visual Design*, for example, Kress and van Leeuwen (2006) explore the many ways in which different cultural images, including those in children's picture books, communicate their meanings. A complex mix of existing cultural concepts, juxtapositions of visual material and conventions such as direction of 'reading' (inherently left to right in western cultures) create out of a simple picture an image that has as much power as dense text. We only have to look at some of the cultural 'loading' in our media (associations with Second World War uniforms, beer-drinking, lederhosen for Germany, for example) to see that we are in constant receipt of stereotypical imagery.

For all these reasons, when evaluating materials for use with primary age children, it is very important that teachers consider their cultural content and the power of the imagery. If a book, DVD, picture material or an online resource makes extensive use of line drawings, clip art, neutral photographs, then its contribution to cultural understanding is very limited and might even be negative. If, on the other hand, it has authentic photographs showing children of equivalent age in natural settings then this encourages children to notice and ask questions about apparent similarities and differences. Many current resources use video extracts to present language and, as with Early Start (see Chapter 10) for example, even a short clip of children eating lunch, being at school or shopping can open up the possibility of culture-based conversations. The short sequence in that resource of a French family eating at midday shows a range of differences which do exemplify some cultural attributes (for example, French children often eating lunch at home in a more formal lunch setting, different patterns of 'courses', collaborative laying/clearing of the table). While there is still a place for cartoon characters in stories and for all the fantasy possible with such images, they should be combined with strong, authentic, culturally accurate representations in any good set of materials.

In the last 20 years cross-over culture has been very strong and this leads to a need to reappraise what we mean by 'culture'. Spain as a holiday destination has continued to grow in popularity and as a result many children are familiar with much of the obvious features of Spanish life, such as some of the food, the climate and coastal landscapes. But we can delve deeper and present more traditional food and issues from the climate and less familiar landscapes if we plan this in carefully. More concrete examples can develop this theme. While food is an obvious cultural aspect of interest, there is much less value now in offering learners of French a French breakfast as an activity, though this was common in lower secondary a few years ago. Our supermarkets offer *pain au chocolat* and *brioche* as standard items as well as *baguettes* in plenty. French yogurts are commonly advertised on television and hot chocolate is a more common breakfast drink than before. We need to look at shopping habits, eating habits and a wider range of food items and to make the point that French food has a strong North African influence rather as ours has (amongst others) an Indian influence, and for at least some similar reasons. In sport, the premier league has brought not just French footballers into common view, but a host of French-speaking players from Africa. Countries such as Côte d'Ivoire and Sénégal are known to older primary pupils, some of whom may have seen scenes from Africa on television through watching African Nations Cup football. Spain and Portugal bring with them strong associations with South America, for example Argentina and Brazil. Access to less superficial cultural material is potentially more manageable if we can build on that initial basic knowledge. The Arsenal FC Education programme has also started creating materials with this aim in mind.

But many might see this as a partial diversion because surely children cannot handle these conversations in the target language? As with everything connected to target language use (and we deal with this in more detail in Chapter Three), we should look hard to find ways in which it might be possible before we opt for the safer English route. Scaffolding can be used to support children's use of the target language and this can take the form of a series of questions which offer language and which support its re-use to express real opinions. By Year 6 this should be possible at a relatively high level.

Example from practice

In a PowerPoint presentation we created, which used some material from Oxfam's on-the-line website (www.oxfam.org.uk/coolplanet/ontheline/ french/journey/burkina/bfindex.htm), a young girl's daily routine in rural Burkina Faso was explored very simply. She had to get up early, then she walked an hour to school, fetched water, had a day's lessons, walked home, helped her mother to cook and clean, and spent the later evening with family and friends making her own entertainment. Apart from some useful French language this was tapping in to Citizenship and Environmental themes. Here is a sample teacher scaffolding script:

'Alors, Mariam se lève à cinq heures, prend le petit déjeuner et elle marche une heure (soixante minutes!) à l'école.' (This sentence is said more than once with the PowerPoint or other visuals in support. The figures '1 hour = 60 minutes' can be written on the whiteboard while pointing at the clock or a watch.)

'Se lever à cinq heures, c'est bon? Marcher une heure à l'école, c'est bon? Ça serait bon pour toi ou un problème pour toi?' (Use mime as well as images, and elicit an answer from one pupil then ask several others so that repetition occurs. Do this in a natural manner with a range of pupils genuinely asked for their opinion – they will, after all, have different opinions so this dialogue is for a real purpose, both individually and collectively.)

'OK, Ça serait un problème pour toi, mais pourquoi? A cinq heures tu es trop fatigué/e? Après une heure de marche, tu es trop fatigué/e?' (Giving vocabulary such as *après* and *trop* in a definite context is important because connectives, prepositions and adverbs often allow children to express more shades of meaning. They need to encounter these words in sentences that have a real purpose and not just learn them as isolated items. Note that the 'push' from the teacher here is to ask for reasons. The question *why* in any target language needs to appear early and be used regularly.)

With these questions it is possible to respond in very simple or slightly less simple ways. This means pupils can self-differentiate but still participate – the emphasis is on communication and finding real answers to questions where the answers are not known in advance.

But it is also very positive to encourage children to experiment with using familiar language in different ways. Here they might want to express something about carrying things to school or the weather. If they are used to you as teacher wanting contributions and supporting making half-sentences into full sentences, then they may draw from previous work and offer: *'j'aime…'*, *'parce que le sac est…'* or *'il pleut…'*. If you then supply a word like *dormir*, *lourd* or *souvent*, they will have the satisfaction of having made an original contribution and have a chance of remembering the new item because they heard it and put it into a real context that belonged to them.

The PowerPoint then led to a more challenging worksheet suitable for older KS2 learners with more depth of language learning behind them.

Culture, then, can be brought directly into the language teaching fabric of the lesson – it can be the lesson and is certainly not an add-on, which the teacher includes from time to time as a topic which gives a change from language work.

 Reflection point

Think of an aspect of life in a target-language speaking country – preferably arising from experiences you have had personally – that would be an interesting cultural element for your teaching. What resources might you look for which would engage children and allow them to explore differences in the right spirit, and, preferably, using the foreign language? Write three questions you might use to help children notice and react to the aspect you have chosen.

Communication

Communication is obviously an essential part of language learning and teaching. Ask most modern language teachers if they have a style or method to their approach and they will reply that they are 'communicative' language teachers (see also Chapter Nine for a full discussion of this theme). The essence of that methodology is that learning occurs through authentic communication – real messages for real purposes using authentic language and authentic stimuli. This involves real menus, real transport timetables, real estate agents' details of houses, real pen-friend letters from real children and real school timetables. The accepted curriculum is survival topics, which for example feature in the modern languages examinations at the national GCSE level, taken normally at age 16 in England, Wales and Northern Ireland.

Clearly primary age children need to learn how to identify themselves and survive (with adult support) during a stay in a target language speaking country. It now seems common sense that we should achieve this by helping them to learn by using the real materials they will encounter when abroad, and that we should allow them to practise dialogue which could take place there. In doing so we should look to techniques from Drama (for example hot-seating or giving participants in a role-play 'secret' circumstances for the dialogue) to make the communication more inherently interesting and enjoyable. Even so, there is a danger in fashioning an entire language-learning curriculum around survival, especially when a concept such as van Ek's 'threshold level' (1975, van Ek and Trim 1991) can become diluted to a syllabus consisting of vocabulary, grammar structures and topics.

Van Ek (1975) listed the themes or topics needed as foreign language knowledge to survive in another country. With these he included the language functions, grammatical understanding, key vocabulary required, but also how the language worked as a system of communication, socially and culturally, and how speakers might compensate when their competence was limited. The 'syllabus' was one for survival, but in a sophisticated, linguistically competent way rather than what might be termed as at 'phrase-book' level.

In fact, in addition to those elements discourse competence, sociocultural competence and compensatory competence all appear in van Ek's work and indicate the inclusion of genuine rather than staged (and stilted or mechanistic) communication. Even if GCSE examination boards maintain that this has been a part of their design, the reality is that it has not been tested at any but the highest levels. Examinations are notorious for setting the standards, objectives and 'feel' of teaching and learning (Volante 2004, Menken 2006) and it would appear that GCSE ML has done this. Ironically the low levels of thinking and creativity, the formulaic demand of role play and prepared questions, the endless listening and reading to spot contrived shades of meaning (that is, the lack of challenge) have resulted in the examinations being perceived as more difficult than those in other subjects. Difficulty in securing real motivation appears to have led to difficulty in fulfilling examination demands. One young secondary learner complained that her foreign language lessons were dominated by the unit tests and in the unit tests they had to learn what they were going to say or write and had no opportunity to respond using their real opinions and experience. This led to a slightly ludicrous situation where she had to write that she had visited the Louvre in Paris, when, although she really had been to Paris, she had not been to the Louvre. The option of writing the truth, that she had been to the Musée D'Orsay, was not allowed!

Of course survival in a foreign country through being able to use the language competently is a vital aim of language teaching and we should all equip our pupils with aspects of that skill, but if this is their only diet it is not surprising that learners in KS3 have often tired of it. So to explore communication more fully, we need to think what it is that learners are communicating *about*. This leads us to the next 'C' and shows us that communication as a concept by itself is limited.

Content

Content is often ignored in language teaching, where there is a tendency for the 'medium to be the message'. In other words the content is the language itself rather than something else learned *through* language. As we saw above, if the content is an abstract global concept such as 'survival' there is a danger that processes can become mechanistic as learners try a range of parallel ways to reach a laudable but intangible aim. So objectives might focus on a list of vocabulary or a grammatical structure, or a skill such as complaining politely or the ability to give directions to a particular place. The problem with this is that it appears to learners as mostly either simply learning something for its own sake (for example, a list of words) or as relatively trivial content, unless a visit is imminent and they can see an immediate real purpose.

Using language is much more important than knowing language or knowing about language. Clearly to use language effectively you need to know some language and have some kind of overview of how it works as a system, but if objectives stop at the *knowing* or *knowing about*, it might be harder then to move on to *using*. If the objective is to use the language from the start, then the other factors will take care of themselves and the *purpose* of language learning will be unambiguous from the first lesson. Dropping a learner into a target language speaking country and asking them to survive *is* authentic and does have a meaningful content. But recreating that in a classroom amongst learners who all share a different language from the one being used and expecting reality to be suspended is less convincing. On the other hand, learning about something else (which may be cultural) has the effect of deflecting attention from overtly practising the language and onto solving a problem or establishing a new concept. An example of what we mean by this follows and the original of the worksheet we are referring to is available in the *A La Française* pack (Tobutt and Roche 2007 and see Chapter Ten).

Example from practice

Les monuments de Paris
Materials

Pictures of la Tour Eiffel, le Musée du Louvre, la Cathédrale Notre Dame

Facts (Formatted in boxes, they can also be cut up and used as a classification activity.)

C'est une église.

C'est un musée.

C'est une tour.

La construction a duré de 1163 à 1345.

La construction a duré de 1887 à 1889.

Il a été construit en 1594.

Elle a été construite par Gustave Eiffel.

La hauteur est 324 mètres.

La hauteur est 69 mètres.

La pyramide à l'entrée est 21 mètres haut.

Il y a plus de 12 millions de visiteurs par an.

Il y a plus de 6 millions de visiteurs par an.

Il y a plus de 8 millions de visiteurs par an.

Ici on peut voir La Mona Lisa de Leonardo da Vinci.

La tour a été construite de 18 038 pièces métalliques.

'J'aime les arts.'

'J'aime l'histoire.'

'Je suis sportif! Je prends l'escalier!'

The activity here is to match the sentences to the monument. The objectives include learning some information about the three monuments, but also aim to broaden the knowledge of the pupils about the kind of historical sights which Paris offers, to reinforce a historical awareness that modern cities have features which originated at very different times. Language objectives are mainly about receptive language (that is, comprehension) and include, for some or all, using contextual reading to infer unknown vocabulary items, using grammatical information (il/elle and grammatical gender). Depending on the level and experience of the pupils, the class could also be asked to reason in French. *'La cathédrale est plus agée que la tour'* / *'La tour est plus populaire que la cathédrale, n'est-ce pas?'* / *'La Mona Lisa est une peinture – c'est dans le musée.'* So, active language use as well as the receptive processing of language can be involved in an activity like this. Pupils will learn something (a non-linguistic content) and will have used language to do so, reinforcing vocabulary, pronunciation and possibly grammar.

 Reflection point

Take any three common language teaching topics and list next to them three dimensions of content that you could involve in presenting the essential language to primary pupils. An example might be:

Colours – What are the primary/secondary colours? Which colours do we use to express different emotions? Survey of colours of family cars or own bedroom walls or pets.

Challenge

Challenge sits in the centre of our list of seven terms. It is especially connected with what we have just said about content and clearly links into the next issue, cognition. But all of the other 'C' words have a link into challenge if we interpret them in that way. Pupils generally welcome being challenged because they acknowledge that they are in school to learn and this process is often more stimulating when it is harder than when they simply coast. This is where excess repetition can be harmful, especially over time. If the content remains trivial and the curriculum is repetitive (the NC and GCSE survival topics have always tended to operate in a spiral which reoccurs at various points), if the activity types consist of short, undeveloped tasks with unsubstantial outcomes, then we should not be surprised if motivation drops. We can challenge our pupils in many ways, and the later chapters of the book will all deal with this as one of the constant themes. The main emphasis should always be on children discovering rather than being told, making for themselves connections which, admittedly, we may have set up for them, using language naturally and creatively and being inspired to go off and tell or teach someone else.

One Y4 boy responding to a questionnaire wrote the comment in Figure 2.2

7. What do you most enjoy in French lessons?

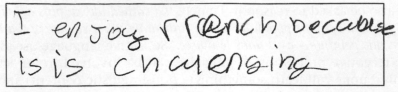

Figure 2.2   Response from a Y4 boy

The type of challenge is of course important and the same boy added this (see Figure 2.3) to a later question (we think 'tingly' might be the intention of the third word).

10. If you chose strongly agree or agree for Question 5, can you write *how French lessons feel different* in this box

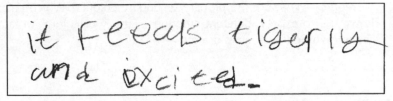

Figure 2.3   A further response

Pupils often like things that are 'hard' rather than 'easy' and one comment that showed this came from a Y3 focus group: 'When things are hard you learn it quicker.' A Y6 boy commented on why he liked to do topic work in French: 'You've got a challenge to do rather than doing just what you already know.' Many good language teachers report comments from parents that children teach parents or siblings foreign language expressions at the meal table or while walking home from school. It is obvious that to do this they must first care about what they have learned and that they must see a purpose in knowing it in the first place, or why would they bother?

Cognition

Cognition then links to this discussion because essentially what we need to do in language lessons is make children think. This is at the heart of the learning process everywhere else so this should not be surprising. Thinking can be at different levels and in different guises. In commonly used language topics, thinking can be rather difficult to engender, because often the way these topics are approached is through fairly descriptive rather than analytical processes. When asking about likes and dislikes, for example, children may want to express more subtle shades of opinion and you may wish to ask them why they have certain opinions. This raises more difficult vocabulary and structures. But we could argue that when languages are linked with other subjects, thinking is easier to manage. It can start at the level where children make a single, simple decision while using language in comprehension mode. Questions which operate like this might be: Did the Vikings have glass? Did they have chocolate? Is this sound from a violin or clarinet? Is this bridge made of wood or stone? Which of these animals is depicted in this collage? This level of vocabulary (that is, single words) does not need to be presented separately, or pre-taught, as the simple format of asking 'Is it x or y?' or 'Was x true, yes or no?' actually teaches that vocabulary while the learners' minds are focused on the question being asked.

Thinking continues in the process where children make meaning from text, often as a group or whole class, as we showed in the example of the French monuments. It is present again when pupils are asked to reassemble sentences or to generate their own simple sentences in response to pictures. If we ask pupils to respond to simple open questions where the answer is personal and not already known by the teacher, we again move away from formulaic parroting of learnt material and back to a child having to think: 'What has she asked me there? How do I respond?'

But thinking tends not to occur when vocabulary is simply repeated or when very tightly controlled pair practice or role-play is used, especially if the pupil's own views or experience are not elicited by the task. The limitations of some common language learning activities are now clear. An example might be flashcard games which have a place in the learning cycle but will become formulaic and tedious if used at the same point in every new topic. Partly this is due to repetition of a format but also partly due to the nature of the format itself. Excessive practice of common topics, for example personal information, is a further example. If we rehearse too often questions to which we know the answer and everyone else in the class knows the answer and the pupil we are asking knows that everyone knows the answer, then the motivation to give that answer becomes minimal. The worst example of this is the type of question which goes: '¿Stephen, cómo te llamas?'. But asking ages in a single year class is similar unless you are investigating proportions with birthdays at different points or establishing an age order, in which case you need years and months. Even asking about brothers and sisters more than once falls into this category and needs another dimension. One good way to sidestep all of this is to ask pupils to take on a different identity and to keep it a secret. All of the same questions can then be asked but none of the answers will be known in advance. If we do not think about this, then, in the worst scenario, any real level of thinking can be absent from the entire learning cycle.

Reflection point

You have used a café menu to introduce a number of drinks. You do not want to play flashcard games with these items now, so need to consider some other activity that will involve some thinking as well as the use of the vocabulary. What could you do?

Collaboration

Collaboration is vital in language learning because language use generally involves some form of communication between two or more people. This might seem obvious given the amount of talk associated with the ML curriculum at all levels. However we do need to think beyond the obvious. Talking to a formula is not strictly collaboration and talking to a rigid formula makes the fact that two are involved in a dialogue almost superfluous. So, by collaboration we mean that a pair or a group of children are working for a real purpose (Oxford 1997, Dillenbourg 1999, Crandall 1999, Fisher 2002). This might be to make something, solve a problem or to exchange information in an authentic way. You might even combine all three if you operate a survey about pets to find out the average number of pets per pupil to create a pie-chart on pet-popularity, and perhaps push a little further by asking people whether they have had a pet who has died. While many children do know some other children's pets' names, colours and bad habits, this still contains a very real chance to find out unknown facts, to use the information for another purpose and to involve a more affective issue, which is all too real for many children.

But we are not just talking about talking. Children nearly always respond positively to questions which ask if they prefer to work collaboratively in general, and within the area of language learning this is especially true of reading. They tend to make much more of a text when reading in a pair or group, and also enjoy the reading more. In a group it tends to become a matter of collective 'finding out', of argument and it carries a greater (because more public) sense of task completion and satisfaction. Reading is also much more immediately accessible as an activity when carried out collaboratively. So we can ask children to read earlier and to read more if we do it this way. In an unpublished thesis (Hood 2000), we looked at lower secondary age children reading individually and in groups and found clear evidence of higher performance in the collaborative mode.

Competition

Very many pupils really love both playing games and solving problems and, in so doing, competing either individually or in teams. Competition can be healthy and can involve high levels of collaboration. We need to be careful only to ensure that the focus does not move so much on to competition that it leads to a desperation to win and shortcuts too much the language and the process of using the language. It can also lead to anxiety amongst some pupils (Oxford 1999, Crandall 1999, Pollard and Triggs 2000, Ortega 2007). Ortega particularly deals with the relationship between competitiveness and anxiety and offers a set of classroom procedures to ensure a healthy ethos. Whole-class games such as identifying vocabulary on the whiteboard as fast as possible have a danger of involving a very small number of pupils and leaving the majority on the sidelines at any one point. When using a whole-class format it is important to issue something (for example, a card with a number or vocabulary item) to everyone and then to carry out a team competition where an item is called out and the first person to stand up, show the card and say it correctly wins a point. This means anyone can be involved at any point. Group-based games have the advantage of involving far more people more continuously. An example of this (available in the *A La Française* pack, Tobutt and Roche 2007) is an envelope game involving euros that has a distant similarity to the TV programme, *Deal or No Deal*. Board games, which can be based on snakes and ladders type formats are popular, but tend to take more time to play. With these it is vital to think about 'surround sound' social language (which will be seen in Chapter 9 as language for learning) and to get as much target language activated as possible. This has to be prepared for and will not happen by itself.

Competition between the teacher and the class is extremely popular. A number of guessing games (with a number of guesses allowed or timed spans for the answer to be reached) can be played in the early stages as directly competitive and this has a certain motivational power, particularly if the class is able to work together. There is also the advantage that if the teacher is trying to guess a cultural object, location or other item that the class has chosen, he or she can use a good range of target language to ask questions and test out guesses to which the class need only answer yes or no. This has the effect of offering a good receptive language experience for the children without making impossible demands on them. Of course when the children start to want to take the teacher role they should be allowed to, even though their quantity of language will be far less.

In summary, we might say that competition which is firmly aimed at enhancing learning works very well. This can often be organised in teams so combining competition with collaboration. Competition, purely for its own sake might be popular for a time and with some pupils or classes, but in the end it will wear thin as a motivator.

 Reflection point

Planning activity

- Take a language teaching lesson plan and evaluate it for *Challenge* by annotating it with examples of the other six Cs from the box on p. 21
- Are any of the Cs absent? Were opportunities missed?
- Could you insert them easily without changing the plan radically or should the lesson be completely re-planned?
- How challenging was this lesson and why do you think that?

From the review of the seven Cs above, we can now infer that the dangers might emerge from too much repetition or restriction of children's natural desire to use language to communicate. If we over-rely on making it fun we may run into fun-fatigue. It is not that natural repetition or some measure of control over language is not part of the learning process and we mentioned earlier how important enjoyment is. But we need to mesh these elements in to the seven Cs to create a truly stimulating environment. To explore this further we will ask another question.

 Reflection point

How can learning another language offer even more to a school (for example, by reinforcing the development of core skills such as first language or EAL, numeracy or reasoning)?

Learning another language has always been seen by teachers as a potential consolidation tool for learners with particular difficulties. For example, in Y7 teachers have often commented that 'doing the time' in a foreign language offers students who still have difficulties with this life skill to gain practice in a non-threatening environment with others who are also learning it for the first time in French, German or Spanish.

If we make comparisons between the core subjects and languages we can see a potential two-way process, where the foreign language draws from the skills established for the core subject but also gives back to them, reinforcing and extending those same skills. This applies to all pupils, not only those with specific or special needs and establishes ML as a truly integrated subject. In this chapter we will look in depth at examples from Literacy.

ML and Literacy

The strands that lead the objectives in the primary framework for literacy (see www.standards.dfes.gov.uk/primaryframework/literacy/learning objectives/Strands/) are as follows:

1 Speaking

2 Listening and responding

3 Group discussion, interaction

4 Drama

5 Word recognition

6 Word structure and spelling

7 Understand and interpret texts

8 Engage with, respond to texts

9 Creating and shaping texts

10 Text structure and organisation

11 Sentence structure, punctuation

12 Presentation

Each strand has separate objectives for each year group so the complete package consists of over 300 separate objectives. Some of these objectives will be difficult to envisage as realistic for ML at the parallel age level, but some can be seen in this way and we will look at two of the strands to demonstrate this.

Speaking

Here is the Y3 set for Speaking, the first strand.

- Choose and prepare poems or stories for performance, identifying appropriate expression, tone, volume and use of voices and other sounds.

- Explain process or present information, ensuring that items are clearly sequenced, relevant details are included and accounts are ended effectively.

- Sustain conversation, explain or give reasons for their views or choices.

- Develop and use specific vocabulary in different contexts.

We can see immediately that beginner language learners at the start of KS2 will not be able to use the language at a level remotely approaching how they use mother tongue or English as an additional language. But it is important to establish what they will be able to do by the end of that year. If the language lessons are sufficiently broadly based and offer enough challenge, they will have encountered simple poems, stories and songs. In joining in with more repetitive elements they will not just get words but meaning as conveyed through intonation and volume, and they will also have a sense of context. This is absolutely true of a class which contains some pupils with EAL. It is important that they are able to contribute by presenting their own work alongside that of their peers. This will often be at a simpler level but they will also learn from hearing more able first language speakers use a similar format with richer vocabulary or more complex syntax. Because it is the same format, they will make more direct gains, as they hear this language in context, and imitation at first will lead on to internalisation and their ability to make the language their own. In an ML class most pupils will be at a similar level so the teacher's encouragement to use richer language is crucial. In a Y1 class of Cantonese speakers in Hong Kong, for example, children who had heard 'We're going on a bear hunt' in a morning lesson were seen in the dinner queue later playing a game in which they chorused 'We're not scared!' in just the right tone and context, and they clearly loved playing a game with the language they had just met.

If the language lessons include a measure of content, for example science, then sequences will be embedded in the work the children cover. Helping plants grow well as a topic offers the opportunity to create simple checklists, combining visuals and text with either simple lists or sequences information. Figure 2.4 shows how such language might be stimulated and what the best pupils might produce at first in spoken form, and later in writing.

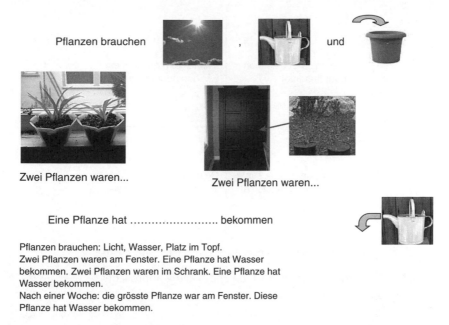

Pflanzen brauchen , und

Zwei Pflanzen waren...

Zwei Pflanzen waren...

Eine Pflanze hat .... bekommen

Pflanzen brauchen: Licht, Wasser, Platz im Topf.
Zwei Pflanzen waren am Fenster. Eine Pflanze hat Wasser
bekommen. Zwei Pflanzen waren im Schrank. Eine Pflanze hat
Wasser bekommen.
Nach einer Woche: die grösste Pflanze war am Fenster. Diese
Pflanze hat Wasser bekommen.

Figure 2.4 Helping plants grow well

Language learning is expected to involve opinion giving. In KS3, levels 3 and 4 mention personal responses and opinion giving. In other words, it is expected that Y7 students have been exposed to this during the first year of learning. Clearly then, Y3 children should be able to meet contexts where they talk about an item of personal interest and give some simple reasons for their preferences. This might involve food and healthy approaches. A simple organiser to prepare for such conversations might be a matrix with four quadrants, labelled as Figure 2.5 shows. By locating foods onto the matrix children are ready to give simple opinions about healthy eating and the more able will be able to add some simple reasons. When this is put together into a paired comparative dialogue or a mini-presentation, we get material relevant to the third of our speaking objectives listed above.

The use of more precise vocabulary is also simple to draw together. Language schemes of work often involve colours in the early stages, but at Y3 level children are already more sophisticated about their colour appreciation to settle only for the major primary/secondary colours with no qualifiers. It is not complex to introduce words for light- dark- and even shiny, fluorescent and so more closely reach the expressions children want to use.

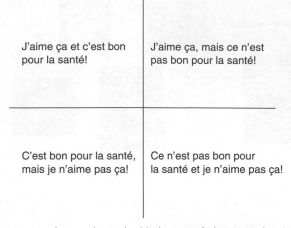

parce que c'est .....(amer / acide / sans goût / trop sucré etc)

Figure 2.5   Conversation matrix for food and healthy approaches

Grammar

Perhaps the Speaking objectives will be felt to be a very easily accessible set for such comparisons. Grammatical strands are no more complicated, as the fact that children are focusing on such issues in English makes it very easy to focus them also in a foreign language. They will naturally seek patterns and comment on what they find. This comparative approach gives extra support to both languages. But we can look for a more complex set to see if the case for a parallel focus between Literacy and ML can really be substantiated.

Understanding and interpreting texts

Here is the Y3 set for Understanding and Interpreting texts – an aspect that people may feel is beyond the beginner language learner.

- Identify and make notes of the main points of section(s) of text.

- Infer characters' feelings in fiction and consequences in logical explanations.

- Identify how different texts are organised, including reference texts, magazines and leaflets, on paper and on screen.

- Use syntax, context and word structure to build their store of vocabulary as they read for meaning.

- Explore how different texts appeal to readers using varied sentence structures and descriptive language.

As we will show later in the book, it is vital that children are exposed to text at a level commensurate with their experience in English from the very beginnings of learning. Again we should remember that an enormous amount of importance attached to text is signalled to them every day in literacy lessons. Therefore it is illogical not to make parallels with French, German, Spanish or another language. So often the 'diet' we give learners is simply accessed by them as individuals at an appropriate level for their current development. Children in Foundation Stage who are really interested in letter patterns through their phonics work and who pick out letters and sounds while listening to stories from a big book that they see in front of them, will naturally do the same in the foreign language. If they have not yet reached that stage in work through English, they will not. By Y3 rhyming patterns in a poem, significant stages in a story, or key words in the description of a town or village will be visible and 'note-taking' (probably orally and collaboratively) is more than possible. Again from the beginnings of learning in F1 or F2 children listen avidly to stories in a foreign language, look closely at pictures, 'hear' intonation and emotion portrayed through the reading and so identify and empathise with characters or situations. At first it may be preferable to talk in English about a story that they have heard in a foreign language, making the most of the foreign language experience of listening. As with the grammatical objectives, learners focusing on text organisation in English will be able to make similar comments about foreign language informational texts and will be able also to use that structural understanding to help them to identify and infer word meanings, so meeting aspects of the third and fourth objectives above.

Perhaps these objectives are best viewed from the point of view of a single theme – an example might be endangered species. The webpage www.linternaute.com/nature-animaux/animaux/dossier/especes-menacees/top-10/index.shtml gives access to short dossiers which a teacher could use to produce visuals and simple facts under a theme of *Sauvez...*!

For example from the card about giant pandas, the 'start text' is:

> Panda géant: Où vit-il?
> Dans les forêts humides et froides qui couvrent les versants des montagnes du Tibet et du sud-ouest de la Chine, dans les montagnes situées au Sichuan, au Gansu et au Shaanxi, à plus de 2000 mètres d'altitude.

The teacher can elicit the real key words through asking the class collaboratively to supply possible endings to the sentence: *'Le panda géant habite...'*. They might offer:

Les forêts; les montagnes; Tibet / Chine; 2000m
Les forêts sont humides et froides

This can lead to poster work – *Sauvez les pandas géants*, where design is informed through the preceding language work and where some Y4 shaping text objectives about persuasiveness are anticipated. Using story books linked to the theme allows it to be located in the child's wider work – even if these are for younger children such as Eric Carle's 'Panda Bear, Panda Bear, What do you see?' told in the target language. For Objective 5, at a very simple level teachers could show, for example through simple poetry, how the language can *sound* different with different intentions. Ideally this could involve poems written by NS children on the endangered animals theme.

The two examples given of ML work associated with Literacy Framework objectives are not contrived to make a link that does not really exist. They demonstrate that a modern language *functions as language* just as English does, that we need to see the role of the language in our teaching, as well as the language, as a teaching end in itself, and that we need to encourage our pupils to communicate in and play with the language as well as to 'learn' it.

 Reflection point

Take the listening and responding strand objectives (Y1 and Y2) from the Literacy Framework. These are:

Y1

- Listen with sustained concentration, building new stores of words in different contexts.
- Listen to and follow instructions accurately, asking for help and clarification if necessary.
- Listen to tapes or video and express views about how a story or information has been presented.

Y2

- Listen to others in class, ask relevant questions and follow instructions.
- Listen to talk by an adult, remember some specific points and identify what they have learned.
- Respond to presentations by describing characters, repeating some highlights and commenting constructively.

Which of these could you imagine being used as ML objectives for a Y3 class by the end of the year? Make a few notes about how you might approach one of them.

What differences are there between 'language lessons' and the experience of a child coming into a school with EAL?

To complete the final point from the previous section – that language should be used to serve our teaching and not be an end in itself – we can make a further analogy with EAL. This is the term used to describe the context of a learner who does not have English as a first language. We will explore the research base to CLIL and EAL in Chapter Eight but it is important at this stage to note that teachers working with children with EAL operate a sophisticated model of scaffolding and differentiation within what is for the children with EAL an immersion framework. Being surrounded by the language and being set carefully planned, purposeful tasks with clear outcomes should ensure a positive learning context for all to gain from it what they can. These skills are very close to what is needed by language teachers and language learning should be as broad as this. The answer to the question is therefore that the differences should be of context not so much of experience. The contextual advantage for teachers of a foreign language is that most of the class will probably know a similar amount of the language as each other, whereas the parallel advantage for teachers of EAL is that they have native or near-native command of English. Clearly the ML teacher with strong competence and who has experience also of EAL has the best of all possible starting points!

Chapter summary

What can language learning offer primary age children and what can it offer a primary school? We hope that this chapter has demonstrated that learning a language can play a very full role in a primary school and in the experience of its children. As ML enters the compulsory primary curriculum, it is difficult to see it as just another foundation subject. It needs regularity of timetabling and this is not a status offered to most other foundation subjects (except Physical Education (PE) and perhaps Personal, Social, Health and Citizenship Education (PSHCE)). The embedding across the day and week in its use in registration, classroom organisation and management, routines, and perhaps through music in assemblies means that it can almost disappear from having an overt focus. Certainly some schools feeling the intensity of time pressure will look to account for a major part of ML provision through embedding, and with only a smaller official time allocation. But this will not serve

(Continued)

(Continued)

anyone's purpose in the longer term. It may sound greedy on our part but the embedding should not be seen as a part of the provision, but rather a way to prove that ML is a legitimate means of communication for real purposes. The way to 'save time' in the longer run is to give more but to ask for more back. ML can contribute to the whole curriculum by taking some of that content in every single subject (including Literacy!) and presenting it to children and asking them to work on it in the target language. But first it has to be established as an aspect of school life which has real status and real support from all staff no matter what their capability. In return the school and the school population should see an increase in confidence, self-esteem and an opening out towards the new horizons, which greater cultural exposure can provide. School linking, backed by two-way language use, is so much more satisfying than the realisation that both sides just have to use English, and that we cannot quite deliver what the other school seems able to do.

The chapter has tried to provide very practical strategies to offer a full range of experiences to pupils in schools. These have not been specific to age, ability or experience but organised to demonstrate the importance of elements such as the seven Cs. The next set of chapters will look in more detail at specific ages or specific stages of development of the language curriculum and of pupil competence in a school.

Key and Further Reading 📖

QCA's 'Big Picture', accessible at www.qca.org.uk/libraryAssets/media/Big_Picture_2008.pdf is a useful overview of how the role of individual subjects is only a small part of something much larger in terms of global educational focus. This is also, conversely, a useful way of showing the breadth and scope of any one subject. We would include Primary ML in this view.

For an interesting view on foreign language materials, culture and tasks (written with secondary learners in mind) see Allford, D. (2000) 'Pictorial images, lexical phrases and culture'. *Language Learning Journal.* 22(1): 45–51.

To see a practical example from an EAL context, look at: www.naldic.org.uk/docs/resources/vignettes.cfm and choose 'Primary Vignette 1'. This shows how a teacher can be sensitive to the language needs of learners without sacrificing challenge and cognition.

3

How might I structure language learning in the Early Years Foundation Stage?

Introductory vignette

Emily (5 years, giving out fruit): *'Une orange?'*

Edwin (5 years): 'Thank you.'

Emily: *'Qu'est-ce que c'est? Merci!'*

Edwin: *'Merci!'*

This short and entirely spontaneous conversation between two children in a Reception class (YR) took place only six weeks after the children had started to learn French. What does it demonstrate? The children are happy to interact with each other in French; they even remind each other of conventions of politeness using the new language. In this case the daily fruit time was used to integrate the ML into class routines very effectively: after only a few weeks of learning the children do not just respond to the teacher's questions but are able to use a complex question form themselves naturally and with clear purpose.

Chapter objectives

- To summarise how children of 3–5 years learn.
- To explore how children can best access another language.
- To establish what makes them successful learners of the new language.

(Continued)

(Continued)

- To offer some sample activities for each Area of Learning.
- To look from a teacher's perspective at how to plan ML into a stimulating curriculum.

Relevant Q Standards: Q1, Q2, Q4, Q6, Q8, Q10, Q11, Q14, Q15, Q18, Q19, Q22, Q25, Q29, Q32, Q33

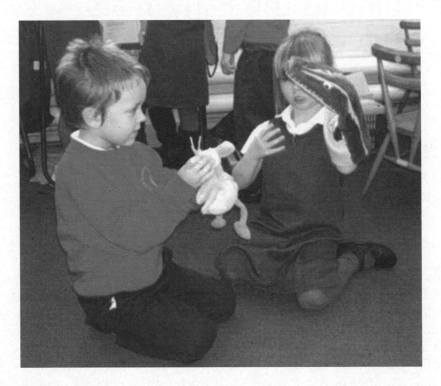

Figure 3.1

 Initial reflection point

What might these children be doing and how might it connect with language learning?

Response

The children are playing with two of the puppets regularly used in French lessons. They are singing a French song together which they have previously learned. The activity is both authentic and spontaneous. They have not been asked to do this by the teacher but have themselves asked to play with the puppets as part of child-initiated play.

How do children in the Early Years Foundation Stage learn?

The Rumbold Committee Report (DES 1990) summarised the relevant characteristics of learning in the Foundation Stage:

- Children are active learners, operating most effectively through first-hand experience.

- Children are naturally curious; their imagination can be nurtured by responding to their curiosity.

- Interaction with others is crucial. Learning should take place in a social context.

- Talk is central to the learning process.

  For the early years educator, therefore, the process of education – how children are encouraged to learn – is as important as, and inseparable from, the content – what they learn. We believe that this principle must underlie all curriculum planning for the under fives. (1990: 9)

The Early Years Foundation Stage Statutory Framework (2008) and *Practice Guidance* (2008) are both available to download from www. standards.dfes.gov.uk/eyfs/site/resource/pdfs.htm. These documents represent the most current government policy on the birth–5 teaching and learning context. Also on the same website is a short research review article on how young children learn (David 2003) which addresses the themes of pedagogy, curriculum and assessment and adult roles. In addition to these documents, works by Edgington (2004), Riley (2007) and Moyles (2007) all deal with approaches to good teaching and learning for the age range and, more importantly, they also address the developmental issues which ground the pedagogy in terms of child psychology. Researchers into the 3–5 stage of education seem to attain a strong unity about values, approaches and desired outcomes and place a strong emphasis on the role of the professional practitioner as the interpreter of attainment.

And what stands out from all of the writing about this stage is the accent on creativity and independence. Far from being vessels to be filled, children in the 3–5 age range in school are given and exercise an enormous amount of choice in how and where and when they learn. The onus on teachers is to plan for this choice. There is an expectation that the whole curriculum can be delivered both indoors and outdoors, for example. Children are expected for at least some of the time to initiate activity, fashioning their own tasks out of the resources they find and so to control their own learning. They are given roles that start to establish collaboration, community and understanding of others. Children need to be engaged by teachers and other adults who have this enormous responsibility to provide stimulating learning environments because at this stage children are not especially gifted in rationalising why they have to do something. Even when there is a strong government dictum, for example over the teaching of reading (Rose, 2006), and material to support this emerges (DCSF 2007), successful progress is highly dependent on gifted practitioners who can make the activities fast-paced, varied and highly active and so draw children into the learning cycle. If the children enjoy the work they will learn to read, but if they do not, they will not. Synthetic phonics by itself is not the recipe. How practitioners use synthetic phonics is the key.

Given that the process of how children learn is as important as the content we should not separate the learning of a new language from the rest of the curriculum but aim for an approach which integrates ML naturally into activities which encourage children's learning. In fact ML can provide opportunities for both whole-class or larger group work, such as singing or listening to a story, and more spontaneous free choice activity, such as activity in the role play area or outdoors which a small number of children might choose to do. In this sense it can perform a full role in the Early Years Foundation Stage (EYFS) curriculum, developing concentration and communal self-discipline at some point and firing children's individual imagination at others.

 Reflection point

We are now going to take a look at a few short activities around the names of colours as one example which is often introduced at the early stages of language learning. What are the children in each scenario doing? Are they actively involved? Are there elements of curiosity? Are the children interacting? Does the learning take place in a social context?

1   In the first scenario the teacher uses traditional language methodology, saying the names of the colours while holding up different coloured flash cards or objects. The children listen and are encouraged to repeat the names of the colours. They might then put the different coloured cards or objects in a bag and pass it around in a circle while music in the target language is playing. When the music stops the teacher asks the child who holds the bag to take a certain colour out of the bag.

2   In the second scenario the teacher chooses two toys, two characters from a story the children have read, and three different coloured bags. The teacher then hides the toys in the different bags, asking the children to try to remember where they are *'Où est le petit chien? Dans le sac bleu, dans le sac rouge ou dans le sac vert?'* The children respond by saying the colour of the bag.

3   In the third scenario the teacher is setting up an art and craft activity for making a dragon's mask. The children start by choosing the colour of their mask with the teacher asking *'Tu voudrais faire une masque rouge ou verte?'*

Response

The third scenario has the most purposeful use of language as this is entirely focused on the art activity and uses language merely to establish how the children are going to start (by choosing the colour of paper they want to use). In the second scenario the teacher is using a 'flow' of natural language to pose a question and is offering a choice of answers so that the children can respond at any level they wish – they might just nod at the right option, or they might say a colour or they might produce the whole phrase. It does not matter which they do as the main purpose is that they understand the language used and understand as well that they can make a choice. In the first scenario there is a real focus on 'fixing' the vocabulary by repetition and at this point there is no real purpose involved except to learn the language. The circle game offers more of a separate rationale as children enjoy playing guessing games and finding objects.

As teachers, we need to be clear in our own minds what we are doing and why. These scenarios might all be used at different points, but we should perhaps ensure that we do find a balance. If we only used the type of activities indicated in the first scenario, the children might lose out on some essential roles of language.

Using the target language

Our aim is very much for children to be able to communicate in the foreign language, and not just recognise and recall lists of words. This can be achieved by exposing children from an early age to rich language and to the use of new language for different purposes of communication.

Since the advent of the National Curriculum (KS3 and KS4) for ML in 1992 there has been a strong recommendation from government, CILT (National Centre for Languages), teacher educators, LA advisors/consultants and OFSTED for teachers to maximise the use of target language in the classroom. This stems partly from the ideas of Krashen and Terrell (1983) that if we mirror immersion techniques we will more acquire (a natural process) than have to learn language (an artificial one). Understandably teachers with lower confidence find this one of the most daunting aspects of starting to teach ML in primary schools. There are two very different but very important ways to address this.

In the first instance, because a teacher cannot suddenly 'magic up' language competence or confidence that he or she does not have, the school should look at resourcing the start-up of the subject with multimedia materials that have audio support. There are a number of options here (see Chapter Ten for examples). The advantage of these materials is that they contain native speaker recorded stories, songs, games and in many cases video extracts, all of which save the teacher from having to manage the language input independently but also provide a model so that the teacher's own target language command can steadily and invisibly improve. The resources can be used via data projector and are colourful, well-paced, lively and provide very good models. The younger the children, the easier they find it to discriminate and produce very good target language pronunciation and intonation. So the resources also have an invaluable role in starting children with very good models.

The second route is one for the teacher to work on. Many native speakers admit that they find it difficult to modify their language sufficiently to prevent confusing children with too much of a rich language diet. Hitting the middle path between stilted, over-repetitive, even unnatural target language use and completely unstructured use of anything and everything that comes out of a native speaker repertoire is vital. We need riches but not a surfeit! Non-native speakers are often far more able to stand in the children's shoes and to select forms which will be more accessible, perhaps because they contain more cognates (words which resemble each other between two languages) and which the children will recognise, make sense of and start to internalise relatively quickly.

So teachers should script out a range of expressions (see below) and use them regularly in a natural rhythm and at a natural speed. All common classroom instructions can be given in the foreign language, introducing a few at a time but then using them often. This can happen throughout the week, not just in the slots where the teacher focuses on whole-class language work.

To make the change between languages clear, it has proved successful to use a puppet which the children can associate with the new language. Whenever the teacher speaks in the ML, he or she can use the puppet to make the change clear to the children. Research into bilingualism (Baker 2006) has highlighted the importance of children associating each language with a certain person (or group of people) who should persevere using that particular language. A puppet can take on this function of indicating the change to the foreign language, in addition the children can familiarise themselves with the idea that the new language might only be used in certain situations or with certain people. If the children then integrate the puppet into their role-play they will understand that they can only use French when they want to interact with the puppet. First they will use greetings and simple songs or perhaps finger rhymes that they have learned. But they will soon feel the need to express more. One boy in a reception class was observed having a conversation with the French puppet, Croco the crocodile, offering different fruits from the shop in the role-play area. Owen (five years) was familiar with the question *'Qu'est-ce que c'est?'* and he knew the names of some fruits in French from his regular exposure to French during fruit time. He now put the two elements together, asking the puppet *'Qu'est-ce que c'est ... une orange, Croco? Qu'est-ce que c'est ... une banane, Croco?'* After a while he came over to the teacher and asked 'How do you say "Would you like" in French?'. The teacher modelled the use of *tu voudrais* but Owen didn't go back to the puppet – Croco had eaten all the fruits he'd been offered and he was full up – so didn't use the new structure this time. He might be able to recover it on another occasion, or he might not remember it. With this age group simply telling them the language is not enough. The important element in this incident is that he realised he needed more language and asked for it. It also shows how children respond when they feel the need to use language for a real purpose and how adding new language can most successfully be based on real communication for real purposes. Only this will, in time, create independent learners and ultimately confident users of the new language. If the teacher sets up the puppet as only speaking the target language then the children readily accept that they need to try to understand what the puppet says and to try to use the target language to speak to the puppet.

The teacher can also use stories and songs as sources of expressions, phrases and sentences to be used elsewhere if the context arises. Similarly 'commentary' language may also be spoken in the target language. For example, some new sand appearing in the sand tray might seem a stronger colour, and to use the foreign language to comment, *'Le sable est très jaune aujourd'hui!'*, reinforces a colour and the words for sand and today without it being a specific learning point. In these circumstances children will often reply in English and this does not matter. The intention at this stage of using strong target language is to set up the flow and the natural process of interpreting.

A vital language skill is to be able to select from a stream the key words which carry significant meaning. This is not easy but unless it is on the agenda right from the start it will become a barrier frighteningly quickly. Perhaps because children are still developing their mother tongue strongly at the 3–5 stage they are unconsciously accustomed to making sense of words being used in new contexts and even of completely new words. They continuously integrate the learning of language with doing something else (hearing a story, singing a song, playing a game) and this is shown by the way they naturally also play with sounds and words at this age. It appears from our observations that children in EYFS find hearing a foreign language much more natural and can cope with the unknown much better than older children can. As long as the global meaning is clear and they know what they have to do, as long as they understand enough of a stimulus 'text' to enjoy it and participate, they do not worry about each individual word. This should encourage teachers to tap into the resources available so children hear a mix of native speaking voices and for teachers to slowly increase their own skills in using the language.

Some practical examples follow of how we might embed our use of language into routines. These tend to have, as we have said above, a teacher initiated, pupil receptive focus. The pupils more often act on the instruction than use the language themselves, but the scope is there for them to start to use the language too. We saw in the introductory vignette and with the incident with Croco that some children will readily use the language for their own play or at those times when they briefly become the 'responsible adult' such as distributing the fruit.

Whole-class routines can include:

- Taking and responding to the register in the new language can be at the level of a simple greeting, but can sometimes be extended to asking how the children feel. One teacher recounted how she met a child coming towards the school office and asked her in French how she was. The child responded in French that she felt ill today – in fact she was coming to lie down as she had a stomach ache. This shows the true communicative power of the work they did on a regular basis – the response to the foreign language in the foreign language was entirely natural.

- General instructions (sitting down, getting in a circle, finding a partner, getting ready for play outside, lining up, washing hands, tidying up) can be introduced and built up gradually. In each case the teacher can use gesture and modelling to support understanding until the children recognise the instructions and will then find the support can slowly be dispensed with.

- Handing out milk or fruit gives children the opportunity to name the item they want in very simple language but also, as we saw, to 'be the teacher' and use some additional target language themselves in those interactions.

- Giving praise. Children will sometimes also imitate this between themselves.

- General display in the classroom with labels in the new language will expose the children to the written form from an early age.

Using these familiar routines, the new language can be integrated in a natural way which the children will soon adapt to. If practitioners feel concerned about confusing the children and, as we explored above, if your primary aim is to use language purposefully, that is, to communicate meaningful content, it should not matter which language is being used as long as the children feel safe and supported.

Reflection point

Take three of the routines listed above and script the language you think you will need to use to ask children to carry out the routine. Consider how long the words and sentences are that you choose and look for ways of shortening them. But keep the language as authentic as possible.

However using the language for the routines is not enough of course – we can go further! The next section looks at how teachers can plan to embed ML activities into the EYFS curriculum.

Embedding ML activities into the EYFS curriculum

The EYFS curriculum is organised into six areas of learning (DfES 2007):

- personal, social and emotional development

- communication, language and literacy

- problem-solving, reasoning and numeracy

- knowledge and understanding of the world

- physical development

- creative development.

These areas of learning provide the basis for all planning and for the children's learning and ML should be no exception but integrated as far as possible into any activities. It is vital that ML specialist teachers working in the foundation stage, but not specifically trained for it, are aware of the EYFS curriculum structure and teaching methodologies in order to adapt their language work and integrate it into the children's learning. The following sample activities for each area of learning should exemplify the type of language activities which could be integrated easily into the curriculum.

Personal, social and emotional development (PSED)

Circle games can be played in the new language. These will encourage children to work in small or large groups and support their social development, such as turn taking and sharing with others. During a simple but very popular circle game, one of the children has to leave the room while one of the other children is hiding a certain object (in this example, sea animals) behind their back or in their lap. The first child is then called back into the circle, where he or she has to find the hidden object by asking the children in the circle 'Have you got the fish?' ('*As-tu le poisson?*'). The children asked can simply reply with '*Oui/Non*' or add more language, for example 'No, I'm sorry' ('*Non, désolé/e*') or by saying that they haven't got it, '*Non, je n'ai pas de poisson*', depending on their level of confidence. The game can be played until the child in the middle has found the object – perhaps count how many children have been asked or decide at the start how many 'goes' each child should get.

Other circle activities could involve counting and simple decision making. Put a range of objects into a bag and two hoops in the middle. All the children sit in a circle and count while passing the bag on to the next child. When they reach a certain number they stop counting. The child holding the bag takes an object out of the bag, hears a question from the teacher and decides if the object should go into the '*Oui*' hoop or in the '*Non*' hoop. The teacher can control the language input in this case by using any relevant question associated with the current topic focus and the object the child has taken from the bag, for example, '*Le lion habite dans la mer? Oui ou non?*' Children can be asked if it is the correct response. Other turn taking could involve children choosing a song which they might sing at the start of a language session, or a small group game such as bingo with mini cards.

A carefully prepared role-play area can provide opportunities for play and learning to experience different cultural backgrounds.

Certain stories with themes around friendship (*Die kleine Maus sucht einen Freund/La souris qui cherche un ami* by Eric Carle) or being frightened in the dark (*Lilou a peur du noir*) can be read in the target language to contribute additional support to children's emotional development in these areas. Children often reveal through their responses just how much they do follow of a story read in this way.

Early learning goals from EYFS which can be supported through the foreign language can include the following. By the end of EYFS, children should

- have a developing respect for their own cultures and beliefs and those of other people

- form good relationships with adults and peers

- work as part of a group or class, taking turns and sharing fairly, understanding that there needs to be agreed values and codes of behaviour for groups of people, including adults and children, to work together harmoniously (DCSF 2008).

Communication, language and literacy (CLL)

Learning a new language can also underpin children's development of skills in English by widening their overall experience of a range of sounds through the foreign language. If songs, stories and rhymes are used regularly and the children are exposed to rich language from the start, they will experience listening to a range of new sounds and a different intonation. Far from confusing them, this will add value to their ability to discriminate and underline how important it is to listen carefully, with concentration. Listening to stories, joining in with songs and rhymes is a familiar style of learning to the children and this offers a completely separate dimension to this valuable activity. Being encouraged to join in when they are ready, the children experiment with sounds during whole-class story telling and singing. Natural repetition in stories will encourage children to participate and they will be able to do this both individually if they are very confident or as part of a group if they are less secure. If you watch EYFS-aged children listening to a story or singing you can see how often they look around to see what other members of the group are doing and then often start to join in. Additionally, the children experience not just the new language but often a different culture first-hand while engaging with a story.

Teachers might want to start using simple stories first, for example, an 'open flap' book such as *Où es-tu, maman?* which uses a comparatively small amount of language but a repetitive structure which invites the children to join in very quickly (*Oui ou non, Où es-tu? Toc, toc, qui est là?*). Children can be encouraged to sustain concentration and active listening by responding to certain words or phrases giving a physical response (for example, touch parts of the body if they hear it while listening to the story *Va-t-en, Grand monstre vert* (*Go Away, Big Green Monster!*), or joining in with the actions and sounds while listening to *La chasse à l'ours* (*We're Going on a Bear Hunt*). A story read in the target language can also provide the starting point for literacy activities such as sequencing pictures of the story, focussing on beginning, middle and end. Teachers should choose a story which fits in with theme as far as possible and should not worry that children might not understand every word as long as they can follow the story line. It is important not to translate but to let children engage with the story, whether in English or in the target language, and to use gesture, mime and visuals to support comprehension. Stories can be used for active listening or simply for enjoyment.

Songs can be excellent opportunities to engage with the different sound system of the new language. Teachers should choose songs which, as far as possible, allow children to be active while singing, for example *Savez-vous planter les choux* (pretending to plant with different parts of the body), *Meunier, tu dors* (slow and fast turning of windmill), *Tourne, tourne petit moulin* (movements of different objects or animals), *Petit escargot* (actions for parts of snail and rain). The words of these songs are all available on the website www.momes.net/comptines/comptines-chansons.html. Some also have midi-file style music with the words so you can learn the tune.

In the early stage of *Letters and Sounds* rhyme is an important device to help focus on sound, because being able to discriminate whether two words rhyme is a good first step towards being able to hear different sounds accurately and younger children in an EYFS setting also really enjoy playing with words in this way. So teachers can also explore in the foreign language rhyming words through authentic songs and rhymes such as French comptines, such as *Bateau, ciseaux*, where the teacher uses pictures to stimulate the use of the rhyming words and can alter the sequence to ensure that the children are actively involved.

We can see then that early learning goals which can be supported through another language can include the following. By the end of EYFS, children should

- sustain attentive listening, responding to what they have heard with relevant comments, questions or actions

- listen with enjoyment, and respond to stories, songs and other music, rhymes and poems and make up their own stories, songs, rhymes and poems

- retell narratives in the correct sequence, drawing on language patterns of stories (DCSF 2008).

Problem solving, reasoning and numeracy (PSRN)
Numeracy work in the new language can support children's mathematical skills. A boy with autism was reluctant to join in with whole-class counting in English. Having learned a finger rhyme and a simple song which involved movement in French, he was observed later counting in French while he was lining up the engines of a train set. This even constituted a basic level of evidence for his EYFS Profile as it was clear that he was counting properly, that is, with a sense of the meaning of number.

Teachers can also use the target language and encourage pupils to use it while carrying out sorting activities, for example of 2D shapes (*C'est un cercle/un triangle/un rectangle/carré*).

There are very many opportunities to use the foreign language during normal everyday numeracy work, such as putting the correct number of fruits and so on into baskets; adding missing numbers to a number line; looking at the colour patterns of beads; finding as many ways as possible to colour in trains with three carriages; using only three colours as part of a simple investigation. Teachers can also use EYFS numeracy websites, such as materials for the interactive whiteboard and simply talk round them in the foreign language. They can play domino games and board games in the foreign language too. In this way the foreign language can be used whenever the teacher (or the children) wish to – it does not have to remain in its set slot.

Examples of French finger rhymes (*jeux de doigts*) for counting include the following:

Using the five fingers of a hand in turn:

Un bonbon

Deux bonbons

Trois bonbons

Quatre bonbons

Cinq bonbons

Miam, c'est bon!

Tapping increasing numbers of fingers on the palm of the other hand:

Un petit doigt qui frappe

Deux petits doigts qui frappent

Trois petits doigts qui frappent

Quatre petits doigts qui frappent

Cinq petits doigts qui frappent

Un, deux, trois, quatre, cinq

Et voilà ma main

Early learning goals that can be supported through a new language include the following. By the end of EYFS, children should

- say and use number names in order in familiar contexts

- count reliably up to ten everyday objects

- recognise numerals up to nine

- use language such as 'greater', 'smaller', heavier' or 'lighter' to compare quantities

- find one more or one less than a number from one to ten (DCSF 2008).

Knowledge and understanding of the world (KUW)

This area contains a range of what we see elsewhere as separate National Curriculum subjects. Science, history, geography, religious education (RE) and information and communication technology (ICT) are all subsumed into this general area. There are numerous ways in which this area can be brought into the foreign language work, depending on the current topic that is being used to plan the curriculum activity. Some examples within the science and geography areas follow.

The teacher can use the target language for instructions and to elicit simple responses, such as through sorting activities (for example, toys according to size – big or small; materials which are hard or soft; liquids which are warm or cold). The children can suggest the correct habitat for different wild animals or different animals for different habitats, for example: Where does the tiger live? Which animal lives in the desert? The children can experience hot and cold by holding ice cubes until they melt and offering reasons, for example, because my hand is hot.

Early learning goals which can be supported through a foreign language are as follows. By the end of EYFS, children should

- investigate objects and materials by using all of their senses as appropriate

- look closely at similarities, differences, patterns and change

- build and construct with a wide range of objects, selecting appropriate resources and adapting their work where necessary

- find out about their environment, and talk about those features they like and dislike.

- begin to know about their own cultures and beliefs and those of other people (DCSF 2008).

Physical development (PD)

This is a good context for the foreign language to be used for instructions for physical activity. This can include basic aerobic type activity such as: walk / run / jump / hop / go faster / go more slowly / stop. Children can count their heartbeat during warming up / cooling down exercises. They are limited as to how high they can count of course but it is possible to monitor if it is 'fast counting' or 'slow counting', which allows them to see the difference. Action songs can be chosen so that children can use movement and drama while singing. Good examples of this might be (in French) 'Le fermier dans son pré' or 'Promenons-nous dans les bois' both of which can be found at www.momes.net/comptines/comptines-chansons.html. Children often like to learn simple dances or clapping rhymes that can also contribute to a more cultural appreciation of a target language speaking country, especially if a video can be shown so that they gain a sense of other elements such as traditional dress.

Early learning goals that can be as well supported through activity in a foreign language as through English are as follows. By the end of EYFS, children should

- move with confidence, imagination and in safety

- move with control and coordination

- show awareness of space, of themselves and of others

- use a range of small and large equipment (DCSF 2008).

Creative development (CD)

If we look at the EYFS Practice Guidance, especially the Early Learning Goals, it is evident that in some respects the creative arts, such as music, art and dance are themselves viewed as languages. Children are encouraged to express themselves through alternative modes and not just through words. Therefore a foreign language can be as easily used to create the stimulus and to give simple instructions as English. Here the teacher should try to provide resources from a variety of cultures, associated with the language, including music, dance and art. Again the teacher can use simple language to set up practical activities and so use language for a real purpose.

Early learning goals that can be supported through the target language are as follows. By the end of EYFS, children should

- respond in a variety of ways to what they see, hear, smell, touch and feel

- express and communicate their ideas, thoughts and feelings by using a widening range of materials, suitable tools, imaginative and role-play, movement, designing and making, and a variety of musical instruments

- explore colour, texture, shape, form and space in two or three dimensions

- recognise and explore how sounds can be changed, sing simple songs from memory, recognise repeated sounds and sound patterns and match movements to music

- use their imagination in art and design, music, dance, imaginative and role-play stories (DCSF 2008).

Example of medium-term planning – integrating a foreign language into a topic

This section of the chapter offers planning for a topic on wild animals. It is important to stress that the class are taking wild animals as their overall topic and the work in the foreign language forms a part of this. In other words it is not a discrete foreign language topic on wild animals, rather activities in a foreign language will be embedded into a broader approach that also involves existing planning for the topic in English.

The following are some typical activities associated with the topic; many of them can be set up in a foreign language and the teacher can use a number of stories. Many of those mentioned here are available in English as well as in French, German or Spanish. It is probably best to use a story in only one language rather than in both.

Area of learning	EYFS learning objectives	Possible experiences	Resources
Personal, social and emotional development	• Be confident to try new experiences	• Play circle games, (hide and seek – *As-tu le pingouin? Un, deux, trois... qui est dans le sac?*) • Play 'Loto' (*Qui a deux chameaux?*) • Encourage children to take turns	• (Finger) puppets for role-play • Toys/objects/'feely bags' for circle games • Bingo game with animals
Communication, language and literacy	• Listen attentively and respond to stories	• Set up role-play area as a vet's practice • Use puppets to act out stories • Use a selection of non-fiction books to find out about different habitats	• Stories: 'La souris qui cherche un ami', 'Je veux ma banane', 'Petites chouettes', 'Bébés chouettes', 'Le petit pingouin' • Songs: 'Tourne, tourne, petit moulin', 'Petit escargot', 'Les petits poisons', Renard, renard', 'Promenons-nous dans les bois'
Mathematical development	• Count reliably up to 10 everyday objects • Use language to compare quantities	• Play counting games • Sorting small/big animals	• Counting equipment • Compare bears large and small
Knowledge and understanding of the world	• Investigate objects and materials by using all senses • Look closely at similarities, differences, patterns and change • Observe, find out about and identify features in local environment	• Place animals in correct habitat (*Le chameau habite dans la mer ou dans le desert?*) • Make ice cubes and let them melt in hand	• Laminated pictures of different habitats (and visuals on interactive whiteboard)
Physical development	• Move with confidence and imagination	• Respond to story 'La chasse à l'ours' • Play playground	• Story: 'La chasse à l'ours' • Song:

Area of learning	EYFS learning objectives	Possible experiences	Resources
Creative development	• Explore colour, texture, shape, form and space • Sing simple songs from memory • Use imagination in art and design and imaginative role-play	game '*Promenons-nous dans les bois*' • Learn songs and accompany with movements and instruments • Make animal mask (*On fait des masques*) • Create 'hot' and 'cold' pictures (*Il fait chaud ou il fait froid? Les couleurs chaudes/froides*) • Paint and weave 'Elmer' patterns	'*Promenons-nous dans les bois* • Songs: '*Tourne, tourne, petit moulin*', '*Petit escargot*', '*Les petits poisons*', '*Renard, renard*', '*Promenons-nous dans les bois*' • Coloured card, paper, glue, crayons, paint, sand, sugar • Musical instruments

Example short-term lesson plan

For the story *Va-t-en, Grand monstre vert – Go Away, Big Green Monster*

Learning objectives

- To listen attentively to and respond to the story *Grand monstre vert* (CLL)
- To know some parts of the body (KUW)
- To create a collage (face of monster) – explore colour, texture and shape in two dimensions, to manipulate materials (CD)

Lesson outcomes

- Children will join in with story
- Children will place cut out parts of body (head/face) in the correct place
- Children will make their own 'monster' mask collages

Sequence of activities

Starter:

Warm-up – singing of familiar songs. Children take turns to choose. Teacher asks: '*Qui veut choisir une chanson?*'

Main activities:

1 Teacher reads the story *Grand monstre vert* for the first time, using mime, gesture, variation of voice, pointing to visuals in the book to support understanding. Invites children to join in with the repetitive phrases: *Partez! Va-t'en!* (supported by gesture)

(Continued)

(Continued)

2   The teacher has an empty head shape on the board and asks the class where the first item (for example, eyes) should be placed. Then volunteers come to place parts of the face in the correct place on board. Teacher asks questions such as '*Où est la bouche? Où sont les yeux?*' '*Viens et mets la bouche sur le visage.*' Teacher asks: '*C'est correct?*' to encourage children to join in, evaluate, be involved even if seated in the group.

3   Half of the group creates their own monsters (free choice for others). Teacher models the process and gives instructions in French: '*Tu veux faire un monstre rouge ou orange? Prends les ciseaux. Prends un crayon et écris le nom. Prends la colle et colle le nez sur le visage.*'

End of lesson:

Children put on their monster mask collages and show them to each other.

In the lesson plan above we can see that the teacher uses specific language at specific times and always with a purpose. The children are generally engaged in responding through action or simple language. An observation of this sequence showed that some children were unsure about where to place eyes or mouth on a blank face, so they were learning this aspect of knowledge while engaging with this material in the foreign language and not just 'doing French'. The total repertoire of language needed to accomplish this is actually quite small. In the starter activity it is the stock question, used always in a warm-up where the children will sing. In stages 2 and 3 of the main activity, there is a mix of commonly used classroom phrases – such as 'Where is?', 'Get...', 'Write your name', 'Stick...' – together with the vocabulary set for this topic, in this instance the parts of the head and face. In the story reading section, the book provides the 'script' of course so the teacher does not have to learn all of that language by heart. In between the teacher might well be using other familiar classroom instructions – such as 'Listen!', 'Sit quietly!', 'All stand up!' – but again this is language familiar to both the teacher and the children.

As we have said before the children may respond on a number of levels. They may simply nod or shake their heads, echo phrases or speak more spontaneously in the target language. This does not matter because the important issue is whether they understand and feel part of what is going on. The teacher should always of course look round the group during a story reading. The children's expressions and reactions and general behaviour will reveal whether or not they are engaged. Their comments, often in English, will show that they are understanding. At the end of the

Monstre vert sequence, where the monster gradually appears and then gradually disappears, a comment (in English) such as 'He's gone now' shows that the sense of what has happened in the story has been fully comprehended, partly through pictures, partly through text. The subsequent activity will use individual vocabulary items from that story and underpin the purely language element of the story, and the monster masks will again reflect the sense of what the class has been working on. If the children subsequently choose to hear the story again (and they often do) the story will be even more meaningful on a second reading precisely because the different linguistic and creative activities have contributed to a richer understanding.

 Reflection point

If you are in a position to plan and teach a lesson using a story, use the planning approach above to embed the story into a lesson which has an outcome for the children like the monster masks. When you have taught the lesson, make evaluation notes about what the children enjoyed and about any issues that arose.

If you are not yet in a position to do this, select a story in the foreign language and make two sets of notes: write suggestions for yourself about how you will read it (think of speed, intonation, emotional aspects of your reading, repetition) and summarise how it might link with other types of work (which could come before or after it).

Chapter summary

In this chapter we have tried to stress the importance of making the foreign language work as part of the overall integrated structure of the EYFS curriculum. We have spoken about how children learn and shown that the children do not easily separate out their experiences into different segments (apart from into enjoyable and less enjoyable categories). We have suggested that children naturally enjoy joining in with songs and stories and that this is often the source of much of their learning. But they can in some cases also be remarkably independent in their language use because they do not feel any inhibitions – language is language and is to be used. We have seen examples of children beginning to use the target language when interacting with each other (during role play, when playing with puppets, during everyday routines such as giving out fruit).

(Continued)

(Continued)

For all these reasons, to make the ML element deliberately 'different' is not really justified. The children themselves speak about their ML experience and integrate it into their wider lives as we see when we hear comments such as these:

'I love this song. I always sing it in the bath.' (Lizzie, five years)

'Isabella always sings French songs at home and she speaks French to her brother who is in Year 8.' (A mother about her five-year-old daughter)

Another mother reported that her daughter was teaching her younger brother, aged two, songs in French!

'I really like playing with *le poisson*.' (Owen, five years, showing that languages can be mixed in a way that is similar to what happens with bilingual children. But that this is not significant – it is a form of playing with language that underpins language learning.)

We have also tried to show through a series of practical examples how, even with limited language, a teacher can achieve this integration. Teacher vision is needed for the planning and for the conceptualisation of integration, in the sense of how to interlock different activities both with each other and with the general ongoing topic. But the language demands are much less than some teachers fear and a good EYFS teacher can be a good ML teacher too.

We must remember that children of this age have an intriguing blend of 'innocence', by which we mean the ability to suspend reality and to use their imaginations, and 'experience' by which we mean the ability to see reality as it is. When listening to a group of Reception children talking about how much they liked the crocodile puppet, we asked the question: 'And can Croco speak English?' Daisy (four years), gave a withering look and replied: 'Well, it's only a puppet. It's the teacher that makes it talk!' We can really enjoy children's creativity and imagination but we ignore their capabilities and their sophistication at our peril!

Key and Further Reading 📖

An interesting document with reviews of five different curriculum approaches for early years can be found at: www.standards.dfes.gov.uk/eyfs/resources/downloads/31672150.pdf. It does not specifically mention foreign language learning at all, but you can read about the roles ascribed to language in general and to the 'different languages' children use, in one case imagining how it would look if a teacher were using a foreign language for part of that curriculum.

An American view on early language learning and its long-term benefits can be found in Stewart, J.H. (2005) 'Foreign Language Study in Elementary Schools: Benefits and Implications for Achievement in Reading and Math'. *Early Childhood Journal*. 33(1): 11–16.

A Norwegian view on English in the kindergarten was published can be found in Elvin, P., Maagerø, E. and Simonsen, B. (2007) 'How Do the Dinosaurs Speak in England? English in Kindergarten'. *European Early Childhood Education Research Journal*. 15(1): 71–86.

How should I begin to offer language learning in KS1 and KS2?

Introductory vignette

Tristan (8 years): 'My favourite lesson is maths and my second favourite lesson is French.'

After pausing for a few seconds, Tristan changes his mind: 'No, my third favourite is French, my second favourite is maths and my favourite lesson is maths in French.'

Comment

This comment by a child in the first year of learning French shows that children's enjoyment of learning languages can from the start be linked to the wider curriculum. When introducing languages we should resist the notion that this is a 'separate' subject. While it might be appealing to create an exotic flavour around French, German, Spanish or other language we are offering, this difference can become counter-productive in time. Add-ons are rarely seen as positively as integral components; rather, like other accessories, they may be discarded or replaced.

Chapter objectives
- **To explore how we might start to teach a language by reflecting on languages in the community, how languages are learned and how to include aspects of culture from the beginning.**

(Continued)

(Continued)

- To suggest appropriate activities for language learning in the first year and to note any differences between ML in KS1 or at the start of KS2.
- To establish throughout the strategies that are likely to make children successful learners of the new language.
- To offer some sample activities.
- To look from a teacher's perspective at how to plan ML into the curriculum.

Relevant Q Standards: Q1, Q2, Q4, Q6, Q8, Q10, Q11, Q14, Q15, Q18, Q19, Q22, Q25, Q29, Q32, Q33

 Initial reflection point

Consider the following description of a classroom activity. What are the children doing? What are they learning?

A group of Y3 children look at a Spanish website showing stationery, for example www.elcorteingles.es/tiendas_e/cda/mt/tv_mt/0,5415,PD 12382!ECI,FF.html or toys, for example www.ludomecum.com/index. php saying in Spanish whether or not they like the items and colours. They also look at the layout of the website, discussing what certain links may be and exploring them to see what is there.

Response

The children may use limited active Spanish while doing this task, but they will gain in other ways. They will have access to the culture of children of their own age and will discover that they have very similar tastes and interests to their own, but that there are also some differences. By exploring the links they will meet some key words in Spanish and use their own knowledge of the merchandise they see to infer some of the descriptive language. They will meet vocabulary which interests them and over which they have some control. Similar websites could be used with Y1 classes, but preferably in a whole-class context with the teacher guiding the conversation, but the pupils still managing the choice of links.

How do we start with complete beginners at Y1 or Y3?

We offer here a suggestion for how you might like to manage the first two lessons. Language learning should not happen in a vacuum, but should be connected to the class context in as meaningful a way as possible. In cities in England children in schools have had access to a number of languages for a long time and that now applies much more generally to all regions of England. From current data, accessible from CILT (www.cilt.org.uk/faqs/langspoken.htm), we see that 14.3 per cent of all primary age children have a language other than English as a first language and that in London schools there are more than 300 languages spoken. Although this book has used French, German and Spanish for its examples, it is very important that we appreciate the languages children already know, and in some schools community languages are chosen to be the languages all pupils learn. Both the KS2 framework for languages and QCA schemes of work for ML suggest building on children's existing knowledge and this includes locating the learning of a language in a context where languages are real, used and vital. In order to develop an interest in the culture of other nations we should acknowledge the interest and insight children might already have gained outside school, either through family, culture, religion or holidays. Even if a conventional European language is the one chosen for the school, a good starting point for the more general appreciation of the importance of all languages is to carry out a survey of which languages are spoken either in the class or in the whole school.

This visible proof that cultural diversity in school is valued and regarded as a source of learning easily leads to a discussion as to why it is important to learn other languages. From there you may also like to talk to the class about how babies learn language in the first place. By eliciting from the children that listening is the key element and that babies have to work out what things mean by watching, listening, thinking as well as imitating, the key components of language classroom activity will start to become clear. Of course this should not be too time-consuming. An abstract discussion either about the importance of language learning or about how we best learn language is no substitute for learning some language and enjoying the process. But it is still vital to find a way to start children thinking about these very important elements as they begin. Leaving it until later will mean that in some cases a restricted view of language learning may be instilled at the start, and later may be too late.

Embedding culture and content into an early lesson plan

One way to achieve a number of these aims from the beginning is to start with a strong cultural focus and this is probably often achieved through a geographical theme for a very early lesson. Look at maps, begin to establish where your target language is spoken. Limit the

Figure 4.1   Satellite image from Google Earth

language, but still use full sentences for comprehension, and also use extensive visual support. For Y1 this would probably just include France, Germany or Spain to begin with, but with Y3 you could extend this to world language coverage. Satellite images are a very good way of demonstrating this, as their reality often excites children. (The glacial deposits in Norway, Iceland and Switzerland usually draw comments.) Using Google Earth to find a specific location is a further progression that reinforces for the children the reality of other countries. A progression from western hemisphere into Europe to highlight the UK and Spain (for Y1), but then back out again to show South America and a focus on the number of countries where Spanish is spoken for Y3 allows the wider importance of the language to emerge for older pupils.

You can then move to showing pictures of places from these different countries but of course avoiding stereotypical images (the croissants and castanets phenomenon!). Pictures of urban and rural and of coastal and inland Spain already offer contrasts and challenge stereotypes. But if you add to that, for Y3, the different landscapes of South America and the urban and rural populations of diverse societies such as Argentina, Peru and Mexico, you have a powerful and exciting montage. Also depending on whether you are working with Y1 or Y3 you can restrict and expand the number of pictures you show and you can do this with the satellite images by building on prior knowledge or teaching something new.

This activity needs to be approached sensitively as we are certainly not suggesting you overwhelm the class with too much too quickly. The associated language can be limited to the names of countries and continents (and perhaps oceans) in Spanish (which all builds on some prior knowledge), some very simple material perhaps using simple description around the images but highlighting adjectives such as *bueno, bello, estupendo, grande, pequeño* and perhaps some colours. Those words that you might use to praise the children can be included in both contexts from the start. For a Y3 class you could introduce some numbers through comparing the time zones and give an opportunity to move from saying *'hablan español'* to *'y yo hablo español'*. There will also be a range of comments and questions in English, some of which you might be able to respond to at least partly in Spanish.

In these ways you achieve at the very beginning of language learning the cultural link, the fact that language is a vibrant medium through which you learn things. Through the questioning and very simple commentary where possible on the pictures, you will also give a sense of joining in and having fun using the language.

How do we start to use language and teach language? What types of activities and what materials should we use?

A book such as this should not set out to recommend any particular commercial material. We have occasionally referred to the resource pack *A La Française* (Tobutt and Roche 2007) for examples of activities because it is mainly authored by one of the writers of this book and therefore exemplifies our own practice. It is important that children starting a language experience a good variety of material and so all teachers will undoubtedly wish to choose resources which offer stimuli that they themselves cannot easily provide. A good example of this is authentic video material and we also referred to the course 'Early Start' in a previous chapter because it centres most units around some material filmed in the country, and because it is available in French, German and Spanish. The use of such video can only enrich language learning and rationalise it for children who perhaps do not actually visit any of the countries where the chosen target language is spoken.

Any resource that offers such video should be considered as an option for classroom use, and we recommend that teachers seeking commercial resources look for this element above all.

The teacher's own use of language is bound to be a very important factor from the beginning if the classroom is to feel connected to the language and the culture, and for that reason we start the rest of the chapter with the language of routines.

The language of routines

The language of whole-class routines can be established gradually from the beginning. When children need to be brought back together to listen or to look during these first lessons, then using '*escuchen*' and '*miren*' with appropriate gestures will establish those words quite quickly. We saw in Chapter Three that the whole structure of the day has potential to be used regularly in the target language, from lining up to go elsewhere at change-points, to giving out fruit (still relevant in Y1 at least), to moving from carpet to tables, to choosing equipment for tasks.

It is important that the children do not simply fall under a completely unstructured blanket of language and that we plan how we might introduce each of these activity types. At the earliest stages it is useful (for both the teacher and the children) that the language used is scripted. For less confident teachers scripting is a means of being secure that in the spontaneity of the classroom you can deliver what is needed at the right speed and with maximum benefit. This is also important for specialist teachers, as it will focus you on what you want to use and prevent the children from being exposed to too much language or too many variants on a theme. Fluency also has its drawbacks.

Basic verbs, such as listen, look, read, write, draw, take, choose, give me, show me, as single word items (in Spanish at least) become known quite quickly. They can be assembled into a wall display for Y3 classes with the visual and label placed together so that pupils can quickly check when they hear an instruction if they need to, although with non-verbal cues this would rarely be necessary. Classroom objects to go with these words are often taught as a topic and you can move into referring to these when you tidy up before the lesson starts. Stationery is often not needed in the early stages of learning but can still be brought into the conversation as most teachers want tables clear of pencils, rulers and rubbers so they will not be a distraction. Your aim is to move towards using only the target language for all areas of organisation and management in language lessons, and to expand this by having bursts of language time at other points in the week. Morning registration could become Spanish time, for example, or fruit could always be given out using the language. By trying out a couple of new instructions each week and ensuring you maintain the non-verbal support for as long as it is clearly needed, you should comfortably achieve your target language classroom within the first half of the year. If you know you need certain instructions, then you also know that you will use them in a purposeful context. Children are more likely to learn to respond, and in some cases use such phrases, if they actually mean something in the reality of classroom life.

Apart from the language of classroom routines, the importance of the children using language for interaction right from the start cannot be overemphasised. Expressions such as *sí/no, me gusta, pasame, por favor, gracias* can begin through natural repetition but children need to be able, even with very little language, to react and interact, not just to repeat what they hear, so the teacher should listen for examples of children using language more spontaneously and praise and reward it.

Using a puppet

As with children in Foundation Stage, the introduction of new language using a puppet who only speaks that language is a useful tool. Y3 classes are often still 'young' enough in ethos and imagination to enjoy this too. Certainly those who have learned a language in Key Stage 1 are reluctant to give up the puppet as they enter Y3. The puppet has two distinct functions. As a 'native speaker' of the language it can introduce new language to the children either directly or through whispering things to the teacher. As a stranger to the school it might not know things the children and teacher do know (for example all the children's names and ages) or it might not be able to read very well (especially if it is an animal puppet of some kind). A crocodile puppet, for example, probably would not know the names of the fruit even in his own language because he does not eat fruit. When the puppet makes mistakes the children tend to enjoy correcting it and of course they have to do this in the target language because the puppet does not speak English. In the early stages this can generate practice in giving names and ages because the puppet can name children wrongly and can be corrected either by the child (*me llamo Chloe*) or by another child (*se llama Martin*). This means that the more mechanistic practice of topic vocabulary, such as personal information through questions that everyone knows the answer to, is avoided. Because the teacher can have a dialogue with the puppet, he or she can model both questions and answers and can encourage children to imitate the questions too. Within this imaginative space some children will be more willing to speak and they will start to internalise the language by using it.

Stories

We have so far indicated the need to limit the language to what is manageable and not too overwhelming for the children, but an important factor in this is the context in which the language is used. Too many or too complex instructions from the teacher, which can cause anxiety because a response is expected, are likely to have a negative effect on confidence and eventually on motivation. But children are much more likely to manage more challenging text if it comes in the form of a story or song which invites them to listen and either join in as a class through singing or not respond unless they wish to. It is through this material (repetitive stories, songs and rhymes) that children are exposed to rich language, and hear or sometimes read more than they can produce. A story can at first engage, stimulating emotion and curiosity, then allow the class to meet new language, then provide a base for further connected but distinct activity within a topic. In this sense we are mirroring exactly how stories are used in English, especially as part of a topic-based curriculum. Alongside this there is the potential to pre-empt literacy development in the foreign language through phonological awareness activities and the following section will pick up this theme separately.

One example of easily accessible story and associated activities appropriate for Y1 and Y3 is Eric Carle's (1979) *Veux-tu devenir mon ami?* / *Die kleine Maus sucht einen Freund* (*Will you be my friend?*). Other Eric Carle books are equally effective and some are also available in Spanish. In KS1 this story can be used to introduce the names of different animals and children are likely to become involved in the story in two ways. Because of the repetitive pattern, where the little mouse asks other animals '*Veux-tu devenir mon ami?*', they will naturally start to echo, join in with and at times even lead the chorus as it appears on each new page. They will also meet and begin to remember and say the names of the animals as single word items. Even if children are not ready to join in with the longer question, the layout of the images allows the children to guess which animal is being asked next. This is also a valid experience as only a fraction of the image is seen before you turn the page and so close observation is encouraged. While going through the book, the teacher can easily use the story to involve the children through simple closed questions such as '*C'est un crocodile? Oui ou Non? C'est un lion?*' before the full picture is revealed on the next page. At this point the animal is named again but in a meaningful sentence as part of the ongoing story. In this case the text is: '*Le lion dit "non, merci".*' which is fully comprehensible and will generate further repetition and probably some imitation outside the context. It is very useful that the children can focus on individual words at some points but not lose the overall flow that this is a story and so has a value outside the learning of some words in French.

After a couple of readings, follow-up activities in KS1 could include the sequencing of the story: the children could place cut out mini cards with pictures of the animals in the correct order while the teacher re-tells the story. Later in the year, this task can also be used by confident children who might wish to retell the story in very simple language using the cards as a prop. An example of a follow-on task, drawing from the same theme, is to use the animals that the children have met in the story and for groups to place them in the correct habitat. If this is done at first visually the teacher can use the language items as part of a collaborative review and so move the vocabulary base to other areas of the animals topic. The fact that the children have made choices about where the animals should go means they will want to know if they are right. If the way to find this out is to access the foreign language vocabulary for these habitats by hearing the words along with non-verbal and visual support from the teacher, they will willingly participate as long as the process is active, lively and comprehensible. So the teacher can ask while showing the appropriate visuals – *'Le lion habite dans le désert ou à la savane? Dans le désert, oui?'* to elicit *'Non, à la savane.'* This process causes children to hear new words, process them and think of a response, but in a completely unambiguous context. If they have placed the animal correctly they will hear the right word and repeat it very happily. If not, they will focus more on content and learn the correct habitat. This is entirely proper as we should not be teaching vocabulary without the concepts being established. This method can do both almost simultaneously.

If the same story is used in KS2, the activities given above could still be used if this happens early in the year. With a Y3 class there might be a greater emphasis on introducing the written word to support the children's literacy development in the new language. You could focus on the 'i' phoneme in French, firstly discriminating the sound and identifying it in words such as *ami, crocodile, lion, souris, petite* before making the phoneme/grapheme connection. If we want children to be able to access language independently we need to make them aware of the different phonetic system which will enable them to decode new words and also develop their ability to encode with increasing independence.

The story can also be used as an introduction to classifying animals into herbivores, carnivores and omnivores, explaining what different animals eat. Again the teacher would need to exemplify this sorting process, using the appropriate language and using extensive closed and then open questions to fix the vocabulary through natural rather than forced repetition. From here, if this material is used later in Y3, the children can use short texts which the teacher might find giving information about the animals, their habitats and their diet.

Songs

Children of all ages in the primary phase seem to enjoy singing as long as the choice of songs is made with an eye to their age, interests and 'maturity'. With Y1 and Y3 children, the important issue is to choose age-appropriate songs that have a real origin in the cultures of the countries concerned. While it can be a useful learning aid to sing language items to the tune of well-known English soap themes or for that matter to the tune of *Frère Jacques*, it is far better to offer them a song which has a story, uses rhythms which they respond to, or which has accompanying actions. Song words can seem very complex, but children can absorb messages and sing with enjoyment without having each of the words in their active vocabulary. It is important that they do not just sing with no understanding of course and this is where modern DVDs can be very supportive. For example, *Mon âne* (Le Notre 1999) is a very popular French resource, which uses animations to reveal the gist meaning of the songs. One Y6 pupil was quite shocked at the 'cruelty' in *Alouette*, for example. She still enjoyed singing it, and was able to draw out key words without needing an exact translation – the key message had certainly been understood!

For Y1 children the very simple songs that were described in Chapter Three are still relevant, and it is just as important in both year groups that pupils are given a chance to choose which song they want to sing. Something very simple like '*Tourne, tourne petit moulin*' for French, (words and tune obtainable from www.momes.net/comptines/comptines-chansons.html) is popular with younger learners because they can perform it confidently after a few practice sessions and it feels good to them not to be 'on the spot' but to be able to sing with the class and enjoy joining in. There are many other websites offering a range of songs including for German, http://ingeb.org/kinderli.html and for Spanish http://pacomova.eresmas.net/paginas/canciones_infantiles.htm (perhaps more suitable for Y1 – there is a link to some songs with video performances on this site). In the first year of learning it is nearly always worth using actions with songs because it appears that for many children melody and movement really do facilitate and consolidate learning, (Davies 2000). The power of music for memory can be demonstrated by the very noticeable phenomenon where children sometimes need a push at the start of a song, with the teacher singing the first line or just the first word, but they are able to continue from there almost word-perfectly and finish it. Y1 language lessons especially benefit from a song as a warm-up to establish that we are now using the target language as much as possible, or as a change activity for a few minutes in the middle, or as a satisfying whole-class way of ending a lesson. Each of these is a valid use of time, helping to promote all of the positive attributes of learning a language: participation, active engagement of memory and focus, active use of the language, collaboration with others, an intercultural dimension and enjoyment.

Phonological awareness activities linked to stories and songs

Developing phonological awareness in the foreign language is an expectation in Key Stage 2 (the Oracy and Literacy objectives for Y3 refer to this activity) but this can, however, be introduced earlier, for example in Y1, especially as now all children are experiencing phonics on a daily basis from age 3 to 7. As a language teacher you can create your own version of phoneme flowers/clouds as part of the classroom display. The flower pattern is especially useful as you can site the phoneme in the centre of, say a daisy shape, and then add words containing that phoneme as petals around the outside. For this to happen the teacher needs to structure lessons which centre on particular phonemes. In such a lesson the teacher will choose one phoneme that appears in a story or a song. Firstly children will carry out discrimination activities, for example repeating the words that contain the phoneme in focus. They can then see the phoneme as a grapheme and identify words from the story that contain that grapheme. Finally they will read independently new words that contain the phoneme/grapheme. Because this is an on-going process, the children's attention can be called to it regularly through the use of the phoneme classroom display and this helps to fix the concepts gradually in their minds.

As we showed in Chapter Two, we can access other materials designed for literacy development in English. The earliest stage of *Letters and Sounds* (DCSF 2007), the synthetic phonics pack, is dedicated to the development of phonological awareness with a whole range of suggested activities, as shown below in the *Letters and Sounds* support document available from QCA at www.standards.dfes.gov.uk/local/clld/resources/letters_and_sounds/phonic_phases_link.pdf:

- Join in with repeated refrains and anticipate key events and phrases in rhymes and stories.

- Listen to others one-to-one or in small groups when conversation interests them.

- Build up vocabulary that reflects the breadth of their experiences.

- Use a widening range of words to express or elaborate on ideas.

- Use talk to connect ideas, explain what is happening and anticipate what might happen next.

- Enjoy rhyming and rhythmic activities.

- Show awareness of rhyme and alliteration.

- Recognise rhythm in spoken words.

- Listen to and join in with stories and poems, one-to-one and in small groups.

- Begin to be aware of the way stories are structured.

- Show interest in books and print in the environment.

- Enjoy joining in with dancing and ring games.

- Sing a few familiar songs.

- Sing to themselves and make up simple songs.

- Tap out simple repeated rhythms and make some up.

- Explore and learn how sounds can be changed.

- Imitate and create movement in response to music.

- Engage imaginative play and role-play based on own first hand experiences.

Clearly most of these activities (items two to five are less appropriate at this early stage of language learning) are also suitable for foreign language classes at Y1 and still at Y3 level. They can be linked to a song or a story very easily with joining in a very natural occurrence and with rhyme and rhythm being picked out for special focus on some readings or 'singings'. The noticing of sound in the target language absolutely underpins phonic skills for English as well, as it is the noticing process that is so important to establish. For most children in Y1 and even more in Y3 this noticing will be well established and the skill will be applied readily to the new sounds. But this is another example of where children with language development issues can only benefit from this fresh and added opportunity to take part in phonic discrimination activity in a non-threatening, collaborative, socially and academically equal context. The fact that there are some new sounds also highlights for all pupils the differences to known sounds and therefore consolidates those known sounds in English at the same time. The more independent stage of singing individually or as a group will demonstrate some mastery over pronunciation, intonation, rhythm and fluency and will be carried out by some children before others. But even this is not necessarily determined by ability, but can be as much linked with enjoyment of music, a capacity for using an ear for sounds and personality.

Games

Children in Y1 and Y3 clearly greatly enjoy playing games. The potential in language lessons is almost limitless, although of course we cannot use anything in the earliest stages which depends on the pupils using a lot of language. We have mentioned several times the desirability of avoiding parrot style repetition, even if we dress it up with elements such as repetition with different emotions or in different voices. But in certain circumstances this can be beneficial and, as with all approaches, if a teacher perceives value for children in using a particular method, then he or she should try it. For example, if a particularly difficult word has come up which the class can see they are having problems with then asking them to repeat it six times as a deliberate device to fix it and as a special method because it is difficult is often successful. Something you might need regularly such as *¡Feliz cumpleaños!* or, in German, *Herzlichen Glückwunsch (zum Geburtstag)* can be usefully repeated as a game when first encountered. The best technique here is to ask for six repetitions that become quieter with each one, ending in a whisper. The reverse is not to be recommended!

On a similar theme and undoubtedly popular is a repetition game where the class have to repeat the word after the teacher if the teacher has said the correct word. The teacher may point to a visual and name it correctly in which case they should all repeat it, and since this is easy there are no points available for doing it! But if the teacher says the wrong word everyone in the class must be silent – if they are, they gain a point, but if even one person repeats the wrong item the teacher gains a point. The first to five points wins, and it is usually the class.

Hiding or finding games are also popular with these younger pupils. This might be an image within a set (the well-known secondary game with flashcards held to the teacher's chest) or it might be an object in the classroom. Of course, further up the school the 20 questions format can be used as by then children will have the vocabulary they need, but at the beginner groups of Y1 and Y3 it is more likely to be a single object. This may be something amongst other objects, for example stationery on the teacher's desk, which is located by the use of simple questions such as: '*Ist es ein Bleistift?*', '*Ist es ein Gummi?*', '*Ist es blau?*' If it is something actually hidden then the limited set questions might be '*Ist es in einer Tasche?*', '*Ist es unter einem Tisch?*', '*Ist es in einer Hand?*' together with '*Ist es hier?*' (referring to a section of the classroom).

All normal guessing games are possible in the target language and usually need no materials. They can sometimes be planned in for specific reasons or can be used spontaneously, rather as we said with songs, because the teacher feels a game would be a healthy way to bring the class together and inject a short change activity into the middle of a lesson. They can also be used as a filler in non-language time, for example just before home-time, giving children more exposure to the target language. One way to consolidate a group of vocabulary items at an early stage is to play *Je pense à (une couleur) / Ich denke an (eine Farbe) / Penso en (un color)*. Although this game is normally started by the teacher (and we explored the competitive aspects of that in Chapter Two), we have noticed how keen some children are to volunteer to lead as they enjoy having a brief moment as the teacher. They can often manage turn-taking very well and this allows you to observe who is really contributing and whether any members of the class are less motivated or less secure in the language.

When pupils can read, chain games are also popular. These work with each class member having a card with an answer and a question on it. When a child hears the question that they think they have the answer for, they stand up and read it out. He or she then asks the question on the card to keep the chain going.

In Y3 an aural discrimination game that has very good potential for progression is the simple idea of a team game where children have a word to listen for (stimulated either by the word on a card or a picture of the item if appropriate). Each team will receive the same set of cards so that when the teacher says the word the first of the two pupils who has the item must stand up and say it. This means all of the class are involved as they have to listen carefully to each new item. The game can be moved on to include the word plus an adjective, for example colours, where now two on each team might have the same noun but a different adjective so concentration is even more important. It can also be moved to sentence level where the word needed must be heard within a longer flow of language.

A version of battleships, which is certainly possible with Y3 and perhaps later in Y1, uses a grid with squares labelled with objects rather

Figure 4.2   Grid for a version of 'battleships'

than letters and numbers. Figure 4.2 gives an example that combines shapes and colours. The children play in pairs and each 'hides' an object in one square and then they take it in turns to call out a 'grid reference'. The first to find the object wins the game.

Beginning to link – working with art and mathematics

When the children are showing an initial confidence with the language of instructions it will be worth trying to achieve a greater impact in their own eyes by taking them through a whole process in the foreign language to achieve a completely non-linguistic outcome. This might happen early in the year if you as a teacher are determined to make it work, or it might be left until later if it seems more daunting. If we imagine an art project with a collage as an outcome and a process involving choosing equipment, following steps and creating a finished work, we can see that there will be a series of short instructions needed to achieve it:

> *Prends le papier et les couleurs.*
>
> *Colorie le papier.*
>
> *Prends les ciseaux.*
>
> *Découpe des formes droites et arrondies.*
>
> *Avec toutes les formes, fais ta composition.*
>
> *Prends la colle.*
>
> *Colle les formes sur le papier.*
>
> *Et voilà, c'est fini!* (*A La Française*, Matisse material, Tobutt and Roche 2007)

This set of instructions needs to remain in the correct order and with a Y1 class the teacher would certainly use them with the class step by step, using realia at each stage so that the children hear the foreign language but follow visually. A great deal of natural repetition occurs when teachers give these sort of instructions as children always operate at different paces, so the class will have a lot of opportunity to hear some key words such as *prends*, *le papier*, *les couleurs*, *les ciseaux*, *la colle*. These words do not need to be pre-taught, as they will be known receptively by the end of this process. With Y3 it is possible to go further towards making the class more independent and a good way to use these instructions is on separate cut up slips, asking groups to establish the order before they start to make the collage. In either case, pupils will have a completed collage at the end which they will have made with no use of English for the instructions.

Art is often used for early cross-curricular work because it tends to involve receptive language as we saw in the example above. But many teachers also use short maths tasks because they can be quick to set up and carry out (this builds on the notion of oral and mental starters at the beginning of the daily mathematics lesson, where the foreign language work can be easily located). Because maths is number based it is also more language-free than some other subjects. Children can see the figures on the whiteboard and can calculate without language then retrieve the language for their response. Of course higher numbers are difficult in most languages so teachers need to be careful, especially at Y1 level, about what they attempt to do. But number bonds to 20 are still worth practising in Key Stage 1 and calculations which have an answer in the range 1–20 could still be sufficiently challenging for Y3, especially if they centre on multiplication and division facts around the times tables which are set for that year group. Examples of such sums might be $45 \div 3 = ?$, $? \times 4 = 48$, $36 \div 6 = ?$, $? + 82 = 100$. Each of these missing elements that the class must supply is still in the range 1–20, and the teacher can talk through the sum asking for the missing number as he or she goes. Through this, especially if worked on quite regularly, the class will also learn higher numbers through hearing them and finding patterns. The Y3 mathematics objectives also include material on 2D shapes and again this is a good mini-topic for a foreign language.

Knowledge about language

There are evidently differences between the capabilities and understanding of children in KS1 and lower KS2. Although children should be exposed to written language in KS1, ML lessons should concentrate on developing phonological awareness, as we showed earlier, introducing and identifying phonemes and so not really looking in detail at any grammatical elements of language. Writing can be given as an extension task, rather than as a norm to all children, and correction should certainly be avoided when children do write in the foreign language because they will still be at the emergent writing stage, perhaps even in Y3. Sometimes children will ask about language elements that they notice and this might include gender indicators such as adjectives agreeing with nouns. There is no reason why a question should not be answered, but in the first year there is little reason to build lessons around grammatical points. The Knowledge about Language strand in the KS2 Framework (DfES 2005) indicates certain themes (mainly addressing sound/graphic correspondence) but also cross-references them to the main objectives within Oracy, Literacy and Intercultural Understanding. (See Chapter Seven for a full discussion of how to use the KS2 Framework.) In other words, particularly at Y3, overt grammar is not officially encouraged. However one of the reasons behind ensuring that children hear full sentences from the beginning is that they are exposed to the major word classes in context well before they begin to examine or discuss them.

Example topic: La Réunion

The full presentational material referred to here is available in the *A La Française* pack (Tobutt and Roche 2007) and consists of a starter PowerPoint presentation which can be used with either Y1 or Y3, although of course follow-up activity after that will be different.

The slides show a series of scenes from La Réunion, a French-speaking island in the Indian Ocean. They are intended to support the class topic, Islands, which often focuses on islands in the UK, using the Katie Morag stories both as a literacy starter and an organiser for the topic that has a strong geography content. The purpose of the initial slides is to identify a possible hiding place for a butterfly who is finally located behind a flower. The question '*Où est le papillon?*' and the follow-up suggestions: '*A la plage? Dans la mer? Dans le volcan? Dans la maison? A la montagne?*' establishes this key vocabulary through natural repetition by the teacher. As he or she puts the question to different pupils (who may have different opinions) there is a chance for those pupils who wish to speak to join in and use the vocabulary as part of this dialogue.

The presentation also includes a map of the island, drawn by a primary age child who lives there. At this point the children can take cards containing photos of the scenes shown on the slides and bring them to the board to place in the correct location on the map. For Y1 children this represents a reinforcement of their map skills which the general topic is developing through English elsewhere in the week. By choosing the correct card in response to: *'Où est la plage?'* and placing it somewhere on the edge of the island where land meets sea, they show they have recognised the French word for beach and know that a map showing an island is laid out as a view from above with the sea surrounding the island and beaches at the point where land meets sea. Similarly, if they place the volcano picture at the point on the map in the area to the east of the centre of the island where there is shading to show higher ground, they are again demonstrating a recognition of some geographical features.

Often in KS1 there are comparisons made between a remote and a more familiar location and this activity also allows the comparisons of the landscape of La Réunion with that of the UK or even with their own local environment. Children could certainly draw their own map of the island and label key features, and as an extension they could write a sentence about its location.

In KS2 much of the same work could be done as an introduction but at far greater speed. The language demanded might be at a slightly higher level (although they are still beginners) and the work could be extended by looking at descriptions of the island written by children from La Réunion and displayed on their school website: http://pedagogie1. acreunion.fr/circons/stleu/9740256K/20012002/ cpce1/reunion.htm.

A poem about the carnival written by H. Jamy for children is available from this site: www.ile-reunion.org/guetali/poeme/poeme.htm.

> **Le Mardi Fou (poème pour les enfants)**
> *C'est Mardi Gras dans notre école,*
> *Comme on s'amuse! Comme on rigole!*
> *Avec nos masques et nos grimaces*
> *Dans le défilé qui passe.*
>
> *Joues rouges, cheveux verts,*
> *Pantalons lâches et chapeaux de paille,*
> *Sur les enfants tout fiers*
> *Qui se tortillent et qui piaillent!*
>
> *Sifflets, flûtes et tam-tams*
> *Cognent, roulent, secouent,*
> *Pour fêter le jour fou*
> *Que tout le monde acclame!*
>
> *Comme on s'amuse! Comme on rigole!*
> *Dans notre école!*

With any such material, which may be pitched above the level of pupils at individual word level, reading in pairs is usually a popular and successful activity. If the children are given a more global task of finding out some information and noticing elements of interest, they are motivated by the challenge and by the fact that the task is open-ended, rather than tightly prescribed or quantified, and therefore does not run a risk of failure. This is a good example of how you can move beyond the narrowly defined topics such as numbers, colours or family and into a context of real language use and real communication. The message it gives, that we will rarely know it all but we can certainly work out some of it if we try, is vital in setting an early expectation of what learning a language is really like.

Y1 children will not be able to cope with reading at this level of course, though they might enjoy hearing the carnival poems read, especially with accompanying pictures. But they can undertake more practical and less language-rich tasks such as making masks and then using them for an authentic dance. This still involves receptive language as, similar to the collage activity introduced above, the teacher needs to give instructions for the Design and Technology activity in the foreign language, encourage pupils to name their choice of materials using colour, material, shape, and then to teach the dance.

At both levels some work can also involve climate and weather. The Meteoconsult website (www.meteoconsult.com/) is a very useful resource for French, German and Spanish (as you can select your language) and is best used on an interactive whiteboard as if gives detailed live forecasts for all parts of the world, and each day can be viewed across four separate time periods, simply by moving a mouse over the map. La Réunion can be located within the site and by clicking a location an even more detailed forecast is available.

Just talking about different weather and climates is a little limited so teachers can look for opportunities to link the idea of more extreme weather, such as tropical storms, through music and drama activities as well as pictures and video if available. Again, in the first year of learning, some material in English that genuinely gives an insight into a different culture is still worthwhile from time to time.

Chapter summary

This chapter has attempted to describe and rationalise the range of activity teachers may wish to include in the first year of learning for either Y1 or Y3. It has shown that from the beginning we can offer children a whole-language experience, exploring richness of both culture and language

(Continued)

(Continued)

where possible, but still with an emphasis on making the experience both enjoyable and non-threatening. We have indicated that the children may be using the language in only very specific manageable scenarios while meeting a much broader range from the teacher and from commercial and on-line resources. We have recommended extensive use of texts and songs to ensure that this happens with the least pressure on non-specialist teachers. We have given examples of games. We have looked at the early development of literacy in the foreign language and at beginnings of linking with other subjects.

Key and Further Reading

A document produced for the USA regarding second language English speakers in mainstream schooling has some interesting points about language learning in general. It gives a good view of the need for language learners to experience some form of immersion in the language. It can be downloaded from www.fcd-us.org/usr_doc/MythsOfTeachingELLs Espinosa.pdf.

5

Where to next? How can I embed the language into the school day and the wider curriculum?

Introductory vignette

Two children in Y4 are learning about the Vikings in French. They practise offering each other a range of artefacts (as photographs on card) as part of a bartering dialogue. After a couple of turns they begin again and one child decides she wants a sword – she has a malevolent intention!

A: *Tu voudrais un verre?*

B: *Non.*

A: *Tu voudrais une peigne?*

B: *Non merci!*

A: *Tu voudrais une épée?*

B: *Oui, oui.* (takes the picture of a sword) *Attaquez!*

The previous two chapters have each approached how to start language learning at particular points in a school and have aimed to provide an initial focus for a new teacher or for a school languages coordinator when starting to organise the teaching. But from the beginning it is important to see also where the subject should be heading. A clear and shared vision for the whole of the school's present and future language provision will considerably enhance that initial teaching. This chapter looks at how initial progression might be viewed, while Chapter Six deals with the aspirations a school might have for language learning at the end of KS2 and transition to KS3.

Chapter objectives

- To consider briefly what psychology research says about the relative roles of ability/aptitude, motivation, attitudes, task setting and learning styles.
- To address the issues of differentiation and personalisation.
- To explore a range of different aspects of progression through examples from practice from both KS1 and KS2.
- To explore a model of progression through four levels of cross-curricular integration.

Relevant Q Standards: Q1, Q2, Q4, Q6, Q8, Q10, Q11, Q14, Q15, Q18, Q19, Q22, Q25, Q29, Q32, Q33

Initial reflection point

In a topic-based syllabus, especially one created by the teacher to fit with the needs of the class, there is a danger that progression will be limited. Each topic tends to start at the beginning with new vocabulary and structures and be practised in isolation from other previous topics. Published schemes of work, for example the QCA Units (2007) or the Catherine Cheater scheme (2006) have addressed this issue to some extent. What is your view on progression? Do you feel that children only need to do different topics across the four years because primary languages is about building a base for KS3, or do you feel that the language classroom in Y6 should be very different from the Y3 classroom? If so, how?

Does progression mean the same for all children?

Primary teachers are fortunate in that they see children across the week and across different subject and skill areas. They gain a more comprehensive view of a child's complex personality and do not just see the child in a limited role. Secondary teachers are perhaps not as lucky, as they may view a class and its children from a perspective which is determined by a time of the day, or an influence from another lesson or teacher, or by the fact that they teach the child a single subject. For this reason, personalisation (rather than whole-class differentiation into, say, three levels of work) is perhaps easier for a primary teacher than for a secondary colleague to visualise (although of course no less time-consuming to put into practice!). This chapter will address ways to personalise and differentiate in its second section, but we need to be clear at the start about how we establish the criteria for any division into levels of work that we make.

Ability

When devising groups for Literacy and Mathematics work good primary teachers currently balance the notion of an 'ability level' with other aspects, such as confidence, a need for support by an assistant, a preferred approach, for example visual or hands-on, or a social special need. Perceived ability is probably still the major factor but our understanding of what that means now includes other aspects. For example, in his review of individual differences (IDs) and language learning Dörnyei (2006: 42) notes that there are five major domains of ID: 'personality, aptitude, motivation, learning styles and learning strategies'.

Although used for some time in the USA the term 'readiness to learn' is now more common in the UK context. It often refers to the social and economic contexts in which children live and to more physical elements that underpin lifestyle. For example, a recent Teachers' TV focus (www.teachers.tv/experiment March 2008) addressed sleep, exercise and breakfast and showed that all three could affect children's readiness to learn. But 'readiness to learn' seems to us to be a useful term for classrooms also because it is often children's overall readiness rather than simply their ability that counts, as we will try to show.

Progression can be tied into grouping insofar as teachers may provide different materials or even programmes for different groups. The government document on grouping pupils for success (DfES 2006) itself offers a range of models and rationales. Some writers promote the use of full mixed-ability rather than ability-based groupings on the grounds that all children learn best when they are able to articulate their understanding and scaffold each other's learning through collaboration, while others support this approach more from a social justice perspective. Ireson and Hallam (1999) challenge ability grouping in the form of sets or bands on a number of counts (including reinforcement of low expectation, unreliability of allocation, effect on self-esteem) and suggest that schools might like to look at different criteria for grouping at different times and for different needs. Nevertheless, it is common in primary schools with two-form entry or bigger to 'band' for literacy and mathematics and then to divide into ability groups within those banded classes.

Learning styles and ability

In the second section of this chapter and in the practice examples we will try to illustrate how learning styles might play a part in securing progression in different ways. There has been a great deal of attention paid to the notion of learning styles in recent years and most teachers mention aspects of VAK (visual, auditory and kinaesthetic input/activity) or multiple intelligences theory (Gardner 1985) if they speak about their approach to planning. Writers such as Sternberg (1997) or Riding and Rayner (1998) have explored learning styles in more detail although a critique of this entire literature was supplied by Coffield *et al.* (2004). Techniques such as accelerated learning (Smith and Call 1999) are popular subjects for school INSET programmes. But the whole debate proves that it is now more difficult to determine why a child should be grouped with others and what the nature of 'ability' really is. In terms of language learning, ability is a difficult concept. What was earlier called 'language aptitude' is now seen as a linked set of different factors (Robinson 2002, Skehan 2002) rather than a single quality that an individual has or has not. Research has shown that learners' actual performance level can vary and be determined by a whole range of elements (and often by these in interaction). For these reasons, we want to give a brief overview here of some aspects of the possible role of motivation and effort, attitudes to ability, and task demands.

Motivation and associated elements

Tremblay *et al.* (2000) showed in a study on young adults that aptitude or ability was only one factor that determined achievement. They also found that motivation and effort, the attitude towards the teacher and subject and anxiety were all significant factors. These other aspects of course can be linked so motivation will be greater if the attitude towards the teacher or subject is positive. While that may seem like common-sense it is important to note that these other elements have been shown empirically to impact on performance as well as on motivation because that makes it even more an issue which teachers should heed. Lepine *et al.* (2004) looked at the interaction of what they termed 'stress' and performance amongst a young adult group and established that stress in the form of 'challenge' could produce a positive effect which enhanced performance whereas what they called 'hindrance stress' impacted negatively. So it is important when we consider progression that we both plan to support children but also plan to offer the right amount of challenge and in the right way. Cury *et al.* (2006), building on Dweck (2000), identified the importance of entity and incremental views of ability (in other words whether learners think they have any control over their own ability levels and so can affect their own performance, the incremental view, or not, the entity view). They found that mastery goals (part of a more personalised and self-developing motivational structure which led to continuous individual development, irrespective of others) were associated with the incremental view and that performance goals (those related to doing well against other members of the class) were associated with the entity view. An entity view unsurprisingly was less likely to generate a high level of intrinsic motivation. In Chapter Eight we will look at formative assessment for learning techniques that are associated with personalised mastery structures.

Teachers sometimes comment that a very bright child who has excelled at the more 'predictable' tasks offered in a subject can become anxious very quickly if the work becomes more investigative, more open-ended and therefore less predictable. Just as a child with learning difficulties can become acclimatised to failure and not believe he or she has the chance to improve, so an able child can become acclimatised to success, but only of a certain kind. That child may not be able to cope with a different and/or more demanding level of work, not because he or she does not have the ability, but because the self-belief is posited on being able to succeed without a real challenge. Clearly this gives us the message that we should find ways to show all learners that they can act to affect their performance and achievement, and that we should not just talk about it, but prove it to them in concrete ways. Their existing view is difficult to change but one of the positives about the fact that no matter how well we integrate language learning, children still often see it as a little different, is that we can set out a new classroom landscape when using the target language where established hierarchies and beliefs about ability are not as valid. If shown consistently that they can achieve children will believe more readily that this is in their own realm of control. Once again this underpins the need for teachers to consider more than ability when deciding what the individuals and the classes in front of them are capable of.

Motivation and how we generate this is clearly crucial. Dörnyei's very extensive work on motivation in language learning (for example, Guilloteaux and Dörnyei 2008, Dörnyei 2006, Csizér and Dörnyei 2005, Kormos and Dörnyei 2004, Dörnyei and Csizér 2002) has shown consistently that motivation is a vital component of success in language learning, that it has personal, contextually situated and temporal aspects and is certainly not a fixed or single entity. Along with Gardner (1985) he identifies what is known as the integrative aspect of motivation as crucial to language learners. This means they identify with a community (target language speaking) into which they wish to integrate and has been shown to be more predictive of language learning success than a more instrumental focus (for example, learning to get a job or impress one's parents). Here we again see the importance of culture as an active and meaningful part of the programme, planned to permeate our materials and not be seen as an occasional add-on, because the culture which enters the classroom is of course more constant as an influence than the culture which lies overseas. The culture of the classroom is equally important – joining in with that is also a part of the integrative motivation spectrum.

In a book on motivational strategies, Dörnyei (2001) addressed at length the importance of generating initial motivation and then maintaining and protecting it. Much of this is a good-practice summary for working in classrooms, but he stresses the importance of clear goal-setting and success criteria, demonstrating genuine commitment to the subject and to the learners, making material relevant but also interesting (for example through the intercultural dimension) varying the task styles and lesson structure, being aware of potential causes of anxiety and acting to lower or remove them from the programme, increasing both collaboration and independence while promoting higher self-esteem through success and opportunities to work actively and with confidence. He also included in this the notion that with the use of learning strategies, modelled by teachers, children could rise above their apparent 'ability' and learn better. It is clear that an enhanced ability to call on strategies will engender greater success, greater motivation and hence positively affect readiness to learn.

Writers on primary language learning will vary in what they think needs to be done to achieve the common-sense goals included here. Some will argue that caution is the way not to lose children from the learning process, and that enjoyment should always be highlighted, while others might say that too slow a progression will be equally problematic. To make sense of this we need now to look practically at personalisation and differentiation techniques.

How should I approach planning differentiated or personalised lessons?

In the first section of this chapter we considered a range of elements that might prompt planning to include different levels of work avail-able in a teacher-targeted or open-choice approach. Clearly no teacher can think of all of these elements when planning differentiated work for a class. A personalised approach is in some ways easier to plan for, as teachers who know a class well will be able to visualise how the whole class might react to certain stimulus materials and activities, and how certain groups of children will be able to collaborate to enjoy and per-form on different types of tasks. Certain individual pupils will come to mind because they need something a little different and this might involve suggesting a certain role within a group task to ensure they can succeed, the allocation of a teaching assistant to support them or even on some occasions to offer something more individual.

The conventional models of differentiation are that the teacher should consider modifications of task, text, support, and content interest, and this has been supplemented by the focus on the three components of VAK (visual, auditory and kinaesthetic input/activity) and to an extent by Gardner's (Gardner and Hatch 1989) eight or nine intelligences. But the emphasis on working under the headings of categories of differentiation has loosened and, for example if we look at the QCA guidance on provision for learners with EAL (www.qca.org.uk/qca_5093.aspx), we will find a total of 14 points each under the planning and teaching strategies, which range from the focuses given immediately above to considerations of the sort we explored in the first part of this chapter. There is a danger in the planning structure with three-level learning outcomes of 'all will', 'most will', 'some will' that teaching can become too rigidly forced into having three different degrees of expectation and pupils will be channelled only into certain types or levels of achievement.

The rest of this chapter looks at concrete ways in which we can build progression into the second year of learning and is written to be supportive also of non-specialist teachers who feel less confident about moving on.

Progression in target language use by the teacher: embedding the language further into routines

Whether we are working with Y1/2 or Y4, a progression into a second year of language learning should feel like a move forward to the children. As we have indicated in the first part of this chapter there will be more of a need to differentiate and personalise the further we progress, and this is entirely normal. But as we have shown, this does not need to come down to three different strands of work that are rigidly enforced. We should find as we move on from year to year that more and more complex school- and classroom-routine language is used, but of course the earlier more straightforward language will still be in use as well, so offering completely natural repetition and reinforcement to all pupils. Because instructional language so often requires pure comprehension and a non-verbal response rather than one that demands target language use (which may generate anxiety), there is less pressure on less able linguists. In many instances they will see the response, in terms of actions, from peers and will be able to follow it. The natural repetition will, over time, enable them to begin to respond automatically and personally to the instruction that will become familiar. We should remember that this progression is sometimes daunting for the non-specialist teacher as well, and the examples given below are also intended to offer scaffolding for this eventuality. What we should be aware of is that the dialogue of the classroom offers countless opportunities to enrich the language experience – this may come spontaneously or may be semi-scripted. If a teacher simply thinks of possible events and prepares a few simple 'follow-up lines' they will be ready when needed.

Using the language in bigger chunks

Some of the 'extra' language will come in the form of aggregation – several familiar elements may be combined. For example, in the early stages of learning you may give separate instructions to get up, go and get coats on and line up ready for playtime, lunch or home-time. You may wait for each task to be completed and say the instruction several times in the target language, using mime to accompany it. In the earliest stages the mime is so clear that you are actually teaching the language through using it, but gradually you will be able to stop using so much mime but keep the different instructions separate and generally simple.

> *Levez-vous!* (mime get up, by raising both hands, palms up) *Bon, Chloe, Bon Paul, Levez-vous! Levez-vous, Daniel et Claire!*
>
> *OK maintenant, les manteaux! Mettez les manteaux!* (mime putting on coat)
>
> *Mettez-vous en file ici! Paul, Daniel, ici s'il vous plait! En file tous!*

By the second year of learning, you should be able to build on the familiarity of such routines by giving such a set of instructions together, and to weave in more personalised comments when needed. This does not need to be done at speed, and there can be repetition where needed of course, but the class in general should be able to absorb the global message and act accordingly. After all, they do know the routine – you are merely prompting it in the target language.

OK, c'est maintenant la recréation. Alors, levez-vous vous tous, allez mettre les manteaux et après ça, mettez-vous en file devant la porte ici. Paul, tu as un manteau? Il fait froid aujourd'hui, n'est-ce pas? Chloe, ne parle pas – tu peux parler avec Claire dans la cour – mets ton manteau, s'il te plait!

Building up the language from the very simple to a more natural expression

Some early instructions which were pared down to a very basic level can ease towards more natural target language use and in this way the language of the classroom will gradually progress towards a richer experience. Again these are often instructions which will be used very regularly so the progression we are suggesting can happen gradually and be very well internalised. An example might be setting up some written work.

Ici le titre – copiez! – Ici la date – copiez! – soulignez le titre! – soulignez la date! (Here the teacher would point at the items and mime the action of underlining.)

We can see from this example that in the early stages the language used would be very clear because it is either visually prompted or close to English or both. If used at this level too much, the children may not actually internalise the language at all because they follow without thinking. But if it becomes part of a more natural flow, this changes.

OK comme toujours, il faut écrire le titre et la date – ils sont ici et vous pouvez copier. N'oubliez pas de souligner, s'il vous plait, comme toujours!

Using the written form

Some language can be added in written form so that children moving around the school keep aware of the presence of the target language throughout the day and the building. Many schools have labelled different rooms, some in a range of languages to reflect the languages used in school by different pupils from different backgrounds, but this can be taken further to include simple notices about conduct and behaviour, targets, school ethos, events (such as sports results). In a way a 'notice' is more of a learning opportunity than a 'label' as pupils are more likely to engage with it, especially if it changes periodically. The disadvantage of room labels is that they sit there permanently and cease to be noticed.

Using assemblies

Assemblies are a real opportunity to build the language experience of the school. As we saw in the vignette that introduced Chapter Two, a head picked out the fact that the children could share that they were learning a language through an assembly piece of music. In another infant school where only the Reception class had French lessons timetabled, the Y1 and Y2 classes had a French assembly each Friday, where they learned songs and heard stories and where they also shared something that younger children were experiencing. Of course we can again build on the fact that children know the routines and will understand them in the target language readily if used in that context. From greetings, instructions, and management to showing work or things brought from home (with a target language or culture connection where possible), and centred on the content of the assembly, a remarkably rich diet proved possible even though the majority of children in the hall did not technically learn French! Again, this centres on the fact that the children are exposed to a manageable amount of the target language for comprehension and are supported in their own use of the language because it arises mainly from joining in with a song or with the repetitive parts of a story.

Managing behaviour

It is generally accepted that classroom behaviour management is more than possible in the target language. Some teachers take the view that a telling off in a foreign language will be clearly understood but will probably not have the same confrontational feel for more disaffected pupils as a stern warning in English can sometimes have, leading to resentment and worse behaviour. This was perhaps well illustrated by a cartoon in a book on target language used by Jones *et al.* (2002). A teacher, speaking to two guilty looking boys cries: *'La prochaine fois c'est la mort!'* One boy says to the other 'I don't know what she said, but if we do it again she'll kill us!' Some critics of this claim that a teacher cannot generate a 'normal' relationship with a pupil in a foreign language and that the use of the foreign language for management is likely to lead to more problems as the pupil may ignore the instructions or admonition. It is perhaps worth considering that some of the people who maintain this still feel that it is very important to use praise in the target language (and yet there is little difference between the two functions, as both concern emotional aspects of the learning process).

Simple instructions can be used from the beginning of learning, and phrases such as listen, look this way, be quiet now, don't touch..., sit down, sit with... will quickly be learned as we saw in Chapter Four. While this is not intended as a general rule (we must not be mechanistic about either language teaching or classroom management), progression does offer the opportunity to go a stage further and name both the unacceptable behaviour and the desired alternative.

Daniel, ne parle pas avec Sean, regarde-moi!

Chloe et Claire, ne parlez pas! Ecoutez!

We can also sometimes offer reasons for the instruction to do things differently, so giving a good model for language use in other contexts too. Here we should still use mime and visual support to make the meaning clear. Five quick pieces of non-verbal language can easily accompany the following management instruction to make it absolutely clear.

Mark, ne touche pas les crayons maintenant, parce que tu dois regarder les images ici sur l'écran.

Language use through dictionary use

A teacher who lacks confidence can promote the use of dictionaries very effectively if a regular classroom occurrence is to look for a word together. Sometimes this will be spontaneous, but if a teacher has had to check a word while planning the lesson, he or she could consciously do this again during the lesson. This is a vital language skill and should not be seen as reflecting any lack of competence by the teacher. Since few classes will have a whole set of dictionaries, this is perhaps best done by the teacher with a different pupil each time. As children become more accustomed to using a dictionary, it can be extended by tasking a pair of pupils to locate a word. It is also possible to use an online dictionary so that the whole class can see and participate in this process. A dictionary for a range of languages is to be found at www.wordreference.com. There is a whole skill involved here of course and the teacher should give guidelines as to what is being checked, and what should be ignored to start with (for example, the grammatical notation which accompanies the entries). Later, perhaps in the last year of primary school, the full extent of dictionary vocabulary can be opened up so that children know whether they have found a noun or a verb, an adjective or adverb.

Raising the bar – drawing children further into the classroom routine dialogues

Another way to instil progression into the language use of the classroom in a scaffolded way is to move on from an acceptance of English in routine questions. Here, of course, a response from the teacher to a question in English should always have been in the target language so the pupil using English still has to process the foreign language to get the desired result. Instead the teacher may start to project an expectation of target language use by the pupil. This means of course turning receptive into productive language. This does not have to be done in that rather negative way of making the pupil say a complete sentence and possibly even repeat it several times before permission or a response is given. The pupil may use the language at various levels and as long as there is a real desire to communicate this should be both accepted and praised. So a fairly common request may range from *'Die Toilette bitte'* to *'Darf ich bitte zur Toilette gehen?'* and each is completely acceptable. But each also gives the opportunity for the teacher to initiate by qualifying permission with something that has to be processed, for example, *'Aber nur zwei Minuten!'* or *'Wenn Chloe zurück ist.'*

Sometimes children will not have the right vocabulary for a particular function – negatives are often particularly difficult for children, for example. But this gives rise to two issues. First we should accept and praise for effort any real attempt to communicate, for example *'Nein Bleistift'* before offering an alternative *'Kein Bleistift?'* (accompanied of course by hand signals to show it is a negative). Other attempts to say the same thing might bring *'Wo ist Bleistift?'* or one closer to what is needed *'Ich möchte Bleistift.'* In these cases, a natural response is what is needed from the teacher. While it is believed that simply recasting a response and echoing it to a pupil does not usually effectively repair language errors, except phonological mistakes (Lyster 1998), we have to balance maintaining a positive learning atmosphere with a gradual move towards the use of accurate language. On seeing that children have started to try to express negative sentences, it would be worth devising a lesson that teaches them in context and preferably in a content- rather than grammar-driven way. The teacher may reveal to the class that he or she has left her bag with pencil case, packed lunch, books and phone at home and therefore does not have some essential items. This could then lead to a confessional (under amnesty of course) where children reveal what they have forgotten on that day.

Moving to more open-ended use of productive spoken language

If we give children opportunities to talk both to us and to each other in the target language in non-threatening ways we slowly create a norm of expectation that the language of the classroom is not English unless absolutely necessary. This can be achieved through setting up short dialogues and role-plays, but in a way that some level of creativity is offered right from the beginning. Children will try to initiate if they have a chance and so we should avoid setting up drill-like sequences where the dialogue is purely mechanistic. We saw in the vignette to this chapter how at even the simplest level of language children will take the opportunity to inject humour and have fun while using the target language. It is important to value even these small instances, because they signal a desire to communicate spontaneously.

We have spoken before about the need to avoid asking questions to which the answer is already well known to everyone in the room. Obviously in a primary class, personal information can fall into this category all too easily. But a lot of practice is possible if you move to taking on different identities and this can be a very good opportunity to move towards more communicative and purposeful use of the kind of language which is often learned fairly early, for example name, age, family, pets, friends, likes and dislikes. One way of making this contained but still spontaneous is to have a set of photo cards of celebrities (and perhaps school personnel) with key facts and to ask a pupil to draw one out and take on that identity. This may start as a whole-class collaborative activity with different pupils forming questions they feel confident of and all as a group trying to guess the identity. More able pupils are therefore better to be the celebrity to begin with as they are likely to be more fluent but can also be paired with a less gifted partner and can work together to provide the answers. From there you can evolve into a team game with competition to guess the identity, then to pairs of pupils being pairs of celebrities – the more unlikely the better, and eventually to playing the game in groups with the whole set of cards in use and more intensive practice for all. An extension of this topic could result in children carrying out a survey. This could be either still on the theme of the assumed identities, and with more people being involved, giving further repetition of questions and responses, or, with some extra unknown information, this could revert to real identities. If this is the case then there needs to be an outcome, for example a whole-class graphic summary of the data produced.

Some KS2 teachers opt to maintain EYFS practice of having a role-play area in the classroom. If this is available, then it can certainly be used for language practice, and would best be linked to the class topic area. Not all children will want to be 'on the spot' in this way but on the other hand some will really enjoy the challenge of picking up a 'scenario card' which gives a situation for them to explain to a partner. The card written in the target language acts as a support in terms of vocabulary, but does not tell them what to say (in the manner of a GCSE role-play task card). If the class is working on habitats for science and humanities, for example, a scenario card might involve a brief vet/client dialogue about an injured wild animal. The beginnings of this might be possible for many pupils by the end of the second year of learning, and we will present a longer example in Chapter Six.

Progression in literacy

We showed in Chapter Four that we should not keep the written word hidden from pupils at any point. Even in the Reception class, more able children are often interested in how we write the words they are learning and may try to use phonics knowledge to do this for themselves. Certainly by Y3 children beginning a language have a very real engagement with Literacy and it will seem odd if they do not encounter text in the target language. Of course different languages make different demands on children with Spanish and Italian perhaps being the least problematic of the four major western European languages, and German being a lot more instantly accessible than French, which rivals English for obscure spelling patterns. There is no reason why from the beginning core vocabulary should not be on display so that children can access it when they are ready. Those with more visual and language-based learning styles will gain a great deal from regular exposure to these key words. But as we progress into the second and third years of learning the displays will be able to fulfil different purposes, more akin to other classroom displays the pupils have available to them. We can keep the core vocabulary that we feel they need but add language from the current topic and move through the regular cycle of display in best-practice classrooms where the content of a topic is presented then harnessed into a more learning-oriented pattern (perhaps through questions and informational responses) and finally to a more celebratory purpose where children's work is displayed. (If you want to explore this topic further in more general terms, carry out a Google search on 'purpose of classroom display' – there are numerous sites to stimulate thinking on this topic.

We can see how this progression might look through a food and drink topic linked to healthy eating. From a display showing a range of breakfast items (Figure 5.1), which still invites some thinking as the pupils need to make the links between the visuals and the labels (coloured string or ribbon can be used to do this physically), they can move to playing with alliteration in the language of opinions (Figure 5.2) and then to considering questions around healthy options through deciding about the health rating of five breakfasts before creating their own (Figure 5.3).

Building on phonic work

In Chapter Four we looked at the need for activities that develop phonological awareness and about how we might teach individual phonemes and their graphic equivalents. As reading increases, children

Die 5 Getränke waren...

Milch	Saft
Tee	Kakao
Kaffee	

Acht Sachen zum Essen:

Corn Flakes	Butter
Ein Ei	Jogurt
Käse	Wurst
Brötchen	Marmelade

Figure 5.1   Classroom display showing range of breakfast items

Ich mag Milch
Tee ist besser!

Saft ist super !
Ich mag Limo !

Kakao hat
Kalorien !
Kaffee hat Koffein

Figure 5.2   Adding opinions to the breakfast items

Ein gesundes Frühstück?

Mach dein eigenes
gesundes Frühstück
hier !

Wenn nicht, warum nicht?

Figure 5.3   Considering how healthy different breakfasts are

will need to be able to decode a wider range of vocabulary, and to be able to read aloud as accurately as possible. When the class hears new words, before seeing them written, they may be asked to think of other words which contain that sound and to say, if they remember, how these words are written. (The class display may contain examples of these phonemes to prompt them.) The teacher might then subsequently use this method for telling the class how something is written by saying, for example about the new word *'seau'*, *'ça s'écrit comme l'eau, pas comme chaud'*.

Use of stories

By the second year there is a great deal more potential for the use of stories. The issue of stories being age-appropriate may begin to have more of a role and every class is different in this respect. The enthusiasm generated by the teacher for a resource can be sufficient to 'sell' it to classes who are becoming more mature, but there is of course a danger in using material that the children will consider babyish. Teachers who enjoy creating their own stories through using PowerPoint or other presentational tools have the opportunity of course to design material which they know will appeal in terms of content and which they know will challenge but be essentially understandable with concentration, collaboration and support where necessary. In the second year you may like to consider the potential of a link between a target language reading stimulus and a piece of writing in English. A story, especially one with some mystery and an open-ended conclusion, may create a starting point for an imaginative piece of writing.

An example of a story available in both French and German is Ruth Brown's (2001) *Une histoire sombre, très sombre* (*Eine dunkle, dunkle Geschichte*). It is not available in Spanish although other works by the same author are. This story, which gradually progresses from the whole country down to a small mouse in a box in a series of snapshots, is clearly understood from the combination of text and visuals, so children do not have problems accessing it. The sentence structure is repetitive which creates expectation and tension and so engages a class very quickly. The same structure also invites the children to join in as they perceive the pattern, so the language moves from the receptive to the productive through the teacher's use of pauses which encourage the class to supply the words before the teachers says them. Sequencing activities that have been successful with this story include:

- arranging the visuals in order

- labelling the visuals with the correct sentences

- arranging word cards with the 'focus' of each page in order (for example, *un pays, une forêt, un château*, and so on)

- extending the above so that extra items appear, for example *une ville* between *forêt* and *château*, or use *grande* and then *petite* with *boîte*

- writing imitatory sentences then follows and even a complete new story (perhaps with photo illustrations is possible).

This can be linked with Geography topics where the big to small focus can also be used (as we suggested in Chapter Four, when looking at the first two lessons).

Use of informational texts (at different levels)

In the second year of learning you can begin to use informational texts on topics the class are engaged in elsewhere in the week. The final section of this chapter looks in more detail at how you might progress with such curricular integration and Chapters Six and Nine give more detail of how and why this might progress further. But at this point we are looking at very simple text to move children on from language topics to a more general use of the language. Just as we saw in Chapter Four that some work is possible in the first year of learning in areas such as Art and Maths, we can see a wider range of opportunity when the children have both more language and growing maturity in terms of study skills. One source of material for short informational texts is school websites. Where the school has included information about class topics and examples of children's work there is more likely to be appropriate levels of language and the motivation of seeing another young person's work. Examples of sites containing many such links for French are http://d.webring.com/ hub?ring=ecolespf and http://doubleau.chez-alice.fr/anneau/listeanno. htm. A major source for German schools is www.schulweb.de/de/deutsch-land/index.html. For schools in Spain, individual areas need to be searched, for example, Andalucia or Catalunya.

An example text from the website of the Ecole primaire publique de la Chabure (see http://pagesperso-orange.fr/ecole.chabure/exposes/sciences/ volcans/eruption_volcanique.htm) is very suitable for whole-class work (see below). The title provides an easy entry into the text. The initial paragraph can be left until later, but Anthony should be introduced of course. A key word search ('*Quels sont les mots importants?*') as a collaborative exercise would identify fairly easily words for highlighting or underlining: *bouteille, cône (en plastique), cuillerées (à soupe), bicarbonate de soude, vinaigre. Bassine* is also a key item, but coming last, will probably be missed. The more complex items, if given as single words can be expanded (for example, with the descriptors and other adjectives such as *grand/petit*) and can also be matched to the visuals. A sequence can then be created: the items needed, images and the actions are perhaps best separated initially. The question of what is missing (if the *bassine* has not been mentioned) can be asked ('*Qu'est-ce qui manque?*') to remind the class that it has to be used from the beginning. The experiment can now really take place with target language instructions given by the teacher, or by groups of pupils, depending on ability.

Une éruption volcanique dans la classe!

C'est Anthony qui a fait un exposé sur les volcans. Il nous a parlé de leur situation sur le globe terrestre, de leur naissance, des différentes éruptions, des volcans les plus connus. Mais surtout, il nous a montré comment simuler une éruption!

Voici la recette:

	*Anthony avait confectionné un cône en plastique autour d'une bouteille de 25cl. Il y a placé 3 cuillerées à soupe de bicarbonate de soude.*
	*Il a ensuite rajouté 15cl de vinaigre (avec du colorant rouge).*
	*Immédiatement, le volcan est entré en éruption!*

Heureusement, il avait prévu de placer son volcan dans une bassine!

Short texts such as in this example can be gathered, laminated and given to individual pupils either in whole-class or silent reading sessions. Teachers should develop a system for differentiating the texts by difficulty (although interest is also a highly significant factor) so that individual pupils can all read something at an appropriate level. This is also a possible source of individual extension work where needed. But reading should be available to all pupils and not be reserved for the more able only.

Developing cross-curricularity: four levels of integration

This chapter has emphasised how both challenge and integration should grow as children become more confident in their language learning and has attempted to set out how teachers could also progress in terms of using a limited but growing confidence and competence at different points. This section now seeks to explore how to manage the progression in curricular integration on a planning and policy level. Chapter Six will continue to present ways of achieving this towards the end of KS2, but the idea behind the progression is presented here as it is important, as we have stated already, that teachers (and children) have an idea of the direction in which they are moving.

We can see this progression in terms of four levels of embedding and integration.

- Surface cross-curricular linking.

- Integrating language while building on semi-familiar content.

- Integrating language and new content.

- Immersion (full or partial).

In this scheme we can see that level three is distinct from level two, where level two work recaps and extends material within a topic and level three work addresses an entirely new topic. But levels two and three of this scheme can also be seen as inextricably linked because we should never simply re-teach something which the children all know in the foreign language and stop there. They will see no rationale for doing this as they have learned it already. We can (and should) recap on familiar material before extending into a new direction in the foreign language and, in doing so, we may use more challenging language when the children are familiar with the content and less challenging language when the content is new. So levels two and three will not always be progressive in terms of language level.

The rationale for the progression is given as we more closely define each stage and, first, Table 5.1 sums up the differences through some practical examples.

1 Surface cross-curricular linking

This is probably where teachers with less confidence in their language competence or with existing language teaching experience with a more topic and vocabulary-based focus will begin. In its level of integration, this stage remains mainly language focused in its style and sequencing. As topics arise which allow some links with another curriculum area, they are explored through the language approach with sets of topic vocabulary taught in a more traditional way through imitation and repetition. The focus is more on the use of familiar activity types and limited language rather than allowing the chosen content topics to define language needs. The children will not learn any new content through this level of integration as the pitch is often on material which they learned some time before through English, but which is now revived so that they can learn the foreign language vocabulary associated with it. There is likely to be a listening/speaking focus predominating, backed up with consolidation reading and writing. It can of course be gradually extended and one way of doing this is to use the question words 'Why?' and 'How?' more frequently, as these questions will start to build a greater demand for more complex responses and more thinking.

Examples of activities that may occur in this curriculum include:

- Basic addition and subtraction sums with numbers up to 30 with KS2 students, which do not therefore use mathematics at their current cognitive level.

- As part of a topic on the geography of a target language country: the teaching of compass points through repetition; the teaching of a basic verb form 'to be situated' and then a drill sequence of questions/

Table 5.1 Summary of progression using practical examples

Subject/Topic	Surface cross-curricular links	Integrating language and semi-familiar content	Integrating language and new content	Immersion (full or partial)
Maths	Numbers 1–31 used in addition and subtraction sums in KS2	Numbers 1–31 used in more complex operations, e.g. ? × 10 = 170; 39 ÷ ? = 3; 45 ÷ 10 = ?; √64 = ? Or in a matching task such as: *Trouve les paires*: 75%; 0.67; ¾; 0.25; 2/3; 25%	Teaching a Y4 class to construct different tabular/pictographic representations of data, using TL stimulus	The teaching of an entire subject through the foreign language, for example all the Art and Design curriculum, across several years. The subject becomes associated with the language.
Geography – an aspect of a target language country	The teaching of 8 compass points through imitation/repetition	The teaching of 8 compass points through a challenge to recognise and arrange them using prior knowledge and cognates or through inference via factual information: *Voici quatre villes en France. Calais est dans le nord de la France, et Perpignan est dans le sud. Strasbourg est dans l'est de la France, et Marseille est dans le sud-est.*	Use compass points in target language as part of a task where certain squares are identified on a grid (superimposed on a map). This in Y4 would be new knowledge.	Comprehension of almost native-speaker language becomes possible. This can be extended to other subjects so that a proportion or all of every day is taught in the target language.
Science: healthy eating	Teaching food/drink items and classifying them as healthy or unhealthy	Identifying healthy and unhealthy elements of sample breakfasts – expressing preferences and negotiating healthier options. *J'adore les pains au chocolat. Je prends deux pour mon petit dejeuner. OK je prends un pain au chocloat et un yaourt.*	Teaching the food pyramid as a new item. The visual uses some food items already known, and adds others, but the concept of the pyramid is new. Pupils come to understand the differing amounts needed of the different classes of food in the foreign language.	

statements locating places on a map; the teaching of weather but at a simple sentence and descriptive, rather than 'forecast' level and a subsequent weather forecast role-play which operates on series of single format sentence level units.

- In a PE link: the use of simple commands such as left, right, forward, backward and parts of the body in aerobics style activity, but without more specialist vocabulary being introduced.

- In a science link: the exploration of the life cycle of a butterfly at essentially single word level, for example, first the egg, then the caterpillar, then the cocoon, then the butterfly; or in healthy eating: the use of the single items, healthy and unhealthy, to classify a vocabulary set.

2 Integrating language and semi-familiar content

This approach moves towards a more content-centred base, possibly through a whole-school topic, that is, drawing from different subject areas. It is unlikely to be used to teach an entire unit in another subject as that would imply substantially more new content. The themes may be chosen with language topics in mind, so vocabulary areas that the teacher wants to include in the languages curriculum can still be introduced at this point. There will be some coverage of content already encountered through mother tongue but it is important to build on this in the foreign language. The task styles may be drawn from both foreign languages and content subject methodologies.

There may still be some 'pre-teaching' of key vocabulary, but not in a conventional languages format. For example, as in Table 5.1, pupils might be asked to identify and arrange correctly the eight compass points from a set of cards randomly stuck onto the whiteboard. This focuses them on the vocabulary but they can only do the task by activating their prior knowledge that compass points exist and form a certain pattern. The compass points may either be introduced through the method indicated in Table 5.1 or with a map and photographs of towns as visual support, and as parts of whole sentences: '*Voici quatre villes en France. Calais est dans le nord de la France, et Perpignan est dans le sud. Strasbourg est dans l'est de la France, et Marseille est dans le sud-est.*' In either method the compass points vocabulary is therefore inferred rather than directly taught. The teacher will still give many examples and engage learners in questioning to provide necessary repetition (rather than chorus-style). He or she will establish whether the forms have been heard and internalised properly and a gap-fill reading/writing task will probably be used to consolidate the vocabulary with older learners. There can also be a development into the use of more complex reasoning but still with simple language structures, for example (drawing in the weather, if known) through such questions as: '*Il fait plus chaud à Perpignan qu' à Paris – pourquoi?*', eliciting: '*Parce que Perpignan est dans le sud.*'

Other examples of such a level of integration include:

- More demanding numeracy activity that reflects recent or even current mathematics objectives. This could involve, for example in KS1, number bonds to 20, simple multiplication sums, identification of shapes. In KS2, numbers from 1–30 might be used as the missing part of more complex calculations, such as: $? \times 10 = 170$, $39 \div ? = 3$, $45 \div 10 = ?$, $\sqrt{64} = ?$ or in a matching task such as: *Trouve les paires*: 75%, 0.67, ¾, 0.25, 2/3, 25%. In these examples the teacher can read out the calculation, but pause for the missing item which the class will be able to offer.

- More demanding geographically situated tasks can involve simple comparisons of features in human or physical geography between countries or the reinforcement of facts about global geography (for example, continents, countries, capitals, mountains, rivers, oceans). If the weather topic is used it is important to address some aspects of climate as well as weather and to use authentic internet sources for weather forecasting which involve the range of vocabulary (noun as well as verb forms concerning weather types). The encouragement to use strategies for example to infer *ensoleillé* from *soleil* is vital and reflects an important aspect of the KS2 Framework.

- In a science context, the life cycle of a butterfly can be addressed more fully and in more complete language forms through the story of *The Hungry Caterpillar* (Carle 1995).

- Healthy eating is another very accessible area through the use of classifications of food by fat or salt content, which are very visual in terms of providing material for thought. As long as the language to be used for the output is scaffolded, pupils will cope both willingly and easily.

- Both the water cycle and photosynthesis are further topics which lend themselves to such a visual approach, perhaps using flash animations, and which can therefore support exposure to richer language used as part of a scaffolded explanation and questioning sequence.

- If language topics provide the starting point for the curriculum, then daily routines can offer both citizenship and historical opportunities through, for example, the daily routine of a child in a developing country where lifestyles are very different or by investigating aspects of the lives of children, perhaps during WW2 (KS2 History Unit 9).

- Finally, a friendship/anti-bullying theme, which often forms part of a whole-school focus can also involve parallel foreign language activities which subsequently contribute to a whole-school display or recording of the week's work.

This level of engagement is clearly manageable for all schools as long as planning addresses the vital issue of scaffolding. Chapter Nine offers more strategies for this in the section on the theory behind CLIL. Moving from the surface level to level two is as much about wanting to do it as about language competence. If you can do this as a teacher you will start to offer the challenge that we are suggesting throughout this book is vital for children's continuing progression and continued interest.

3 Integrating language and new content

When we introduce new content in the target language we need to be especially mindful of the language demands we are making. The previous level could in some ways be more challenging linguistically because it was using previously learned content as its base, but taking on a new topic in a foreign language is of course rather daunting. It will take time and confidence before many teachers can easily move into this level of integration, although for a specialist language teacher, the move can be made as soon as the children are ready. But it is important to remember that this is a curriculum focused principally on content objectives via content subject methodologies. It is truly a CLIL framework and if multiplied sufficiently will become an immersion framework (see below). It will take linguistic issues into consideration when framing the ways in which learners meet the concepts and develop the subject skills. Learners will understand more language than they can use productively but they will be able to demonstrate that understanding through tasks that are supported and demand less language.

It is likely that some revision of a previously learned content topic will begin a unit, but new material will then be included, probably with a focus on a target language speaking country. Table 5.1 shows ways for our previously mentioned topics to be extended in this way. It can happen at any level but of course needs to reflect the actual new content the children are scheduled to meet in that year group. Ultimately it is the introduction of a new concept that sets it apart from the level before.

Other examples of topics which may occur in this curriculum and which can still be linked to a relevant languages topic, also ensuring survival language progression, are:

- An extension from a familiar topic taught in Geography or History to a new context. This demonstrates a natural progression between integrating semi-familiar content to integrating new content. For example, a historical character in a target language speaking country can be described and analysed after similar work has been covered in a revisited content context (for example, work on Henry VIII leading to work on Napoleon). This would also link to personal information/ descriptive work in the languages scheme.

- A new topic taught in the foreign language because there is a rationale for this, for example, part of the mountains unit in KS2 Geography taught in French or German with an Alps focus, or in French or Spanish with a Pyrenees focus. This will also link to the world around us/ environment topics in the languages scheme.

- A new topic which centres on practical activity for its understanding, for example a science topic with a strong experimental basis where data rather than abstract explanation provides the material which establishes knowledge and understanding, or areas of the expressive arts, PE, Design curriculum. This will link to the free time, house and home, food and drink, travel/transport or holidays topics in the languages scheme.

4 Immersion (single subject, partial or full)

This approach will also use largely content objectives and content subject methodology, framed with linguistic issues in mind and with an expectation that comprehension will exceed production in scope. The aim of the single subject model (most likely in the UK context) is to teach the National Curriculum content of one subject fully and to facilitate language acquisition through a high level exposure to authentic (although carefully controlled) fluent language. When more subjects are added the model becomes partial or full immersion. A large focus is placed on making the content comprehensible through the use of supporting material and teacher interpretation. Tasks are tightly structured to support the use of language individually and collaboratively, and thereby to internalise the content and language simultaneously. A pure language focus will be needed at some points to consolidate and rationalise language use, for example through grammatical explanation, to ensure learners can manage the complexity of language demanded by the content.

Examples of subjects that may occur in this curriculum are:

- Initially, areas of the expressive arts, technology and PE curriculum which emphasise doing rather than abstract knowledge and where the products can be to a certain extent 'language free'.

- Subsequently, areas of the curriculum with a high visual/tabular content, such as Geography, Mathematics and Science.

- Finally, any subject.

 ### Chapter summary

The chapter has tried in several different ways to offer:

- a rationale for progression (children need to see a deepening of focus or they will become bored)
- a discussion about how we manage that progression in terms of differentiation and personalisation
- concrete examples of how progression might look in linguistic terms, using both receptive and productive skills, oracy and literacy
- a concrete scheme for the progression in content terms, specifically through different levels of cross-curricular integration.

This has been an attempt to provide a signposted and differentiated route towards progression that does not simply operate on a language knowledge, language awareness or knowledge about language model. In this way we have also attempted to ensure that language teaching and learning are pitched in both enjoyment and seriousness, in both fun and challenge in a similar way that other subjects are defined by teachers and perceived by children.

Key and Further Reading 📖

The DfES document, *Grouping Pupils for Success* (2006), gives an indication of the issue from the perspective of Primary Strategy priorities. It is available to download from www.standards.dcsf.gov.uk/primary/publications/literacy/group_pup_succ/ns_grp_succ_0394506.pdf.

Carol Dweck's work on children's perspectives on their own ability is important to bear in mind when addressing issues of ability and progression. Dweck's article with Heidi Grant is a recent work that looks at how self-evaluation and target setting can be used to offset a more negative self-view. Grant, H. and Dweck, C.S. (2003) 'Clarifying Achievement Goals and Their Impact'. *Journal of Personality and Social Psychology.* 85: 541–53.

Rosamund Mitchell and Peter Dickson's report on progression within KS3 offers some food for thought about the nature of learning in ML classrooms ten years ago and underpins some of the messages about rich language input. It is available at www.ioe.ac.uk/mtcg/articlesforcritique/mitchelldickson1997.pdf. Mitchell's more recent work is looking at a similar theme in KS2 and will be very important when reported. Look out for individual reports on each of the three years as they emerge.

How do I make sure I really challenge the older learners?

Introductory vignette

Y6 children talking about learning French:

'If you're in big business you have to travel the world, and if you went to France you could speak French to the people you were doing business with.'

'Some people come over here to work and you need to speak their language when you meet them.'

'It's good that it's quite hard, because if it was too easy we'd fall asleep and it would be boring.'

'You can join in more in French.'

Comment

By Y6, children are much more likely to see the potential instrumental gains of learning another language. They can often also see how they might be able to use it to make friendships with children of their own age. These children were still in their first year of learning French so challenge was not greatly developed at this stage. But they were already indicating that when it was hard, that was a good quality, as was the collaborative nature of the work. Other parts of this focus group interview emphasised the last two comments further as they identified various competitive, collaborative and problem-solving activities as the things they like the most.

Chapter objectives

- To present a unit plan aimed at Y5 or Y6 which demonstrates how far language learning might develop in a 3/4-year programme.
- To suggest additional activity types which can build on established knowledge and skills in creative ways.
- To explore the range of ways in which language teaching and learning might play a part in the life of the school at Upper KS2.

Relevant Q Standards: Q1, Q2, Q4, Q6, Q8, Q10, Q11, Q14, Q15, Q18, Q19, Q22, Q25, Q29, Q32, Q33

 Initial reflection point

If your Y5 or Y6 class has been learning the target language for two or three years, how much language are you now using for routines? Is it enough? If it needs to be developed, how could you increase it? How much do the children use the target language for their part of routine conversations? How might you increase this?

Response

The previous three chapters have each dealt with the theme of target language use, with a view to suggesting a natural development: first of the teacher language, then of the pupil language involved in instructions, management, organisation, resourcing and the questions which arise in classroom life. This chapter will not feature this specifically but has asked the questions in the reflection point deliberately to encourage you as teacher to audit the extent to which the language is now embedded into your routines and has become natural and expected by the children. If you have inherited a class who are not used to this way of working, or the children in upper KS2 have only just started language learning, then the sections in Chapters Four and Five on classroom language should be useful.

Planning for Y5/Y6 topic: *Tudor explorers – Les grandes découvertes*

The first section of this chapter explores the next stage of progression in both content and language through a series of activities in the target language, directly linked to a whole-class topic.

The following planning grid uses French (as that is how we have used it so far) but it could be re-created in German, Spanish or Italian, as it is not specific to French history but belongs to a more general western European historical context. It was used as part of a whole-phase topic which classes in Y5 and Y6 worked with for half a term. The language content is approximately five hours in total, but of course this will vary depending on the class, the amount of time they have learned the language and on the needs of individuals.

Learning objectives	Learning outcomes	Teaching activities/ language	Resources
To ask and answer questions (O5.1)	Identify geographical features and learn about places in different countries	Children see a series of images from francophone countries and note which ones are in France.	Images from French-speaking countries around the world
To recognise similarities and differences between different places (IU5.2)	Understand and name the continents and some countries	*C'est en France? Oui ou non? Pourquoi? Pourquoi pas? C'est où? C'est en Europe/ Afrique/Amérique du Sud/Australie?*	
To understand question forms and negatives in spoken and written language (KAL)		Display cut-out shapes of the different continents. Say their names for children to repeat, e.g. *l'Europe, l'Afrique, Amérique du Sud, l'Amérique du Nord, l'Asie, l'Australasie Phoneme focus: que, ie*	Cut-out shapes of continents
		Display large map of the world. Call out	Map of the world

(Continued)

Learning objectives	Learning outcomes	Teaching activities/ language	Resources
		names of continents and invite children to identify them on the map. *Où est l'Afrique?* etc.	
	Use language cues to produce a practical outcome	Give a small card with a name of a continent to each child. Children walk around the room, finding other children belonging to their continent. *Qui a l'Asie?*	Pieces of card with names of continents
		Place one group of children in a certain place. *Ici c'est l'Europe.* Then ask other groups to find their correct place, reconstructing the map of the world. *Où est l'Afrique?*	
		Show satellite image of the world. Ask children to identify certain continents and features. *Où est l'Australie? C'est quelle continent?*	Satellite image of the world
To listen attentively and understand more complex phrases and sentences (O5.3)	Develop understanding of past and present, historical change. Use and analyse a historical source. Make notes	Then show a large image of a Tudor period map of the world. Let children look at copies in group	Copies of map from Tudor period

Learning objectives	Learning outcomes	Teaching activities/ language	Resources
		with a task: *Quelles sont les differences? Faites une liste*	
To make simple sentences and short texts (L5.2)		Then repeat questioning as before, including: *Où est l'Amérique? L'Amérique n'est pas là*	
To practise new language with a friend (LLS)		Write year of origin of the map on board (e.g. by Henricus Martellus, 1489) *L'Amérique existe, mais en Europe, on ne sait pas ça! L'Amérique n'a pas été découverte, n'est-ce pas?*	
To use context and previous knowledge to help understanding and reading skills (LLS)		*Quels continents ne sont pas là? L'Amerique du nord, l'Amerique du sud, l'Australie*	
		Then ask groups to look at the map again with these questions: *Où sont les pays de l'Europe? Quelles sont les autres différences?*	
		Ask in plenary for the location of a range of countries – include also more difficult items,	

(Continued)

Learning objectives	Learning outcomes	Teaching activities/ language	Resources
	Read and understand short passages and identify key elements of a short text	e.g. *Où est l'Inde?* Introduce some explorers, giving an image and a short description.	Map of the world with navigation routes of different explorers
To read and understand the main points and some detail from a short written passage (L6.1)	Recall and practise personal information Practise and use third person singular	*En 1492 Christophe Colomb découvre l'Amérique. Il arrive sur le continent américain le 12 octobre 1492, après 70 jours de navigation.*	
		En 1534 le navigateur français, Jacques Cartier, part à la recherche d'une route vers l'Asie. Il découvre le Canada.	Short descriptions of explorers' routes
To use context and previous knowledge to help understanding and reading skills (LLS)		In pairs children identify navigation route on map and colour code different routes of different explorers	
	Work collaboratively	Children work in groups to produce notes from the texts used in previous activity for a class timeline, e.g. *En 1492 Christophe Colomb découvre l'Amérique. En*	

Learning objectives	Learning outcomes	Teaching activities/ language	Resources
		1534 Jacques Cartier découvre le Canada.	
To make simple sentences and short texts (L5.3)	Recognise, understand and use language about explorers' lives	Children work in pairs to classify statements about two different explorers, e.g. Columbus and Cartier.	Cut-up statement of two explorers
Prepare a short presentation on a familiar topic (O5.4)	Recognise and practise use of third person singular	*Il s'appelle... Il vient de France/Genova. Il découvre le Canada/ L'Amérique. Ses bateaux s'appellent La Grande Hermillon/Santa Maria, Nina et Pinta.*	
Write sentences on a range of topics using a model (L6.4)	Plan, prepare and present a short presentation		
Apply knowledge of language rules and conventions when building short sentences (KAL)		They then prepare and present a short presentation of one explorer to the class	
Perform to an audience (O6.2)			

In this approach it is important to note that the topic mixes levels two and three of the four-stage scheme presented in Chapter Five. Some of this material builds on (presumed) prior knowledge about the world and the continents, and some on the ongoing work that the children were doing in English. But there are also elements which are new and the text material around the explorers and their lives was unknown and was not being covered at all in the part of the scheme delivered in English.

It is equally important to note that the topic is built up from early confidence boosting activity that is neither linguistically nor conceptually challenging and which is designed to settle the class into a positive and anxiety-free mindset. The first activity expects that children will be able to recognise that some scenes in the pictures are not in France. This is then linked to some basic knowledge of the globe, with the names of continents and some relevant countries on either side of the Atlantic Ocean. The names in the target language can be taught through use and not as separate vocabulary items especially as they are cognate with English and will be related to prior knowledge by a majority of learners. However, not all learners will know accurately the make-up of the globe and the physical relationships between these areas, so there is both some consolidation and some teaching of new content here, depending on individual pupils. With all new content-based topics it is important (and also reflects standard good practice) to begin in this way, re-establishing prior knowledge and as close a level playing field for all pupils as possible. But it is equally important to raise the game, conceptually, quite soon.

This scheme first does this by using an original source, the Martellus map, to provide an important piece of 'new' information, that is, that in the late fifteenth century no Europeans knew of the existence of America. Because the map is visual and is linked to the immediately preceding work, the new concept is established without language (the children see the image and see that America is missing) and then with language. (Having gained the new concept, the language is then mapped on to that piece of knowledge and from that context any new words become meaningful immediately.) Both American continents and Australia are missing in the map and this can be established through questioning. It also gives an easy opportunity to practise some of the countries that will be needed as origins of the great voyages. The European section of the map is mostly very recognisable so identifying the UK, France, Spain, Portugal is easy. But the teacher can also ask about other differences between this map and modern versions – this is an important historical skill, to identify that things change and that original sources help us track these changes.

The next stage is to introduce some text. In effect the teacher has done this aurally through questions that have produced statements about the map. But the class has had this heavily scaffolded because the questions have been prompts for answers that together have produced a series of statements which constitute an aural text. Now the use of written text, which requires reading, makes the work progress and involves literacy in a different way.

It is vital in all of this to use group work to allow children to pool knowledge and scaffold each other. The role of talk in learning is established beyond any contention and whether we look to overriding mental schemes such as Vygotsky's (1978) zone of proximal development, or more activity-focused interpretations such as Wells' (1999) dialogic teaching or Mercer's (1995) talk types, we know that asking children to talk together in a focused way will be valuable. If the overarching task is given in the target language and they need to report back in the target language, then even if the dialogue is in English, the learning will be secured and they will need to formulate their thoughts in the target language as part of the activity. So for the group work on the map or on the text, we should ensure that the way we set up the task and the way we 'harvest' the work that they have been doing uses the target language and is manageable for the children. If we do this, their language will be enhanced and they will also be thinking in the ways they do in other subjects.

The use of short texts in this unit is designed to introduce a range of new facts to the children and to allow them to internalise this new knowledge by engaging with those texts and manipulating the information. But, importantly, this is done with the overall purpose of producing a short presentation for the rest of the class. Because different groups of children will work on slightly different texts, each of these presentations will also hold new information for some class members, and so can be designed as listening tasks, ensuring still further exposure to the key language in context.

The scheme is arranged with the teaching activities and language areas covered in the third column. These were the driving factors in the planning of the topic, and the cross-referencing to the KS2 Framework came afterwards as an audit for breadth and to check that progression in terms of Y6 objectives was being addressed. Chapter Seven deals with the planning process, using the Framework in detail, so this aspect will not be commented on here.

The topic was then developed further by moving into a study of Canada, comparing features such as size, climate, wildlife, favourite sports between the UK and Canada and so linking to geography. This no longer reflected the work in English, but was directly derived from Cartier's discovery of the country and its resulting bilingual nature. The children appreciated the opportunity to use language that would be useful to them (for example, relating to weather, animals and spare-time hobbies) in other contexts as well as just for the topic.

Reflection point

Try to find some simple text material using the internet which would support one of the themes mentioned above for the Canada topic. (If you are teaching Spanish, you may like to do this for a Spanish-speaking Central or South American country; if you are teaching German, you may like to look at Namibia). How difficult is it to find this material? Have you found images, tables or diagrams as well as text? Is the text in long sentences or short bullet points? Have you found any material on websites of schools in the target countries?

Response

Searching for material is an inevitable (and perhaps unenviable) burden on language teachers. But when we find good material we are always extremely pleased that we can offer children something more targeted to their interests and to developing a better understanding of language and the target environment. School websites can be useful as they sometimes offer material, written by children, at or near the right level. In text searches generally, it can be fruitful to search using a small sample of the kind of text you are looking for, as this can throw up less obvious internet sources. Using image searches is also important as you need visual material as well as text. Do not rule out target language versions of Wikipedia as it often contains tabular material, or sites such as YouTube as they can offer some (appropriate) surprises!

The remainder of the chapter looks at the different types of work you may wish to include in your language learning scheme, either in addition to the topic work as described before, or instead of it, if you are working separately from the rest of the curriculum.

Songs

We mentioned earlier that even at the top of KS2, songs were still a very popular element of language learning according to the survey of the primary school reported in Hood (2006). By Y5 and Y6, although many children still actively engage in the authentic action type songs we have been advocating right from EYFS stage, pupils will all also appreciate something closer to youth culture if we can offer this. There are singers who are frequently recommended by teachers such as Henri Dès for French, Detlev Jöcker for German and Rosa León for Spanish. (All of these have their own websites and CDs can be bought fairly easily through Amazon, for example.)

We have found in our French teaching that there is a very useful source in the singer Ilona Mitrecey who started recording at the age of 12 and has therefore genuine pop (techno-flavoured) music with a younger approach than is normally evident in chart-based music. You can hear songs such as 'Laissez-nous respirer', 'Dans ma fusée' and 'Retourner à l'école' at:

www.youtube.com/watch?v=5v16cDk8vt4

http://uk.youtube.com/watch?v=gO4FLHRdw_Q

http://uk.youtube.com/watch?v=C8RKAEajybM&feature=related

The first item actually includes a YouTube discussion (Autumn 2008) about the grammar of the French in the title, which is certainly testimony to the motivational power of the music! At the time of writing, the singer's own website is no longer active, but there are numerous sites related to her including the very important lyric sites.

Singing is not only popular but, just as for younger pupils, also supports learning, and teachers will want to encourage the use of songs for this as well as for cultural reasons. Mnemonic use of singing is very common amongst primary language teachers and there are a number of commercial resources available which have songs especially created for language learning, centred around topics and functional sentences. Teachers vary in their enthusiasm for such resources but the rationale behind using singing of whatever format is not disputed.

Stories

Stories continue to engage learners at ten and eleven and although their reading in English is reaching quite sophisticated levels which cannot be replicated in the target language, it is important to keep an eye on the age-related aspect of material we offer them. Cook (1997) and Ellis and Brewster (2002) clearly show how and why stories are important for language development. In their full-length resource book, Ellis and Brewster explore the ways to read and tell a story and how this can impact on language learning in L1, EAL and FL terms, and they offer many concrete examples. In general, as with the songs, children are often very willing to read 'younger' texts, especially if the work that spins from it is more obviously age appropriate. (See Chapter Seven for a scheme based on *Handa's Surprise*, for example.)

Mercer Mayer's books in translation have been used successfully with the age group. A good example is *There's an alligator under my bed* (1998)

(*Il y a un alligator sous mon lit* / *Da liegt ein Krokodil unter meinem Bett*, or in Spanish, a parallel book is available: *Una pesadilla en mi armario* (1992)). This book is intended for younger readers but the language level is enough to challenge upper KS2 children and the teacher can evoke their memories of being scared as younger children or their reflections on their younger brothers' and sisters' fears now. This injects some humour into the reading.

From a linguistic perspective the story has three obvious features: it contains food vocabulary; it is a narrative of events with a selection of first and third person verb forms which allow consolidation of the pronouns 'I' and 'he/she/it' through acting out, sequencing, retelling, and recasting into a different story sequence; it also has a selection of prepositions making it a useful contextual way of signalling how to say under, in, on, next to and behind. As always the story should be read for enjoyment first and foremost. It falls into three sections with the initial problem (the alligator under the bed), followed by the solution (the boy entices the alligator into the garage) and finally the next problem that arises as a result (Father will find the alligator in the garage when he goes to work the next day!). This makes it easier to focus on the text in more detail after the initial reading, and by Y5 and Y6 we can read more intensively word by word, not through the entire story but with a real attention to certain sentences and perhaps to some language forms, such as the first and third person pronouns. Pausing between sections allows some prediction and some summary in the target language (both with support frames offered by the teacher). After some more detailed reading, alternative story-lines which are heavily based on the original, can be created by pairs or small groups, and can be read or acted for others in the class.

Some non-specialist teachers feel that stories are quite daunting at this level and worry about issues such as their fluency of delivery, pronunciation or ability to cope with questions that arise during reading. A good solution to this is the use of electronic stories that are often part of larger courses. One popular set of such stories are 'Talking Big Books' obtainable from www.earlystart.co.uk/bb/index.htm#guide. These are available in French, German and Spanish and contain the stories, teacher notes, interactive activities and electronic flashcards. Using resources such as these enables less confident teachers to gain enhancement of their own pronunciation and intonation and to learn new vocabulary while working on these elements with the class. The story should remain the essential part of the activity and all of the techniques which primary teachers would list to characterise good story reading should still be used with such resources. The accompanying activities are a bonus which will support further consolidation of the vocabulary, although an eye to the issue of cognition and challenge may be necessary for upper KS2 pupils if the teacher feels these are missing.

Books with a very small amount of language can still sometimes provoke thought and emotion. A good example of this (although only available in French) is *Mon cochon* by Jean-Pierre Blanpain (2001). The pig at the centre of the story does not like being pink so imagines how he might be a range of different colours (*'Il aurait aimé être bleu comme le ciel … ou rouge comme une tomate'*). At the end he reveals the reason why he does not want to be pink (*Le rose, c'est la couleur du jambon –* because it is the colour of ham). The story is completely understandable because of the key words and the pictures but contains a useful structure – he would have liked to be – which can also be transposed to first person and used to encourage some creative writing by the children who have read the story.

 Reflection point

Choose a good storybook for use with an Upper KS2 class. If you do not have easy access to material in your target language, choose an English resource which you might be able to find in a translated version (check www.amazon.fr/www.amazon.de/www.casadellibro.com). Why might this be a good resource to use and what might be the pitfalls? How would you read it, with what specific focus? What kind of activities might lead from it? How might it link with a wider topic?

Poetry

Poetry is both a good source of short texts to read and a stimulus for simple but fulfilling and imaginative writing as a follow-up. Finding the right poems is not quick or easy, but two useful French websites are www.momes.net and www.tact.fse.ulaval.ca/fr/html/nathalie/poesiefinal. htm. Momes has a great deal of material to offer and is a superb resource – the poems can be found under the comptines section. The second site is one where younger children have either written poems or selected one they like and have drawn a picture of it. Searches in German or Spanish will reveal similar sites – one small selection in German, for example, is at http://theodorschule.lspb.de/Kinder/ Gedichte/index.html#NACH_TITELN. These are poems written by children either as *elfchen* (consisting of eleven words) or *rondell* (a round where the first two lines are repeated as the last two). Having a structure, like these or using *haiku* form, or perhaps going to an acrostic pattern, helps to make pupils think about their choice of words and limits in a positive way how much and how they write.

Because the children in Y5 and Y6 are accustomed to a variety of written material and to reading for information and for pleasure through English, they are often much more able to use strategies to make sense of material in the foreign language as well. This means that poetry reading is something very appropriate for paired or group reading. The texts are short and should be linguistically manageable although preferably with food for thought or something that will generate an emotional reaction of some kind.

'Sommerglück von Louisa' is available at the website mentioned above:

> Es ist schwül.
> Das ist kaum mehr auszuhalten.
> Ein Eis hilft dagegen.
> Es ist schwül.
> Die Sonne strahlt.
> Bei so einem Wetter gehe ich ins Schwimmbad.
> Es ist schwül.
> Das ist kaum mehr auszuhalten.

This poem has some keywords that are instantly recognisable, such as *'Sommer'* (summer) in the title, *'Eis'* (ice cream), *'Sonne'* (sun), *'Schwimmbad'* (swimming pool). It contains an expression, *'Das ist kaum mehr auszuhalten'* (It's hard to bear it any longer) which will be unknown and is not easily guessable, but which could be a useful expression to know and could be used as the centre-piece of a follow-up poem written by pairs or individuals. The word *'schwül'* (humid, oppressive) will not be known but could be given as a clue and might help to unlock the longer sentence, especially as both are part of the repeated sequence.

How much a pair or group would be able to make of the whole poem's literal meaning depends on their strategy use. If the class has learned *'Hilfe!'* (Help!) they may guess the end of line 3. They should be able to guess *'strahlt'* (shine or beam) because that is what the sun does and it is a poem about summer heat. Similarly, *'bei so einem Wetter'* should emerge clearly from the context. You might ask pairs to perform the poem, taking a line each so it becomes a dialogue. You might ask them to create an alternative version by giving them the phrase *'es friert so'* (it's freezing) to use instead of *'es ist schwül'* and to substitute where necessary other items to make it read sensibly. They could also perform it as a dialogue. Finally, more able pupils might manage to create a non-weather version by retaining the long sentence of the repeated couplet and thinking of another situation where it is hard to bear it any longer. An example of a new version which shows how effective a small amount of language might be is: '*Fünf zu null / es ist kaum mehr auszuhalten / ich möchte ein Tor! / Fünf zu null / Sie spielen so gut / Wir spielen so schlecht! / Fünf zu null / es ist kaum mehr auszuhalten.*' (5–0 / It's hard to bear it any longer / I'd like one goal / 5–0 / They're playing so well / We're playing so badly! / 5–0 / It's hard to bear it any longer.)

Other resources

We can also be creative at this older level by using existing 'language free' resources for foreign language teaching. A very frequently used item from the Literacy Framework is *The Piano* (by Aidan Gibbons) downloadable from: www.standards.dfes.gov.uk/primaryframework/ library/Literacy/ict/ictks2. This very moving two-and-a-half minute animation of a man playing a piano while reminiscing about his life, which has been known to reduce children (and even teachers!) to tears, is intended in Y5 Literacy to stimulate discussion about both its content (not completely defined so open to interpretation) and also its technique (the filming, especially use of camera angles). Like any language-free resource we can make of it whatever we wish, but given the realistic limits of language at Y5 or Y6, we suggest two approaches that have been successful, both used after the class had seen the animation during Literacy time. There is a time-line which can be inferred from the piece but is not obvious, and which can serve as a group-based language activity. Children can at first match sentences in the target language to the scenes of the animation and hold them up as it plays. They can subsequently arrange these in the order in which they might have appeared in the man's life (which is not the same order as the animation itself). The emotions evoked by the different sequences are another potential topic although, to do justice to the resource, we cannot simply use basic feelings such as happy and sad, as the level of discussion that would be produced in English would be much deeper. Here you might encourage children to ask for words that they wish to use to express what they think the subject is feeling and to locate these together using an online dictionary on the whiteboard. This clearly is a more demanding activity for both teacher and class, but could result in a collaborative paragraph written together to sum up the way that the class has reacted to the animation.

There is a German story, *Opas Engel* (Bauer 2003) (also available in a Spanish translation *El angel del abuelo*) which traces a similar and also serious theme and which could be a very strong follow-up to using *The*

Piano with a Y6 class. Again the language is in short and simple sentences, is limited to a few words on each page and so is manageable and yet still thought-provoking.

Non-fiction material

An ideal source of non-fiction material might be a partner school in a target language speaking country because you could specify exactly what you are looking for. Certainly such a link could be used to activate material for a classroom display on a theme, which is one very good way to present and highlight for attention some key language around an informational topic. We will look at school-to-school linking in a later section of this chapter.

But without such a link the best source of non-fiction material is real books or magazines that you find during holidays in the countries (or through online bookshops which show sample pages). They generate texts of all types that you can use (by scanning them) for whole-class work, but are still available for groups to handle as books for more personalised reading tasks. Magazines are particularly good as they can be broken up and used as single pages, laminated or in plastic wallets. The internet is of course a further source if you have the time and optimism to surf.

Using non-fiction material tends to highlight initially the skill of reading for information, the inference of unknown words from context and the learning of new information through the language. Reading challenging text in a second language and the use of reading strategies has featured in the work of many researchers, for example Barnett (1991), Grabe and Stoller (2002) and Koda (2005). All of these writers agree that a self-awareness of why we are reading and how we might read are important elements that contribute towards success. The sophistication of the objectives in the Literacy strand Understanding and Interpreting texts at Y5 and Y6 level gives an indication of the mother-tongue or EAL expectations made on children. You may not want to work with more complex texts in another language as a whole class too often because it can be very challenging, but it undoubtedly enhances language learning if you set it into that context. If you do find a variety of short texts, the approach also works very well as an extension activity for more able pupils and for groups who enjoy the 'problem solving' aspect of reading. In gathering this material it might help to consider Figure 9.3 in Chapter

Nine which raises the notion of different types of text and their difficulty levels. Adaptation is of course sometimes necessary as what you find is often not exactly what you want.

For French, two sections of Momes can be used to locate non-fiction material although there will usually be a need to modify it a little as it is really intended for native French speakers:

www.momes.net/dictionnaire/minidossiers/archives.html

www.momes.net/education/introduction.html

The German online school web server is at www.schulweb.de/de/deutschland/ index.html?region=de. By choosing a region and the type of school (*Grundschule*), you can access a range of school sites some of which have texts written by children and teachers that can be adapted for your purposes.

An example of a children's site in Spanish that has a range of material is www.holachicos.com/6a9/index.html. One item in the ecology section of this site lists reasons why animals might be in danger, and we will use this to suggest how quite challenging text might be used at Y6 level.

> *¿Te interesa saber cuáles son las principales causas de peligro?*
>
> *La persecución y la matanza por el valor de sus pieles.*
>
> *La caza y la pesca por la comercialización de las carnes.*
>
> *Las grandes empresas que realiza el hombre como represas, autopistas, etc.*
>
> *Contuminación de los mares cuando hay derrame de petróleo.*
>
> *Invasión de otras especies.*
>
> *Contaminación con uranio, polonio o cualquier elemento radioactivo.*
>
> *Erupción de volcanes, inundaciones, catástrofes en general.*
>
> *Incendios.*

The best approach to a text such as this is a combination of work as a whole class with groups finding out and reporting back. It can be presented as a real problem-solving challenge so the children know they are not expected to find it easy. Although the vocabulary is difficult, a keyword identification task, highlighting words which children think they may be able to guess would start to produce a first level of understanding. The theme of the list itself acts as an advance organiser and the use of prior knowledge is clearly a support for this kind of reading. Pupils can also, for example, be asked to check the initial words on each line to start with – this gives several cognates that more able children will know and which will start to be shared within mixed-ability groups. It is important to show children that they can get something out of complex texts, but also to give support at the right point. So a checklist in English of parts of these reasons (for example motorways, floods, furs, radioactive elements, oil-spills), given after the first level of work, will start to focus the readers on further identification of vocabulary. After main meanings have been established for each sentence using this combination of group-base and whole-class detection, the teacher can take stock and perhaps even reveal a translation, in random order as a checklist. Follow-up work which is less challenging might include the making of a display on the theme *'animales en peligro'*. This would enable the list to be recycled with groups producing a good illustration or diagram for each one and then labelling it carefully. The reasons could also be arranged in hierarchical order for England or Spain according to which are the most likely threats to species in our countries, again a task that involves reading and thinking before re-organising the sentences.

There is a link from this page to specific animals in danger, one of which is the jaguar.

> *¿Cuáles son sus territorios?*
>
> *El Yaguareté habita todo tipo de ambientes, lugares casi desérticos, áreas selváticas o zonas elevadas. Se cree que en las zonas desérticas de california está extinguido pero no se lo puede aún confirmar, ocupa las altiplanicies de México, las áreas selváticas de Brasil y la zona montañosa de Bolivia y Argentina, no superando los 1800 metros de altura.*
>
> *Se cree que quedan unos 10.000 ejemplares en todo el continente.*

This might be attacked as a whole-class task. If children are told that they will find three different types of habitats in which jaguars can still be found (and one in which they think it no longer lives) it is possible that even if they cannot be sure about the precise meaning of these words they will be able to identify those which they think are the key words for a dictionary check. Groups can each choose a key word, write it on a mini-whiteboard and hold it up. The teacher can then check the three most popular choices first (if possible using an online dictionary, for example www.wordreference.com) and then go back to the text to see if more has been unlocked as a result. There may be some English in this discussion, but if the focus and concentration is firmly on making meaning from the Spanish the effort is worthwhile. It is often interesting to ask for a general summary of a text at the beginning and a further one at the end of a task such as this. In this way children can see clearly how much they have gained from the process linguistically, and can also identify some new knowledge that they did not have before.

 Reflection point

If you have less experience of using text in this way, try to locate something online about a current topic you are teaching to upper KS2 outside language time. Use the text in the ways described above. Talk to the children about the process and find out how they feel about challenging material.

Talk activities

In Chapter Five we commented that one way to encourage more spontaneous speaking, which goes beyond simple dialogue tasks the teacher may set up for pairs or groups, was to use a role-play corner similar to that normally setup in the EYFS and, increasingly, KS1 classrooms. For upper KS2 classes, it might be appropriate to use a transactional focus, including a counter, brochures of various sorts and a till. The introductory vignette showed that children of this age are more likely to consider the career applications of languages, and this is clearly a very flexible setting. A travel agency or tourist information centre would probably offer the most potential to practise the language that appears in this stage of language learning. Dialogues on countries, transport, entertainment facilities, times and costs feature in both scenarios. As we mentioned in Chapter Five, scenario cards are probably the best way of stimulating dialogue. They should still be very clear and in simple language, which will prompt the dialogue without either setting translation tasks (keep them in the target language) or giving all the language needed so that they are merely scripts to read out.

Vous êtes une famille de cinq personnes (et un chien!). Vous voulez faire des vacances sur un camping en Normandie. Une personne adore l'equitation, une personne adore la mer et une personne adore lire. Vous avez €1500.

It is worth having some core phrases on display in the role-play area; testing is not the purpose of the activities here, but fluency development is a definite aim. *'Je voudrais'* clearly needs to be there, but other examples might also include: *'Ça coute combien?'*, *'Pardon, je n'ai pas compris'*, *'Vous êtes serieux/se?'*

Encouraging an injection of humour from the children participating is a very positive aim as it acts as a strong motivator for them to return to the area again and 'play with language'. Tarone (2000) and Bell (2005) both found that humour enhanced language learning amongst adults, as the language processing was more memorable when associated with something humorous. Cook (1997) extolled the virtues of language play, making connections between first and second language learning. This underpins the use of jokes or word play for receptive listening or reading work as a potentially productive part of the teacher's repertoire. It is evidently more challenging to visualise this with children involved in language production and it may be more likely to happen with the more able. Nevertheless, ensuring mixed ability pairs and threes work together is obvious good practice and sometimes it is the personality rather than the language ability that creates a potential humorous moment, which can then be built on collectively. In the role-play area, recognised characters from TV advertising might be suggested as 'role models' or you may like to overlay an unexpected context on one of the roles: the travel or tourist agency worker may be extremely tired or new to the job, or the customer may be in a hurry to get the business done and meet another appointment. Children might exaggerate costs, offer unpleasant sounding options or try out catch phrases from TV comedies (*L'ordinateur dit "non"!'*). Of course it will not appear from nowhere – the desire to be funny will be there but before suggesting this angle to dialogue work, the necessary language must be prepared in other types of work.

European Languages Day – possible roles for older children

Each year on the 26 September, or as near to that date as possible, a day is designated as European Languages Day. UK information about this can be accessed at www.cilt.org.uk/edl/index.htm and www.nacell.org.uk/ideas/edl.htm but it is also interesting to see a wider European perspective at www.ecml.at/edl/find.asp. Events are tailored for all age groups learning foreign languages but a number do relate to primary learners and the most important intention of the celebration is that individual schools or local authorities can arrange special events for their own children. This is a good opportunity for the involvement of all pupils in the school in different ways. A video clip on one school's range of activity is available at: www.primarylanguages.org.uk/Leaders/planning/European-Day-of-Languages/. Children in Upper KS2 classes can contribute by devising and taking part in the sort of active culturally-based, fun-based and inclusive language activities which form a part of these events. But this can also offer the older children a chance to help plan and run activities and add a different dimension to their experience of the day, especially if they have come through the school taking part regularly. One feature of many of these days is the celebration of the different languages present amongst pupils attending the school. Younger children who have a community or other language and who want to share this will find it difficult to structure a teaching activity to offer others, but older pupils can support this, drawing on their greater experience of learning a language to suggest ways of choosing language to teach and then having an appropriate activity to achieve this. Younger classes who want to run a café or to sell items they have made which have a target language connection can advise both about the practical aspects of this and the language that might be used. Older children can have a real role in greeting and accompanying visitors and ensuring that languages are used to do this to make the whole experience memorable for everyone. Since language learning, in terms of the lesson experience, often has such a positive effect on children's self-esteem, it is thoroughly appropriate to enhance this still further through activity which is possible because of a languages and intercultural curriculum, but is in areas also outside that.

Advantages of school linking

A school link is often best organised with a strong focus on the upper KS2 children simply because they have a little more language and are slightly more independent. There is also more of a chance, perhaps, that they might travel to the country and meet their partner school. The best access point for a new school link if the LA does not have a partner authority in the country is to use the Global Gateway's Find a Partner facility at www.globalgateway.org.uk/Default.aspx?page=0. This gives both a search facility and a great deal of advice about school linking and other international activity in schools.

Many school partnerships start with a single class-to-class link with either letters, e-mail messages, an audio or videotape or video-conference event. In many ways, the more traditional letters are still very positive as they give children a chance to experience real handwriting on real paper (often squared from France and Germany) and to know that another child has created this for them to read. The simplest letters still bring a great deal of pleasure and the teachers can negotiate about the language/s used. It can be a good policy to start by letting children use their own language but to encourage them to think carefully about the needs of a reader who doesn't have much of that language when they construct the letter. From there a mix of languages or an attempt to write in the target language can be planned in – frequent exchanges, although time-consuming to organise at first, are certainly profitable in that they quickly build the relationship and the expectation towards making other kinds of contact seem desirable to the children. The link can be further developed through whole-class activity and some of this could even take place in English rather than foreign language lesson time. For example, two parallel objectives within the strand: Creating and Shaping texts in the Primary Literacy Framework are:

Y5: Create multi-layered texts, including use of hyperlinks and linked web pages

Y6: Integrate words, images and sounds imaginatively for different purposes

Similarly Programme of Study Objective 3b in the KS2 ICT National Curriculum reads:

to be sensitive to the needs of the audience and think carefully about the content and quality when communicating information [for example, work for presentation to other pupils, writing for parents, publishing on the internet].

These objectives can be met within the Literacy/ICT allocated time by a class working together on the best format for a written presentation about the school, created as webpages and made accessible to the partner school via the internet. Because the language will need to be restricted, the use of images and sound files could be crucial in designing something which is comprehensible to the children in the partner class. Working in this way validates the partner school communication as a general curriculum activity and not just a foreign language task. As importantly, it also highlights the role of intercultural understanding as a whole-school issue. To make sure that other classes recognise that the link exists and see what can be gained, the materials received from the partner school, re-formatted electronically if they do not arrive in that form, can be presented through an assembly by the class that receives them. This may take two or three weeks of foreign language lessons in its preparation, but the range of language skills involved (listening to and reading the original source, extracting and summarising material, perhaps into a PowerPoint presentation, creating and then rehearsing a spoken script, performing in assembly) more than warrants the time. The effect on the self-esteem of older pupils when they achieve this kind of presentational level is enormous. The message it gives to younger pupils about the progression that is in-built into language learning is wonderful.

Chapter summary

This chapter has set out to establish the range of activity that is possible by the end of KS2. It is not intended as a compulsory checklist and clearly different classes will have different interests, capabilities and preferences in terms of activities and materials. We have shown that stories can still play a central role in how children meet new language and can spark very positive follow-up work even at Y6. We have stressed that age-appropriateness is an important consideration and that this will determine the way you use a resource even if sometimes the resource is not at first sight aimed at this age group. We have shown that teachers can be very flexible about how children use new language and that 'making it real' in as many ways as possible is even more important than with younger children. Chapter Seven will show in more detail how the KS2 Framework has some quite challenging objectives by Y6 and we have tried to echo this in this chapter.

In summary, we firmly believe that four years good teaching, even of just one hour a week, can bring children to levels of receptive and productive ability which will give secondary colleagues the opportunity to plan exciting and challenging lessons in KS3, and which should ensure we overturn the so-called 'national language barrier' which still persists in the perceptions of some groups in the UK even in the twenty-first century.

Key and Further Reading

The most recent OFSTED survey of languages across schools is available at: www.ofsted. gov.uk/Ofsted-home/Publications-and-research/Education/Curriculum/Modern-foreign-languages/The-changing-landscape-of-languages. Sections that are especially worth exploring are 'The Executive Summary, Recommendations', paras 1–10, 34–47 and 89–117. This conveys OFSTED's perspective about what they feel should be present in language learning at both K32 and KS3 that can then be compared with the factors that this book recommends from a teaching and learning perspective.

7

How do I use the KS2 Framework?

Introductory vignette

Language learning should be planned as an integral part of the whole curriculum, adding a new dimension, rather than a 'bolt-on' extra. The Framework exists to enable schools to build motivating and imaginative teaching plans and units, which deal with content of real interest and relevance to children. (DfES 2005: 8)

Comment

This quotation from the KS2 Framework makes clear the importance of planning activities which are integrated into the wider curriculum, and stresses the need for the actual content and style of language units to be exciting. The KS2 Framework should act as an audit tool for teachers which ensures that their planning achieves two major elements: firstly, a good coverage of a range of objectives across the four language skills, intercultural understanding, knowledge about language and the beginnings of an ability to draw on language learning strategies; secondly, a sense of progression across the four years of learning from age seven to eleven.

Chapter objectives

- **To investigate the different strands set out in the KS2 Framework for ML.**
- **To present and discuss a unit of work planned with the KS2 Framework.**
- **To consider the wider context of language learning when planning with the Framework.**

Relevant Q Standards: Q7a, Q8, Q14, Q15, Q22, Q23, Q24

Initial reflection point

1 Read the following sequence of activities and reflect on what the children are doing and learning.

A class of Y3 children are listening to the story *Le bonhomme de neige*. The teacher encourages them to join in with storytelling by miming the actions every time they hear a weather expression. When they hear certain weather phrases for the second or third time, some children join in with the words as well as the actions.

Having met the new language through a story the children practise these expressions through a variety of activities, such as '*Jacques a dit...*' or '*Répétez si c'est vrai*', a simple repetition game to reinforce pronunciation. The teacher chooses the '*oi*' phoneme as a focus to develop the children's phonological awareness, making links already familiar words such as '*moi, toi, trois*'.

At the end of the session they look at a series of images showing different weather conditions in a variety of French-speaking countries and the children describe the weather, selecting a written phrase from a word bank displayed on the interactive whiteboard.

Throughout the week the children take turns in updating their classroom calendar, changing the date as well as the weather. Later during the week the children paint hot or cold landscapes, adding a short description of their art work in French.

2 In Framework terms the following objectives were met – match up each of these to one or more of the activities above:

- O3.1 Listen and respond to simple rhymes, stories and songs.
- O3.3 Perform simple communicative tasks using single words, phrases and short sentences.
- L3.1 Recognise some familiar words in written form.
- L3.3 Experiment with the writing of simple words.
- IU3.2 Locate country/countries where the language is spoken.
- IU3.4 Make indirect or direct contact with the country/countries where the language is spoken.
- KAL Identify specific sounds, phonemes and words; imitate pronunciation of words; hear main word classes; link sounds to meanings; notice the spelling of familiar words.
- LLS Use actions and rhymes and play games to aid memorisation; use the context of what they see/read to determine some of the meaning; use gestures to show they understand.

What does the Framework offer teachers?

The Framework should be seen as a support, not a constraint: a climbing frame, not a cage (DfES 2005: 4)

This statement is crucial in interpreting how to use the Framework. We mentioned above that it is a means to audit your provision and it offers a very strong and well-organised model for achieving this. But in many ways it is not the starting point. As our sample scheme will show, later in this chapter, it is difficult to simply plan a series of activities around these objectives and to meet them neatly one by one – that is actually not the intention of the Framework. Like all current government frameworks there is a great deal of support on the website (it is all downloadable from www.standards.dfes.gov.uk/primary/publications/languages/framework/) or in the hard copy folder. There is cross-referencing between different objectives and sample activities, so it is important to become familiar with what is on offer. It is deliberately designed to support both experienced primary teachers, taking on a language teaching commitment, and non-primary languages specialists from other sectors.

Before discussing further how we might use it, here is a summary of its essential features:

- It does not prescribe the content (no 'topics').

- It is non-language specific.

- It is skills-based and with progression built into each strand.

The strands are linked and it is important to see them connected and complementing each other, and not as isolated skill areas, especially not as four separate skills as in GCSE or the Languages Ladder.

The three core strands are:

- Oracy (listening and speaking)

- Literacy (reading and writing)

- Intercultural Understanding.

In addition there are two cross-cutting strands:

- Knowledge About Language (KAL)

- Language Learning Strategies (LLS).

The inclusion of Intercultural Understanding as an equal strand to the language skills and the pairing of listening/speaking and reading/writing into a model recognisable by primary English teachers was highly significant when the Framework emerged in 2005. It marked a departure from the secondary model and signalled a change of emphasis from the KS3 Framework that was already in existence but is now under review. The manner in which the two other strands were to be seen as cutting across the major three, and informing and supporting them but not having a separate existence, indicated that 'grammar' and 'learning to learn' were important but only when integrated with other skills in a context which made them real, purposeful and directly relevant to language use. We will now look at the issue of progression, using the Oracy objectives over the four years to illustrate how the principle works.

Progression in the KS2 Framework Oracy objectives

Year 3

O3.1 Listen and respond to simple rhymes, stories and songs

• Identify rhyming words

• Perform finger rhymes and sing songs

• Join in with storytelling

O3.2 Recognise and respond to sound patterns and words

• Listen with care

• Identify phonemes which are the same as or different from English and other known languages

• Speak clearly and confidently

O3.3 Perform simple communicative tasks using single words, phrases and short sentences

• Recall, retain and use vocabulary

• Ask and answer questions

O3.4 Listen attentively and understand instructions, everyday classroom language and praise words

• Repeat words and phrases modelled by the teacher

• Remember a sequence of spoken words

- Use physical response, mime and gesture to convey meaning and show understanding

Year 4

O4.1 Memorise and present a short spoken text

- Learn finger rhymes, poems or a non-fiction text

- Learn and say several sentences on a topic

O4.2 Listen for specific words and phrases

- Listen with care

- Use physical response to show recognition and understanding of specific words and phrases

O4.3 Listen for sounds, rhyme and rhythm

- Identify specific sounds, e.g. rhymes, letters, phonemes, words

- Compare different sounds

O4.4 Ask and answer questions on several topics

- Practise asking and answering questions with a partner

- Develop and perform simple role plays

Year 5

O5.1 Prepare and practise a simple conversation re-using familiar vocabulary and structures in new contexts

- Focus on correct pronunciation and intonation

- Ask and answer questions

- Use tone of voice and gesture to help convey meaning

O5.2   Understand and express simple opinion

- Agree and disagree with statements

- Understand and express likes and dislikes

O5.3 Listen attentively and understand more complex phrases and sentences

• Understand the main points from speech which includes unfamiliar language

O5.4 Prepare a short presentation on a familiar topic

• Plan and prepare – analyse what needs to be done to carry out a task

• Answer in their heads questions asked to other people

Year 6

O6.1 Understand the main points and simple opinions in a spoken story, song or passage

• Listen attentively, re-tell and discuss the main ideas

• Agree or disagree with statements made about a spoken passage

O6.2 Perform to an audience

• Present a short piece of narrative either from memory or by reading aloud from text

• Develop a sketch, role-play or presentation and perform to the class or an assembly

O6.3 Understand longer and more complex phrases or sentences

• Re-tell using familiar language a sequence of events from a spoken passage, containing complex sentences

• Understand and express reasons

• Understand the gist of spoken passages containing complex sentences e.g. descriptions, information, instructions

O6.4 Use spoken language confidently to initiate and sustain conversations and to tell stories

• Participate in simple conversations on familiar topics

• Describe incidents or tell stories from their own experience, in an audible voice

Clearly the major progression occurs in the following:

- *the amount of material* a child is expected to marshall and use, from remembering and using single words and short sentences to performing a sketch or role-play to an assembly

- *the complexity of types of material*, from finger rhymes, words and phrases to pieces of narrative and conversations

- *the interaction of receptive and productive skills* from repeating modelled phrases and remembering sequences or words to re-telling, agreeing/disagreeing and expressing reasons in reaction to language heard.

- *the independence* with which the child manages this, from identifying, joining in and repeating to planning, developing and participating

- *the fluency and confidence* with which he or she expresses language, leading to the fluency necessary for performance.

This entirely accords with our presentation of progression through the central chapters, where we have tried to show a need to build in these same ways, from more receptive to more productive, from more language oriented to more integrated curricular models, and from more limited to more open-ended sources of input either from the teacher or from other sources.

 Reflection point A

Take one of the other major strands (Literacy or Intercultural Understanding) and write a few bullet points summarising the progression between Y3 and Y6 in a similar way to the above summary of the Oracy strand.

 Reflection point B

Using the Framework for planning allows teachers to reflect on different strategies as to how children learn languages and how they acquire necessary skills to be successful language learners. Four short teaching sequences follow. The first, which we are using as an example, has the Framework objectives listed immediately afterwards. It is important to see all the possibilities as we have done here, not in order to break a world-record for objective linking, but because all of the objectives represent worthwhile focuses for the language teacher. Having a clear overview of those objectives in action will shape the teaching towards more purposeful activity and more focused plenary review.

After reading the example, try to make a parallel list for the other three activities, considering all five strands.

1   In Y4 the children have been studying the geography and climate of Canada. They now look at the most popular sports. In small groups they are matching visuals of sports and simple phrases (*'J'aime faire du ski.' 'Je n'aime pas jouer au hockey.'*) and then discuss how these sports are placed in order of popularity (*'C'est numéro 1?' 'C'est le sport le plus populaire?'*).

In this activity the children match phrases and short sentences to pictures or themes (L4.1), they listen with care (O4.2) and ask and answer questions (O4.4). They also learn about some aspects of everyday life and compare them to their own (IU4.2). In terms of KAL the children recognise categories of words, use question forms, they apply phonic and whole word knowledge in order to decode text. They also use a range of LLS to carry out the task: they use context and previous knowledge to determine meaning and pronunciation, they practice with a friend, use gesture and mime to show they understand and practice saying new words aloud.

2   A Y3 class is watching a short video of children performing a finger rhyme, sent by their partner school in France:

Voici ma main

Voici mes doigts

En voici un

En voici trois

Le petit rentre chez toi

Le grand rentre chez toi

Et toi mets ton nez là.

(For more finger rhymes see www.comptinesetjeuxdedoigts.com/index.php and http://descomptines.free.fr/comptines/jeux_de_doigts.htm.) They join in with the actions, then try to imitate the pronunciation and join in with both words and actions. The teacher draws their attention to a certain sound and the children identify words that rhyme with the initial word. Then the written from is displayed, children spot the words which rhyme. They might segment the phonemes of *toi*, then the teacher could set them a reading and a writing challenge with simple words containing the phoneme *oi*.

3   In Y5, children read descriptions of penfriends sent from partner school and carry out a 'guess who' activity, identifying them from the pictures and pen portraits on a poster (these included favourite sports, other hobbies, clothes, and so on).

4   In Y6, working in pairs, children sort statements into groups. The classification included forms of *aimer* and *avoir*, positives and negatives, but these categories were not given to the children. The teacher then asked the pairs to say how they had divided up the statement cards (that is, according to content or language forms) and why.

Planning with the Framework

As we saw from the initial vignette quotation, the Framework intends to enable teachers to plan interesting, creative lessons. If a teacher has a topic in mind and starts to plan the activities that seem to best fit the topic and the class (as a whole and as individuals), then he or she can match those activities against appropriate year group Framework objectives, and so audit the range of planning to ensure it has sufficient variety. Sometimes the objectives will themselves act as a stimulus for planning (see section and website reference below) and sometimes the 'organic' nature of the topic planning will produce a set of tasks which will only be matched up later.

The Framework website has suggested activities linked to the objectives, for example see www.standards.dfes.gov.uk/primary/publications/ languages/framework/teaching_activities/?year=3#1204015 for the Oracy strand. This facility means that teachers need not worry if they are using the objectives as a starting point and cannot think of suitable tasks. In some cases there is a wide range of suggestions which means that meeting the objective on a regular basis (which of course is inevitable) need not become over-repetitive in terms of the classroom experience. But it is still a worthwhile aim to personalise these suggestions and especially to try to let the topic and the content drive the kind of work you plan, as that way the activities will have purpose and the learning will be better. We give a detailed example of such planning next and will comment on it afterwards.

Planning example: healthy living using *La surprise de Handa*
A school chose the topic 'healthy living' for all its children and decided to integrate KS2 French into the topic as fully as possible. The main starter resource chosen for French for all years was the story: *Handa's Surprise* (*La surprise de Handa* / *La sorprese de Handa*) (Brown 1994). Also produced and used were instructions for PE lessons, healthy meals at lunchtime, and canteen menus in the target language. Some activities were designed to be used with the whole school, some were specific to year groups, as the grid below shows. The learning objectives, as they appear in the scheme, are presented in the first column and the parallel

Framework learning outcomes are in the second column. The key column in terms of what the teacher and children are actually doing, and which was the first part of the plan to evolve in this case, is the third column. The resources needed for the activities appear in the fourth column in order that teachers wanting to use or adapt the scheme can have an easy checklist of what would be necessary.

Year 3

Learning objectives	Learning outcomes	Teaching activity/language	Resources
O3.1 Listen and respond to simple rhymes and stories O3.2 Recognise and respond to sound patterns and words	Listen and respond to familiar spoken words, phrases and sentences (O)	Children hear story, hold up laminated pictures of fruit when their one is mentioned	Story 'La surprise de Handa' Laminated pictures of fruit, basket
O3.4 Listen attentively and understand instructions, everyday classroom language and praise words KAL: Identify specific sounds, phonemes and words; hear main word classes; understand that familiar things have different names in different countries LLS: Use gesture or mime to show they understand; use a physical response; play games to help to remember; use context of what they see/read to determine some of the meaning		The teacher calls out different fruits which children place into a basket Focusing on pronunciation the children play a simple repetition game (Répétez si c'est vrai)	
L3.1 Recognise some familiar words in written form		Pictures of fruits and word cards are given to individual children who have to find their partners	Word cards with names of fruits

Year 3

Learning objectives	Learning outcomes	Teaching activity/language	Resources
O3.1 Listen and respond to simple rhymes and stories L3.2 Make links between some phoneme, rhymes and spellings, and read aloud familiar words KAL: Identify specific sounds, phonemes and words LLS: Remember rhyming words	Recognise a children's song, rhyme or poem well known to native speakers (IU)	To extend knowledge of fruit vocabulary and to focus on rhyming sounds (*abricot, trop*) the children learn French comptine *'Pêche, pomme, poire, abricot'*	Comptine *'Pêche, pomme, poire, abricot'* (phoneme focus silent consonant at end of word, e.g. *abricot, trop, avocat, vert, fruit*)
IU3.2 Locate country/countries where the language is spoken	Communicate with others using simple words and phrases and short sentences (O) Identify the country or countries where the language is spoken (IU)	Display pictures and words of fruits mentioned in story and a map of the world. Ask children to place fruits into country of origin through guided questioning (*la mangue vient de...*)	Word cards with names of fruits to support writing
L3.3 Experiment with the writing of simple words KAL: Recognise how sounds are represented in written form; understand how far letters/letter strings are both similar to and different from English	Write some familiar simple words using a model (L)	Children design their own fruit basket (*La surprise de...*), writing a list of the fruits included (*Dans mon panier j'ai une orange...*). Children are encouraged to use plurals	
	Read aloud in chorus, with confidence and enjoyment, from a known text (L)	Shared second reading of story. Teacher leaves out some of the words (*fruits, bonjour, surprise*), fill in missing words	

(Continued)

Year 4

Learning objectives	Learning outcomes	Teaching activity/language	Resources
O4.2 Listen for specific words and phrases L4.2 Follow a short familiar text, listening and reading at the same time IU4.2 Know about some aspects of everyday life and compare them to their own LLS: Use prior knowledge of text types in English and other languages; Apply previous knowledge and language cues to help understanding and pronunciation	Listen to and identify words and short phrases (O) Follow a short text while listening and reading, saying some of the text. Compare aspects of everyday life at home and abroad; Identify similarities in traditional stories, building on relevant Y2/3 National Literacy Strategy *Framework* objectives (IU)	Children hear story, hold up laminated pictures of fruit when their one is mentioned	Laminated pictures of fruit Story *La surprise de Handa*
LLS: Play games to help remember		They play '*salade de fruits*': sitting in a circle the children are each given a name of a fruit. When their fruit is called out they get up and change places.	
O4.4 Ask and answer questions on several topics O4.3: Read some familiar words and phrases aloud and pronounce them accurately KAL: Recognise negative statements; use question forms LLS: Practise saying new words aloud	Communicate by asking and answering a wider range of questions. (O) Read and understand familiar written phrases;	Fruit tasting: children taste a range of fruits mentioned in the story, invites children to express likes and dislikes (*Tu aimes des mandarins? Tu aimes la mangue?*) Children offer different types of fruit to each other, asking whether they	Real fruit Prompt cards to support role-play scenarios

Learning objectives	Learning outcomes	Teaching activity/language	Resources
		like them or not. *'Passe-moi … s'il te plaît.' 'Voilà!' 'Merci!'* or *'Tu aimes…?' 'Oui, j'adore…/Non, je n'aime pas…'*	
L4.4 Write simple words and phrases using a model and some words from memory KAL: Apply phonic and whole-word knowledge to write simple words and phrases LLS: Use spelling strategies appropriately	Write some familiar words and phrases without help (L)	They then fill in a grid, giving their opinion for each of the fruits tasted. Finally they conduct a class survey to find out the most popular fruit and convert the information into a bar chart. Throughout the week they fill in their healthy eating record *'Mangez 5!'* (*Lundi, je mange une pomme, des carottes… Je bois un jus d'orange*)	Grid to note findings of fruit tasting Healthy eating diary

Year 5

Learning objectives	Learning outcomes	Teaching activity/language	Resources
O5.1 Prepare and practise a simple conversation re-using familiar vocabulary and structures in new contexts O5.2 Understand and express simple opinions KAL. Recognise that languages borrow words from other languages	Enjoy interacting even when they hear unfamiliar language (O)	Children are given a range of visuals of food items. Classify them into groups (*les fruits, les légumes, la viande, les produits laitiers etc.*) Focus on fruits, ask children to select the tropical fruits (*les fruits tropicaux*). Call out fruits, ask children to hold up the correct one	Laminated pictures of food items

(Continued)

Learning objectives	Learning outcomes	Teaching activity/language	Resources
L5.1 Re-read frequently a variety of short texts IU5.1 Look at further aspects of their everyday lives from the perspective of someone from another country	Read and understand some of the main points from a text (L) List some similarities and differences between contrasting localities. Recognise how symbols, products, objects can represent the culture/cultures of a country. Recognise how aspects of the culture of different countries become incorporated into the daily life of others (IU)	Read story, ask children to join in with names of fruit and colours, some will join in with repetitive phrases. Children make predictions where the story could be set. Locate some French-speaking countries in Africa. In pairs children list aspects of story which are similar/ different to their own everyday life	Story *La surprise de Handa* Text of story photocopied
O5.1 Prepare and practise a simple conversation re-using familiar vocabulary and structures in new contexts O5.2 Understand and express simple opinions KAL: Understand and use negative statements LLS: Use a physical response. Integrate language into previously learnt language	Join in a short conversation (O)	Children classify different food into healthy/unhealthy discussing in pairs *'C'est bon pour la santé ou c'est mauvais pour la santé?'*, teacher tries to elicit why? *'Pourquoi? C'est trop sucré?'* Whole-class play word class game (different actions for different word classes called out). Then in groups make sentences using word cards to practise position of adjectives and to reinforce adjectival agreements	Picture/word cards of food items

Learning objectives	Learning outcomes	Teaching activity/language	Resources
L5.2 Make simple sentences and short texts KAL: Manipulate language by changing a single element in a sentence. Apply knowledge of language rules and conventions when building short sentences; Recognise some basic aspects of agreement where relevant, e.g. gender, singular/ plural, pronoun/ verb, adjectives. LLS: Apply grammatical knowledge to make sentences; Recall, retain and use words, phrases and sentences	Understand how a simple sentence is written. Write words, phrases and a few sentences using a model. (L) Make a short presentation using a model. (O)	Children write fruit poems, including adjectives from story – *délicieux (-se), juteux(-se), sucré(e), rond(e), crémeux(-se), rouge, jaune,* etc. Practise reading poems in pairs for performing in assembly	Word bank to support writing of fruit poems

Year 6

Learning objectives	Learning outcomes	Teaching activity/language	Resources
L6.1 Read and understand the main points and some detail from a short written passage L6.2 Identify different text types and read short, authentic texts for enjoyment or information LLS: Make sensible guesses based on cues.	Read and understand the main points and some detail from a short written passage (L)	Show children a recipe of a fruit salad. Ask them to identify the text type. Focus on fruits, ask children to select the tropical fruits (*les fruits tropicaux*)	Recipe of fruit salad on IWB

(Continued)

Learning objectives	Learning outcomes	Teaching activity/language	Resources
L6.1 Read and understand the main points and some detail from a short written passage KAL: Apply knowledge of word order and sentence construction to support understanding LLS: Apply previous knowledge and language cues to help understanding and pronunciation;	Read aloud with confidence, enjoyment and expression, in chorus or individually. (L)	Children read the story in pairs, highlighting the names of fruits while reading. Shared reading of story, children encouraged to join in, continuing reading of words left out by teacher	Story 'La surprise de Handa'
O6.3 Understand longer and more complex phrases or sentences LLS: Work out the meaning by using a range of cues. Analyse what they need to know in order to carry out a task.	Listen to and understand the main points and some detail from a short, spoken passage. (O)	Teacher reads out recipe, gives jumbled up instructions of how to make a fruit salad to children; working in groups of four, the children reconstitute the recipe, then collect the correct equipment and follow instructions to make salad.	Instructions for recipe cut up. Equipment and ingredients for fruit salad

(Continued)

Learning objectives	Learning outcomes	Teaching activity/language	Resources
L6.4 Write sentences on a range of topics using a model O6.2 Perform to an audience IU6.3 Present information about an aspect of culture KAL: Use knowledge of form, including plurals and notations of gender to improve access to a range of texts. Apply knowledge of word order and sentence construction to support understanding LLS: Analyse what they need to know in order to carry out a task; Recall, retain and use words, phrases and sentences. Apply grammatical knowledge to make sentences.	Give a presentation in a clear audible voice. (O) Develop a short text using a model. (L) Demonstrate understanding of and respect for cultural diversity; Present information about an aspect of another country. (IU)	Using the internet, children search for recipes from different French speaking countries. Each group presents their recipe with some short information about their country to the rest of the class.	Access to internet and dictionaries

In addition to the activities above, during a whole-school assembly children presented work they had completed and this included from KS1 classes a play – a version of *The Enormous Turnip* (Lewis 1999) (*Le navet géant / Die Riesenrübe / El nabo gigante*) with teacher reading, children acting and joining in with the recurring sentence *'Ils ont tiré, tiré, tire, mais le navet n'a pas bougé'*. There was also whole-school singing, for example the song *Savez-vous planter les choux*.

Progression in the whole-school topic

The scheme given above clearly shows progression in the types of categories we introduced earlier in the chapter, notably in areas such as independence and in the complexity of the ways the language is linked to the content and in the level of language function demanded. The younger children are engaged by the story and then begin to use the language at a simple level, responding to what they hear, repeating words and phrases and focusing on sounds. In this way they gradually learn the vocabulary for the fruit items and then later begin to consider an intercultural perspective through a task on where the fruits originate.

By Y4 children are being more active from the start, for example the *salade de fruits* game demands more concentration. They link to the general topic through tasting and then responding to the fruits and by sharing opinions with each other. The language of likes/dislikes, questioning and polite requests is all included here, bringing together material learned in other contexts and teaching any new items needed through the situated topic and purposeful activity of tasting and reacting.

By Y5 the children are using knowledge of fruit and other foods to carry out a classification task before hearing the story and are then focusing on fruit, and subsequently tropical fruit, so that they are primed for important detail before it is read to them. By classifying through visual images with labels they are beginning to learn vocabulary without going through a teacher-led presentation session, and the task requires thinking as they classify, so the concentration on the items should help learning. As we indicated earlier, children need the language to accompany the tasks the teacher uses regularly (in this case, the languageof discussion while making classifications, such as, 'I disagree, because that is a ...', 'Isn't that a ...?', 'Yes that's right.' etc). If they have used this before, the classification task becomes a more language-rich experience for them.

The Y5 children are also asked to identify possible locations for the story after the reading, bringing in an intercultural element which reflects existing knowledge or gives new ideas about where French (or Spanish) is spoken in the world.

By Y6 the class is working from a recipe for a dish which they will later actually create. They are reading the story in pairs and they also hear it read by the teacher, but by then there is an expectation that they can join in and take over if he or she pauses or misses words.

Towards the end of the scheme for each year, the children are being active and productive in different ways, also reflecting the progression in amount or complexity of both the material they use and the style of their production. In Y3 the emphasis is on controlled sentence writing along with creative activity (drawing a fruit basket) and gap-fill oral production when the teacher reads the story again. Y4 manage a class survey using simple questions and also list their 'five a day' intake. Y5 move onto more creative writing through fruit poems and later perform these in assembly, while Y6 follow instructions to make a recipe and also search for other recipes with a connection to different French speaking countries. Again, they present findings both in the class and in assembly.

This brief summary shows how important it is to consider the children's age, prior world knowledge, thinking and reasoning capability, independence and ability to plan and carry out oral presentations to different audiences, in addition to planning from a starting point of language knowledge or language skills competence. The framework considers all of these elements, perhaps not overtly, but in the way it has identified progression across so many fields.

Primary teachers know well how individual year groups manage the demands made by different styles of work – they often stay with a year group and so become accustomed to planning to raise capabilities within their year and sphere of influence. An incoming new class teacher does not necessarily have that overview, but will need to gain it for a specific year group and reflect it in the ML planning he or she undertakes. An incoming language specialist who may be teaching a range of groups needs to balance the two strands of over-all skills and capabilities, and of language knowledge and compe-tence. Language capabilities may not be progressive across the year groups, if for example a whole key stage is starting a foreign lan-guage at the same time, but the other core abilities will be in place and do need to be reflected through the planning. We have seen examples in Chapters Five, Six and Seven of how we might reach higher levels of language activity through careful scaffolding and the use of prior knowledge to help make new language clear. It is through this way of approaching our planning that we can avoid a situation where Y6 children are still learning language (even if a new topic) at the same level as Y3 children and are practising and manip-ulating language using the same activity types (in terms of games, dialogues and worksheet formats). The Key Stage 2 Framework and the Literacy Framework both show clear types of approaches, using different strands, and both reflect ways of using language to learn. As we showed in Chapter Two, it is possible to make associations between the Literacy strands and approaches to foreign language learning and use, as long as we keep the level of expectation man-ageable. However we plan, a clear progression focus will make the subject vibrant, stimulating and challenging, without losing any of the fun.

 Reflection point

If you have an existing plan for a ML unit that relates to a whole-year or whole-school topic, audit it against the KS2 Framework and then review it against the sample scheme given in this chapter. Would you alter it if you teach it again? If so, how and why?

If you have no existing plans, take a different whole school theme, which you know you will use this year, and plan activities appropriate to different year groups. Audit this plan against the KS2 Framework.

 Chapter summary

In this chapter we have presented the key features and qualities of the KS2 Framework and have tried to suggest ways in which it can be used to start planning or to audit medium-term schemes for breadth and progression.

We have identified the nature of the progression contained within the Framework through comparing objectives at different levels and analysing the range of skills it seems to suggest.

We have presented a scheme of work which shows how the objectives could look in practice and how they can be used to audit a workplan which has coherence in itself, but which can be checked for breadth and progression by such cross-referencing.

How do I know if the children are learning? How can I help them to progress smoothly to KS3?

Introductory vignette

Y3 focus group discussing learning French:

Y3 Pupil 5: The colours is hard, *rouge* is red, *jaune* is yellow

Y3 Pupil 4: *Noir...*

Y3 Pupil 5: No *noir* is black.

Researcher: That's funny, because you said they were hard and then you told me three colours in French.

Y3 Pupil 5: (proudly) Yeah but it's hard!

Comment

Learning a language is in many ways much more of a continuous process than learning other subjects. Despite the use of a topic-based curriculum it is harder to box off knowledge into neat files than it can be in, say, Science or History. And where this is done in language learning too rigidly we find that content such as vocabulary does not always transfer between topics. As a result children are often uncertain as to what they *do* actually know. This makes it all the more important that we both monitor their learning (for our own information and for planning) and enable them to see their own progress too. For this reason this chapter looks at both the teacher's and the pupil's roles in assessment and transition.

Chapter objectives

- To remind the reader of the important issues surrounding different forms and types of monitoring and assessment.
- To address how to establish 'what we know' without a test – and how to use plenary in a language class to consolidate, extend and assess.
- To address the means of assessment of 'language in use' – content, communication of content, pronunciation/intonation, creativity/spontaneity, accuracy.
- To focus on the potential of peer- and self-evaluation and to show how success criteria can be used to help children to improve their competence and set targets.
- To explore models for managing transition between KS2 and KS3.
- To suggest recording formats for the children to use and how these may be involved in giving children more ownership over the transition process.

Relevant Q Standards: Q11, Q12, Q13, Q26, Q27, Q28

The previous chapter dealt with the KS2 Framework as a planning tool and showed how teachers might set up learning objectives for communication/language learning and for the other elements that are involved in the wider curriculum taught through the chosen foreign language. This chapter reviews how you might want to undertake assessment activity, based on the objectives you set and reflecting, amongst other issues, KS2 Framework objectives.

The chapter also deals with transition issues and as part of that mentions the Languages Ladder structure which is introduced as an example of a more formal assessment structure. Tests linked to this are commercially available from a company called Asset Languages. You can find out more about their material at www.assetlanguages.org.uk/ but it would be inappropriate for this book to deal with that in more detail.

Initial reflection point

How do you measure your progress with language learning? Whether you class yourself as a beginner or have a high level qualification, think back over a recent period of time and try to establish what you have learned and how you know this? If you find you cannot evaluate this easily, try to think of ways in which you could monitor and measure future learning.

Definitions of terms and rationale for changes

Assessment practice has changed enormously over the last 25 years. One of the perennial debates (each August) concerns whether the improving results in examinations such as GCSE and A-Level reflect a 'watering down' of standards, a different examination focus or methodology, or a strong improvement in teaching and learning. Some changes are easily identified, others can be guessed at, while others are more the projection of a political view held by a proponent.

The older O-Level and previous incarnations of A-Level examinations were usually negatively marked and the results produced through norm-referencing. This means that papers had marks for each mistake made taken from a 'starting total' and that when the overall scores were produced they were ordered into grades by means of a distribution curve. Therefore there was approximately the same number of grade A, grade B, and so on, each year. The justification for this was that on large populations there should not be much deviation in attainment across several years so this was a fair system for producing a cohort's results. Details of scores were not made available so it was difficult to know how papers had been marked, but anecdotal reports suggest that in O-Level foreign language writing papers, for example, the average mark for more open-ended writing tasks such as a picture story was 0! Certainly the culture seemed to be more on what people could not do rather than what they could.

The first big change, then, was to *criterion-referenced marking*. This system rewards candidates for successes in defined tasks. So in writing tasks the new GCSE papers gave a brief for a communication (message, postcard, letter, story, and so on) and listed areas of content that needed to be included. Marking was done on a content basis first and assessors simply had to decide if a sympathetic native speaker would understand the message without any trouble, would be able to piece it together, infer it or would not understand it. This was decided for each task on a 2–1–0 basis. Then a score was given for the range of language used to communicate the message and finally a mark for accuracy. In both cases there were descriptors for the examiners to use which defined how a piece of writing could score, say between 10 and 12 marks or between 6 and 9, and so on. This meant that a reasonably accurate, reasonably appropriate message gained a majority of the marks available even if the niceties of grammatical accuracy were missing. This produced a contrast with the previous system where the smaller errors would still have been counted and therefore the mark would have been lower, even if the message had been fairly clearly communicated. The other difference is of course that as many candidates gained the top grades as met those criteria and the 'norm' curve was no longer used to fox grades. When the change happened it was in fact not a 'watering down' of standards but rather a redefinition of language assessment priorities. Instead of grammatical accuracy being the single important element, communication of 'real' messages was now the focus, reflecting the changes in teaching objectives, syllabuses and materials. (See Chapter Nine for a fuller discussion of these changes.)

As early as 1984, Ames and Ames wrote about the preference for a task-mastery structure where a learner's past performance was used to structure goals for future improvement, not in a competitive class-based scenario but on an individual basis. A focus on what had been dubbed *formative assessment* by writers in the 1960s (Scriven 1967, Bloom 1968) began to develop on both a theoretical basis and through classroom practice. This brought together two different groups: writers on motivation, for example Dweck (1986), who argued that *summative assessment* demotivated learners, and assessment researchers. Of these, for example, Sadler (1989) argued for the need for authentic evaluative experience for the learners so that they could identify high quality work and measure their own progress toward it. Cohen (1994) brought a language learning perspective to the issue, specifically, recommending formative activity alongside classroom tasks so that teacher could better understand their students' skills and competencies. Following Black and Wiliam's work (1998) a major government initiative on assessment for learning was launched. The work of Clarke (1998, 2001, 2003, 2005) is often used as an example of how this approach is realised in primary classrooms.

Clarke herself (2001) presents the *differences between summative and formative assessment* in the following way:

> If we think of our children as plants, summative assessment of plants is the process of simply measuring them. The measurements might be interesting to compare and analyse, but, in themselves, they do not affect the growth of the plants. Formative assessment, on the other hand, is the garden equivalent of feeding and watering the plants – directly affecting their growth. (2001: 2)

The argument for formative assessment is that it does not interrupt teaching and learning but is an integral part of the process. So it need not take longer, as some state by way of objection. We mentioned in an earlier chapter the implications for motivation of a learner being told what she had to say and write in a language test, irrespective of whether it included her own real experience. Clearly such a scenario does not make learners feel that the testing they are undergoing has value either. There is sometimes in the secondary sector the rather dubious practice of formally testing each unit as it is finished, and of 'retro-structuring' the teaching accordingly. So the focus is very much on preparing for the test that is to come (sometimes by copying down the vocabulary and structures that should be learned) and, before that, teaching the material that the teacher knows will feature in the test. This makes language learning a mere process of setting out a perfectly spaced line of very similar hurdles, practising jumping over each one several times and then running the race, finding a remarkably predictable outcome. The problem is that for some children it does not work and they only achieve a string of failures. For others the hurdles are structured so that the runner can simply take them in her or his stride with little effort and their regular placement and predictable appearance means that no particular thinking focus is needed to evaluate how best to jump each one. In neither case does the particular group of learners benefit. But worse than that, of course, unfortunately, regular lines of hurdles are rarely seen in target language using countries. So even those who reach the finishing line successfully unit after unit find themselves stranded when real communicative situations appear.

Formulaic summative testing, then, is not the answer, and especially not in the primary phase, but nevertheless teachers do need to know how children are progressing. We now need to address how teachers can use classroom activity to find out about children's knowledge, understanding and skills. We should never forget that monitoring and assessment are as much intended to inform teachers about their own teaching and support their future planning as they are intended to inform children and their parents about achievement. Assessment is not about judging children but is about making their future learning opportunities as good as possible.

How might we find out what the children know without a test?

We can start to set out a general set of principles by looking at the findings of two research studies (Gattullo 2000, Zangl 2000) which looked specifically at how children aged between 8 and 12 might be assessed in their English lessons in Italy and Austria respectively. Gattullo highlighted the type of assessment she wanted to explore in the following terms:

> For the next phase in the research, a broad definition of 'classroom assessment for formative purposes' was adopted as a starting point. The following are identified as the main traits of this type of assessment:
>
> • it is an ongoing multi-phase process that is carried out on a daily basis through teacher–pupil interaction;

- it provides feedback for immediate action; and

- it aims at modifying teaching activities in order to improve learning processes and results. (2000: 279)

After her exploratory study Gattullo noted that:

> The classroom data analysed to date suggests that some formative assessment actions are more common than others (i.e., questioning, correcting, judging), at the expense of those that could be considered more beneficial for learning (e.g., observing process, examining product, metacognitive questioning). (2000: 284)

We will take up this point later in the chapter as we examine examples of assessment practice.

Zangl similarly set out her beliefs in her introduction, maintaining that:

> Oral testing in playful situations with the integration of visual and tactile stimuli can be used ... to elicit valuable information about the learners' foreign language development. (2000: 251)

Her conclusion contained three major considerations with regard to assessment objectives, that teachers should try:

1. to assess the learner's proficiency within a multi-component framework, comprising not only domain-/structure-specific items but also the use of language within the social context of the classroom;

2. to capture both the learner's individual profile and the performance level of the class as a whole; and

3. to trace the learner along his or her developmental path where time and experience act as constructive factors. (2000: 257)

The government's most recent statement on primary languages assessment taken from the *Languages Review* (DfES 2007) highlighted the need for some summative assessment at the end of KS2, but stressed this was still intended for formative purposes.

> There should be informal classroom assessment of every child's learning near the end of Key Stage 2 by reference to the Languages Ladder, so that the Key Stage 3 teacher is well informed about the pupil's learning standard and needs. We recommend use of the ladder because it provides the teacher with assessment at the level appropriate to the child in each of the four strands of learning: speaking, listening, reading and writing, and because it is to a common national standard. Its purpose is different from the SATs, which in the past have been essentially a summative means of assessing a school's performance with all pupils taking the same test. The assessment we recommend is formative in purpose, fit for the individual child, not aggregated, and should not be the basis for any league tables. (2007: 10)

The Languages Ladder structure is intended to cross-reference to the *Common European Framework of Reference for Languages: Learning, Teaching,*

Assessment (Council of Europe 2001). This is a very detailed document that gives both the background for and detailed descriptors of language competence at all levels from basic use up to mastery. The two levels associated with basic use are (globally) as follows (2001: 24), although much more detailed individual descriptors associated with the four skills are also available.

Basic user	*A2*	Can understand sentences and frequently used expressions related to areas of most immediate relevance (e.g. very basic personal and family information, shopping, local geography, employment). Can communicate in simple and routine tasks requiring a simple and direct exchange of information on familiar and routine matters. Can describe in simple terms aspects of his/her background, immediate environment and matters in areas of immediate need.
	A1	Can understand and use familiar everyday expressions and very basic phrases aimed at the satisfaction of needs of a concrete type. Can introduce him/herself and others and can ask and answer questions about personal details such as where he/she lives, people he/she knows and things he/she has. Can interact in a simple way provided the other person talks slowly and clearly and is prepared to help.

The Languages Ladder system is designed to make assessment consistent across the country and to help provide reliable transfer documentation between sectors. We include here material accessible at www.teachernet. gov.uk/languagesladder/ in the form of a general summary and an exemplar of the first two major stages, Breakthrough and Preliminary for Speaking competence.

There is a 'can do' statement at each grade in each of the four language skills and they form the basis of the assessment system. These statements can support assessment for learning in any language, providing short-term motivational goals for the learner. The Languages Ladder scheme has three assessment strands: an informal model – the 'can do' statements can be used to benchmark achievement for formative, peer or self-assessment; a teacher-assessed model leading to a Grade Award in any skill at any grade; and external tests available at the end of each stage leading to accredited national qualifications.

Grades 1-2-3 Breakthrough

1   I can say/repeat a few words and short simple phrases.

2   I can answer simple questions and give basic information.

3   I can ask and answer simple questions and talk about my interests.

On completing this stage:

- You should be able to use a basic range of everyday expressions relating to personal details and needs.

- Your pronunciation will not always be completely accurate but your meaning will be clear.

- You should be able to understand and use a few simple grammatical structures and sentence patterns.

- You should be familiar with the sound system of the language.

- You should be aware of how to address people both formally and informally as appropriate.

Grades 4-5-6 Preliminary

4   I can take part in a simple conversation and I can express my opinions.

5   I can give a short prepared talk, on a topic of my choice, including expressing my opinions.

6   I can give a short prepared talk, on a topic of my choice, expressing opinions and answering simple questions about it.

On completing this stage:

- You should be able to use and adapt learned language relating to a range of predictable everyday matters.

- Your pronunciation should be clear and you should be able to maintain a simple conversation using strategies such as asking for clarification or repetition.

- You should be able to recognise the difference between past, present and future events and be familiar with simple forms of the verb tenses.

While the system is very new and is certainly not being used yet as a standard tool even at the end of KS2, there is certainly a value in having a structure. But it would be wrong in our view to see the assessment of language learning throughout the primary phase in these terms. Although there is at www.qca.org.uk/qca_1910.aspx an ML version of the P-Levels (Pre-Level 1 of the National Curriculum), we are also less than convinced that this is the approach that teachers should use. Just as we stated in the previous chapter that the KS2 Framework is something which our work with children should be referenced to, and should not be a starting point for planning, so here all of these descriptor-type assessment tools may offer a useful way to review learning at periodic intervals but should not be a frame which defines what or, even worse, *how* language is taught. Nevertheless it is important that these instruments become familiar to teachers and that they are used when the school and the teacher feel it would be appropriate to take a snapshot of progress.

 Reflection point

Return to your notes from the initial reflection point. Look at the Language Ladder scale which best suits your level of language competence. Take one of the four skills and check a) where you think you are, and b) what you would need to do to progress to the next level. How useful is this as a way of monitoring your own learning? How often could you use it?

Initial thoughts on monitoring learning

Monitoring is a complex practice. When considering how to assess language more formally we usually break it down into separate skills (as does the Languages Ladder) and so find ways to test specifically listening, speaking, reading and writing. This is of course unnatural in real language use as the skills are inevitably interlinked – an obvious example of this is that a normal conversation demands both listening and speaking skills to be activated. But language learning does often involve differential abilities in these skills so there is some logic behind single-skill testing.

When monitoring we need to remember that children will normally understand more than they can produce. (If they do not, a teacher needs to review how he or she is exposing the children to the language.) Logically, a primary age child, especially at the younger end of the age range should be able to listen and understand to a greater degree than he or she can read and understand (although of course this will never apply to 100 per cent of any class). Similarly the majority of children will be able to understand language better than they can produce language and in the production process will generally be able to speak more readily than they can write.

There is a small body of pupil work in KS2 French available on the National Curriculum in Action website at http://curriculum.qca.org.uk/ key-stages-1-and-2/assessment/nc-in-action/index.aspx?&fldSubject= Modern+foreign+languages&fldKeyStageYear=3%2c4%2c5%2c6&page=0 if you would like to see some examples with a commentary, but of course the work in your own classroom is the best starting point to review as you read the rest of this chapter.

Receptive language

Let us consider first how we might monitor children's receptive language development, in other words how they cope with the language they encounter through hearing or reading the target language. This is not, however, the same process as is used in GCSE Listening and Reading tests, nor is it really assessing in the same way.

Remember that we are using in-class activity as an assessment source. We first need to consider non-verbal responses as a useful methodology. If we track back through Chapters 3 to 6, we will recall activities such as the Reception age children making masks, the early starters making a collage and the more advanced learners following recipes. In all of these cases there was an outcome which showed that the children had comprehended the instructional language used, had followed those instructions and had created an art object or a dish. At one level and in one respect, then, they had demonstrated their ability to understand what might be quite complex instructional language without the need for a 'test' on that particular set of vocabulary.

When children regularly hear a stimulus foreign language utterance (no matter how quickly spoken or how grammatically complex it is) which prompts a real classroom action and is a familiar element of classroom life, it is easy to forget that they are acting intuitively and that language is a mere vehicle. Over a period of time the languages teacher should build up a wide range of language that children hear, understand and act on. This will include, as we saw in Chapters Four and Five, the language of:

- greeting

- checking (genuinely) on children's well-being

- organisation of the classroom

- management of behaviour

- routines such as getting ready for other activities such as assemblies, playtime, lunch, fruit distribution, getting changed for PE, getting ready to go home, (in faith schools) saying a prayer

- assembling the materials and parameters for work (equipment, date, topic)

- establishing prior knowledge and familiar language

- asking questions about routines.

In all of these areas over a period of four years children should become completely at ease with the language. They generally have to respond non-verbally and spoken responses can be made at a variety of levels which all children will manage in time as long as they are not 'tested' by being 'demanded'. When they do this, without fuss, in a natural way they are operating in the language as a native speaker would. We cannot state too strongly that where this happens it is a major achievement of primary language learning. It sets children at the beginning of KS3 a clear advantage over 11-year-old beginners not just in what they know but in the fact that they can operate naturally, can cope with a wider variety of language, hopefully spoken at near natural speed, and most importantly, it does not seem like a chore or something difficult. In other words they are equipped to keep operating in the language and to learn more and more how to cope with authentic language that they might meet abroad. This is sometimes never achieved by learners starting at 11 who have two or three scattered hours per week.

However if we tried to test this same language of instructions in a traditional way (perhaps through a vocabulary test) then we might find that some learners would not score very highly. Yet if we regularly use such instructions and the children do what we have asked them to do, why should we 'test' them? At primary level we do not need to convert everything from receptive into active language and children will best remember, use and operate in the language if they see a clear purpose and context for doing so. If we do want to discover whether those phrases and structures have become an active part of their knowledge then a more positive alternative to a test would be to play a game where a small group of children have responsibility for giving instructions for a day. This contextualises the demand you are making on them and is also potentially an enjoyable and humorous activity. Often children do not in fact produce these commands very well because they only have a need to understand them, but it may be a good extension for more linguistically able, more confident children.

So far we have considered the language accompanying routines and instructions and the language used to set up other activities such as Art or Technology or PE where language production may not be required at all. There are also of course receptive contexts where the language that has to be understood is intended to become active because it is the topic content. Whether or not the language is the content or the language is being used to teach another content (for example, something cultural about the target language speaking country or an element of another school subject), the teacher needs to know that what is being in some way presented to or encountered by the pupils is comprehensible.

We have seen the way in which we can build content through a series of smaller steps (simple decisions, responses chosen from a limited range of possibilities, the use of natural repetition through asking a question which has genuinely possible different answers to a range of children, the review of key words from time to time). These are all ways for teachers to monitor as they teach, without needing to stop and assess, and clearly we need to use our 'normal' classroom assessment techniques to do this. These techniques might include:

- mini-whiteboards (used individually and by pairs)

- think-pair-share activity (where individuals formulate thoughts and share with another child and then with another pair before they respond as a group)

- asking for agreement/disagreement with a response given by a pupil

- the naming of children to answer as well as using volunteers.

All of these techniques are just as valid in a language lesson as in any other. This means we are essentially using routine (but well-planned and carefully implemented) teacher questioning to monitor learning. This can be formalised into a review process, perhaps on the carpet, where the teacher has a clear agenda of wanting to find out what the class and perhaps certain individuals know and understand, but can be more opportunistic and more flexible.

Productive language

If we turn towards the monitoring of production, it is firstly important to recall that even in formal assessment the communication of content is prioritised and so teachers should always do everything they can to understand what the child is trying to say. This is a vital part of the motivational process referred to early in Chapter Five and whether or not we are 'testing' we should always give a child making an effort the maximum credit that we can. If a child feels he or she has failed to say the right thing, issues of self-esteem begin to come into play and anxiety levels in a parallel situation (in other words any speaking turn the child might have thereafter) will become raised. Too many experiences like this will lead to the child withdrawing from participating and this will in turn lead to a lessening of focus and concentration. At this point the whole downward spiral begins. But showing interest and encouraging children does not affect our own conclusions we make from the monitoring process and the impact this has on our future planning. So objective monitoring is a different issue from the motivation of the class and individuals in it.

In working out where children are in their language development, it can help if we try to distinguish between children using a simple stimulus-response, consciously recalling the vocabulary or structure for a response before making it and what we might term 'operating in the language'. The simpler items will not be easy to interpret, for example when a child hears ¡Hola! and repeats ¡Hola!, is it a programmed response or are they naturally using the language. But even a slightly more complex item, ¿Qué tal?, can be revealing. We should always look to avoid any language becoming merely a routine stripped of meaning and should remind ourselves of that particular detached tone which takes over a school full of children at the start of assemblies when they respond to a 'Good afternoon', with a chorused 'Good afternoon Mrs... Good afternoon everyone!' So a response to ¿Qué tal? of ¡Muy bien! from an entire class smacks of 'When we hear ¿Qué tal?, we all say ¡Muy bien!', rather than 'She's asking how we are, now how do I say OK?' and is certainly not '¡Mal!' or even better, 'Tengo dolor de cabeza'. The incident narrated earlier of a child clutching her stomach but still replying to her headteacher's question in French is a good example of that in action. If we do think that the responses are becoming mechanistic, we need to alter our use of language for the routines which are causing the problem.

Associated with assessment is the correction process. In a useful brief summary of the different types of correction, Loewen (2007) makes the point that we might use correction which is simply in the form of a recast which does not call attention to the mistake directly, we might be more explicit that it is an error, we might prompt for a correct form, or we might overtly discuss the grammar of the mistake. Different researchers make claims for different approaches but we should always remember that different learners respond differently to different techniques so we should perhaps look carefully at the needs and responses of our pupils when choosing the best method. Generally there is consensus that some kind of focus on form is needed if we want accuracy to be developed. This means that we can decide on a 'level of error', perhaps governed by successful or unsuccessful communication. If the mistake is so great it jeopardises understanding then correction is certainly desirable, and could be explicit. Often at primary level it is pronunciation or choice of word, rather than grammar that impedes communication, so a response consisting of the correct version and perhaps asking for a repetition is justified. By upper primary these corrections are normally perceived as support and used accordingly. Younger pupils may not be able to correct in spite of all teacher efforts – if they are not ready, they will simply not do it. If a mistake is minor, often a recast with no indication that it is wrong is all that is needed. There is evidence that recasts do also have an effect on language competence, although it is usually at a slow rate, with less than half of recasts being noticed and acted on.

 Reflection point

Take a plan for a forthcoming language unit. How might you assess both during and towards the end of that unit? Will there be an outcome of some sort at the very end? Make some initial notes and then read on and add to them as you go.

When should we assess? Blurring the edges between 'learning activities' and 'plenaries'

All teachers tend to be very conscious now of the importance of plenaries and if you are reading this as a student teacher you will find that across all of your subjects the use of plenaries is heavily featured. The National Literacy Strategy suggested the pattern of a three-part lesson and defined the plenary as a very vital part of a process that sought to maximise learning and continuous progression. After some use, and with the natural professional development that teachers always seem to create for themselves, the rigidity of the three-part lesson structure began to break down as teachers saw a need for several smaller 'checkpoints' within a lesson and mini-plenaries began to emerge. Current thinking seems to be that teachers should always seek to move on and develop progression within a lesson but only when they are sure that the class is ready. In other words, we should always both plan and monitor with this two-pronged focus: learning should always develop and challenge should slowly grow, but learning should always be checked. Progression is vital but not as some form of mechanistic automatised process. In the above section on children meeting new language and content we showed that there is a continuum with the teacher controlling the demand for more production carefully until confidence and familiarity begins to build.

One use of a mini-plenary is to retrace the steps of a PowerPoint presentation, selecting key vocabulary and concepts and checking them. This is where the classroom can sometimes become bilingual. A teacher asking a question in the foreign language may elicit a response in English because a child wants to explain something but just does not have the language to do so. If the teacher picks up from the child's points, cross-references them visually to elements of the presentation and paraphrases the child's response into simple target language, then the use of the foreign language for learning has not been compromised and the children will have been exposed to further examples of the key language in use.

Teachers do not of course spend the whole time with children on the carpet questioning and monitoring learning. So how and when can we assess at other points? Children need to spend time working independently and together. They need to practise speaking the language in a non-threatening and purposeful environment, with a task that engages their interest and makes them think. When children are so occupied it is easy for the teacher to monitor the talk and form a view on how well both the class as a whole and the individuals within it have internalised the content and language for the topic they are learning. It takes time to do this and no teacher can assess a whole class during each speaking activity, but a well-organised approach and an easy recording method makes it possible, manageable and not too stressful.

Imagine a common teaching topic, buying some basic food and drink in a café. This topic contains some active key vocabulary in the form of nouns (food and drink items), some politeness functional language ('hello', 'please', 'thank you'), some structures ('Do you have?', 'I would like…', 'Can I pay?') and some more receptive language ('What would you like?', 'That's … amount'). If the teacher sets up role-plays, these may be differentiated with an easy task being followed by a more complex interaction. It is important to teach children to monitor their own and each other's learning and to know when to move on to a more challenging activity (see next section on self- and peer-evaluation), but we also need to know that they can do this by monitoring what they are doing. A grid can be used for such monitoring which allows a teacher to eavesdrop and very easily and quickly note strengths and development areas.

For the café topic, the grid might look like this:

Name	Drinks	Foods	Greetings	Politeness	Ich möchte	Haben Sie?	Zahlen bitte	Pronun-ciation issues	Other issues
Adam									
Briony									
Callum									
Chloe									

The standard grid would have the class list on the side and then blank boxes at the top (apart from the last two) so the relevant items could be inserted for different topics. A simple tick would mean the child was using the item properly. A question mark could be used to indicate a lack of confidence and a cross that the child appeared not to know the language needed to express this function. At this stage accuracy can be interpreted through the tick/question mark structure. If a teacher aimed to monitor a third of the class on any particular activity (if more proved possible, so much the better) then he or she would gain a picture of the whole class in action fairly regularly, even if across a spread of activities. If monitoring just a third showed a pattern of any sort, it would still give a prompt for the teacher to take appropriate action and to consolidate or extend language. The last two boxes allow for more precise notes to be made where relevant.

Pronunciation can be impacted on very successfully at primary level, and whole-class discrimination and articulation games can be used to enhance pronunciation, focusing either on single sounds or tricky words, where teacher notes have highlighted a common problem.

So should the teacher intervene while monitoring or simply use the grid? As always the answer is not a simple one. If children are working well and there is a level of both engagement and fluency emerging in the dialogue then intervention is probably not justified. If one partner is struggling for words, then clearly it is appropriate to support and model. This might be the teacher taking over the role briefly to show how it could be done, or it might be that the teacher suggests a couple of vocabulary items but lets the pupil take it on immediately. Very poor pronunciation, especially if it might mean a native speaker would struggle to understand, should be corrected through a recast (the teacher saying the word or phrase) and possibly a request for both partners to repeat it. But smaller-scale errors should be noted but not corrected there and then.

Should we test this sort of vocabulary in a 'conventional' format? What we can be sure of is that knowing a set of nouns or short phrases for a test does not automatically mean they can be used in real situations. It might even be that not knowing them for a test does not rule out them being retrieved in a real situation. Testing of vocabulary at primary level, especially in the first two years of learning, is probably best done as a whole-class interactive game, using an electronic whiteboard. In other words, it is better to practise language through a game than to test it by a test!

We have not so far addressed the assessment of grammar as a specific item because, again, we are not convinced that grammar needs to be separated from the use of language. A quick scan of the Knowledge about Language strand in the KS2 Framework shows that the major specific grammar issues addressed are plurals, gender agreements and word order. So we are not talking about learning verb conjugations or the accusative case, although, as we said earlier, some pupils might see the German form *den* and ask what it is and why it is so. Similarly pupils might notice a range of verb endings and they may encounter a past tense in a text. They can be told about these things, but certainly do not need to learn them as a class and absolutely do not need to be tested on them! A reminder that, as we pointed out in Chapter Seven, you can see the links between KAL and LLS and the three main strands of objectives at www.standards.dfes.gov.uk/primary/publications/languages/framework/learning_objectives/?year=3& fieldset=kal#oracy. This puts 'grammar' into a language use perspective.

Peer- and self-assessment – the role of success criteria

Before any meaningful peer- or self-assessment can take place, children must understand what they are assessing and how to do it. This means teachers must set success criteria and help children to become aware of how to understand and use them. Because of this, success criteria might as well always be couched in child-friendly language from the start – there is little point in having two sets.

For the café activity this might include:

- I know three drinks and three food items.

- I can say hello, please and thank you.

- I can ask for my food and drink politely.

- I can ask to pay.

- I can say the words properly.

- I can take part in the conversation without hesitating too much.

The first four criteria can be judged by the pair working together fairly easily. Assessing a dialogue activity in this way effectively combines self- and peer-evaluation as the judgement is made on both partners by both partners. The last two criteria are harder for them to evaluate but this tends to come with practice and can be drawn to the teacher's attention if there is disagreement between partners.

Clearly peer- and self-evaluation are not substitutes for teacher monitoring but, organised properly, have advantages in that they can sit alongside it as another evidence stream. Far more importantly, however, they help children to understand their own learning better and that enables them ultimately to make greater progress. Any targets teachers feel are needed are much more likely to have impact if they are negotiated and, for negotiation to be successful, children need to understand the starting point, a desirable next step and how to reach this. There is an element of language learning here which might need to be worked through more in English. Learning to learn involves some complex ideas and complex words. As long as we signal to the class that we need to use English for a special reason, we can come out of target language mode and enter 'L2L time'. Whole-class work can be tailored towards individual or group targets too, simply by the teacher reviewing the need for attention to be paid to certain aspects, with the lead-in being: 'Those of you working on improving your pronunciation of the *ch* phoneme (in German) should pay special attention to this game now, and should be putting your hands up to answer.'

Feedback on simple writing

Primary teachers know from literacy planning and the policies that apply across the curriculum that the correction of written work and the feedback that is given need to be managed carefully. We also know about the types of features that signal writing at a comparatively low level of attainment for KS2. At www.standards.dfes.gov.uk/primary framework/downloads/pdf/sf-asf-enw-Stephanie_l2_y4.pdf is the Level 2 writing profile of a Y4 pupil. The annotations show that this level is signalled by inaccuracies connected with knowledge about language as well as a still developing ability to organise thoughts. It gives a clear message that we should not be too demanding in our expectations of emergent writing amongst primary language learners. However, explicit correction can improve second language capability as we saw in the section on speaking task assessment. Feedback is best centred on key language items in focus at that time and comments about how to improve are very important. Neither simply correcting nor simply praising effort will be successful in bringing about improvement, whereas a targeted comment and a suggestion for a way to improve, plus some kind of encouraging message, will together have a potentially positive impact.

Transition to KS3

As children start to learn languages in KS2, transition issues are raised and year on year become more acute. It is problematic enough when a group of children have learned a language for a year in Y6 and then join other Y7 students who have learned a different language or no language. But soon we will have the situation where children have learned a language for four years throughout KS2 and will present secondary colleagues with a wide range of knowledge, skills and understanding. Of course this is a normal scenario for other secondary teachers. It has only been with languages that the 'blank canvas' argument has ever been used. This 'convenient' view has always masked a reality which was that the incoming students were rarely completely 'blank' as regards their exposure to foreign languages and their cultural awareness. They were also far from equal in terms of aptitude and attitudes at that comparatively late starting age.

It is relevant to start with a brief discussion of some general transition issues. Languages transition needs to be seen in a context of the problems pupils may have on a social and personal as well as an academic level and in the context of other existing practice. In most secondary schools there is now a very strong focus on the need to bring new children in each year with a measure of established familiarity with the buildings and facilities and routines of the 'big school'. Many secondaries have liaison teams who visit partner primaries, and they hold open and induction days, also involving students who transferred a year earlier to give a peer perspective to the newcomers. Some departments have well organised subject liaison procedures and most attempt to make handover information as useful as possible. Of course the urban myths will always persist and each child preparing for transition will hear some variant on the 'horror stories' of secondary school life. The notion of specialist teachers and specialist facilities is often a big attraction for the move, but it is easy to forget that children are used to just one or two teachers with whom they generally work out a productive relationship. Suddenly finding a need to relate to more than ten teachers can be very daunting and can lead to a regrettable pattern of associating a subject with the teacher and not with the content and skills it encompasses. 'Which subject do you like best at the moment then Tom?' 'I like French best because Mr ... is awesome.' may be a pleasing reaction when it is our own subject, but it is a worrying one nevertheless. In fact, in many cases where KS2 Languages is taught by an outreach or PPA cover teacher or even by another member of the school staff, this person is perhaps in a strong position to talk about transition in a generic way. Because he or she already represents a process (that is, the need to relate to a less familiar teacher figure) which children will have to face many times over in a very short period at the beginning of a school year, he or she will be able to talk more convincingly about how to manage that difficult stage.

Many children are also anxious about losing the power to determine how they are placed both in classes and in learning spaces within classes, so forcing them to relate to a whole host of new peers with no friendship circle to fall back on. Essentially, they want to manage this big change by undertaking it with friends. Demetriou *et al.* (2000) found evidence that children have quite sophisticated understanding of who they should work with as opposed to who they like to socialise with and that secondary schools should perhaps trust students' views of this a little more. The practice of seating students boy/girl was especially disliked at this stage. Parallel to this, in a study of attainment rather than attitudes Gibbons and Telhaj (2006) found that the general prior peer group attainment had little effect on the attainment of individual students, so again perhaps familiar pairings continuing through to Y7 would not have any negative effect on attainment.

But against this list of negative aspects we have now made, we should also note that Lucey and Reay (2000) write about the dual nature of the transition experience, which they characterise using Giddens' (1991) phrase, 'anxious readiness'. They assert that much in the transition literature deals with the negatives of the move from primary to secondary schools, but that in their experience most children have a mixture of emotions. They explain this in their conclusion as follows:

> We would argue that the prospect of going to 'big school' presents children with a dilemma central to the experience of 'growing up'; that in order to gain freedom and autonomy from adult regulation one must be willing to relinquish some measure of the protection which that regulation affords. ... Despite the very great fears which children at times expressed in relation to the move from primary to secondary school, and challenges which the new environment will present to them, there was much evidence to suggest that most are able to call on hopeful feelings that on some level, at least some of the time, that move will be a benign one, populated by people who will be willing and able to support them through the changes. (Lucey and Reay 2000: 203)

In the transition report by Galton *et al.* (1999) the focus is on general attainment across the curriculum and the tendency for levels to fall at crucial change points, such as Y3, Y7 and Y8. They noted that at the time of writing the social and personal issues were being addressed effectively in many cases, but that curriculum continuity remained a problem. One of their conclusions, the tendency for work to be repetitive and unchallenging after a transition, is a particular concern for us as ML teachers. There are many anecdotal stories of Y7 students starting again and indeed this was highlighted as a central reason for the failure of the 1960s Primary French initiative (Burstall *et al.* 1974, Hood 1994). The systems for transfer of information and the establishment of mutual understanding of teaching styles, resources and assessment patterns are largely still in the future. Galton *et al.* (1999) also noted that able boys were particularly vulnerable at Y7 to a dip in attainment across the curriculum and, given the gender issue that applies to language learning by older students, this would be a matter of real concern to us if it were true also for languages. In the very good CILT report (O'Hagan 2007) on transition, the interplay between Galton *et al.*'s general findings and ML specific issues is addressed in some detail.

Overall, the transition to KS3 clearly represents a very major change for all 11-year-olds and we should bear in mind this more global context when we focus on language learning and teaching issues. Transition is developing very quickly because it clearly is a very urgent agenda. The NACELL Best Practice project recently published two reports specifically addressing transition.

The first was developed by the London Borough of Richmond upon Thames LEA (www.nacell.org.uk/bestpractice/pdfs/Guidance%20on% 20transition.pdf) and contains views from secondary teachers after teaching incoming Y7 pupils with primary language learning experience, case studies of liaison between schools and a range of proformas used to assess primary age pupils and act as transfer documentation. The Borough suggested a framework and scheme to describe the areas that the primary schools could cover and encouraged activity designed to increase intercultural understanding. This was an innovative programme, coming before both the KS2 Framework and the current developing transition activity that has adopted many of the ideas mooted in this report. There is a sense in the document that the secondary schools had, to a large extent, the power to set the agenda and that is certainly an issue that each LA is currently having to discuss. The more primary schools teach languages and develop the way they teach languages, the more secondary schools will find they need to adapt their practice to meet the primary schools' agenda. Some local authorities will let the primary teachers use the KS2 Framework in their own way to teach in as much breadth and depth as they wish, while others will still wish to set a bar and limit progression to a level which the secondary teachers find acceptable.

The second report, from the International Learning and Research Centre, South Gloucestershire (www.nacell.org.uk/bestpractice/pdfs/Planning% 20for%20continuity%20and%20progression.pdf), documents a curriculum project that linked Y6 and Y7 in work involving French and literacy with what might be termed simple Geography. The KS2 classes were following a curriculum based on the first nine units of the original QCA Schemes of Work for KS2, and the KS3 students at the end of Y7 were sharing with Y6 peers the level they had reached after a year at secondary school as part of a positive process which communicates aims and objectives for progression before transfer. Clearly this facet of transition planning can only be good as the pupils were at the centre of the activity and the benefit to the Y6 children is evident. The evaluation of the project raises the issue that the level of communication both between the two schools and between the ML and Literacy staff at each level needed to be enhanced. This appears to point to the importance of physical meetings and collaborative work rather than simple communication by document and messaging. Sharing schemes is very necessary but it is only a beginning to a much more intense and personal process.

CILT's most recent transition project (O'Hagan 2007) is reported at www.cilt.org.uk/transition/index.htm. Here a summary document and also a series of six (at the time of writing) LA project files detail a very varied series of steps, most of which include some collaborative work across the phases which now seems to be the most highlighted facet of good practice measures.

The importance of transition is signalled as early as the teacher-training phase in some cases. Clearly, if new teachers enter the classroom with a deep understanding of these issues, good practice can be maintained where it already exists and established where it is not yet in place. At Liverpool Hope University, the ML specialists on the primary and secondary PGCE courses join together for some tasks. Their work on transition includes, as well as university-based discussion, some collaborative cross-phase work between secondary and primary PGCE students and they have some ambitious future plans (Rowe 2008a):

- Y7 audit as part of subject training plan and feedback to department
- changing timing of primary placement for secondary trainees.
- a week of 'shared placement'
- collaborative design of 'bridging units' and 'taster days'
- joint mentor training.

Such a coherent programme sets a standard for Initial Teacher Education (ITE) courses by ensuring real and focused contact between the teachers operating on either side of the 11+ gateway.

In a task used by these student teachers (Rowe 2008b) some statements about transition are reviewed (see Figure 8.1). The intention is that they are ranked and a sample selected for more detailed discussion in terms of the logistics, responsibility and accountability and the potential benefits. These statements can be used as a checklist of good practice in transition as we will shortly show. Every one of these statements is a purposeful activity and we can see that they fall into several different categories (see Figure 8.2) which offer a useful guide to the sheer range of approaches we should be considering. Of course not all of these are possible for everyone but the use of at least some activities from each of the categories represents a very real step towards good practice.

In Figure 8.2 we have offered six categories of activity, ranked in what we feel is a logical order of steps, which together involve all three 'constituents': the LA, the secondary schools and the primary schools. It is immediately apparent that the onus falls on the secondary schools to ensure that transition is effective. The specific secondary column includes a series of actions that ask the school to look carefully at the incoming students and to carry out a range of measures to ensure progression for all.

Collaborative teaching in Y6 and Y7 between primary and secondary colleagues
Observation of Primary Modern Foreign Language (PMFL) lessons by secondary colleagues
Exchange of documentation between phases e.g. Schemes of Work
Transfer of PMFL assessment records from primary to secondary
Adaptation of Y7 Schemes of Work to take into account prior learning of children
Development of 'bridging units' within a cluster of primaries and feeder secondary schools
Development of strategies for revisiting language learnt in primary in new contexts at secondary
Taster lessons for Y6 in secondary prior to transfer
Enhanced strategies for differentiation in Y7 Modern Foreign Language (MFL) lessons
Cross-phase MFL working groups and meetings
Observation of Y7 lessons by primary colleagues
A named PMFL coordinator in every primary school who can liaise with feeder secondary schools
'Fast-track' groups in Y7 for those with PMFL experience
A 'change of language' policy in Y7
A common LA scheme of work for PML

Figure 8.1 Transition statements (Rowe 2008b). Our grateful thanks to Jan Rowe for sharing this resource with us.

The adaptation of schemes of work is key to the whole task and should be informed by taster lessons, the observations by secondary colleagues and any joint teaching activity carried out between schools. Only then (if needed) should the re-visiting agenda be considered in order that no unnecessary revision takes place. The need for differentiation or fast-track groups will follow logically if the previous steps are carried out well. A change of language is a way of side-stepping the issue in terms of the content which is known by children, but still their existing skills must be evaluated and the right level of engagement with a new language implemented. And of course the reasons for a change of language at 11 years must be clear and accepted by the family of schools if resentment and frustration are to be avoided. The real challenge now is to make sure that the children involved in transition have a role, a voice and some ownership over the process. The activities given above will work even better if we can also evolve a pupil column of action.

The duty of the primary phase is to teach children as well as they can and to follow any agreed course which has been negotiated (and not

Primary school	Secondary school	Classroom liaison	Document liaison
A named PMFL coordinator in every primary school who can liaise with feeder secondary schools	Taster lessons for Y6 in secondary prior to transfer	Observation of PMFL lessons by secondary colleagues	Exchange of documentation between phases e.g. Schemes of Work
	Adaptation of Y7 Schemes of Work to take into account prior learning of children	Observation of Y7 lessons by primary colleagues	Transfer of PMFL assessment records from primary to secondary
	Development of strategies for revisiting language learnt in primary in new contexts at secondary	Collaborative teaching in Y6 and Y7 between primary and secondary colleagues	
	Enhanced strategies for differentiation in Y7 MFL lessons	Development of 'bridging units' within a cluster of primaries and feeder secondary schools	
Liaison through meetings		'Fast-track' groups in Y7 for those with PMFL experience	**LA**
Cross-phase MFL working groups and meetings	A 'change of language' policy in Y7		A common LA Scheme of Work for PML

Figure 8.2 Transition statements by category (adapted from Rowe 2008b)

imposed!) between the partners. A PMFL coordinator is a very clear and obvious need and should not be contentious. In fact, when we look closely at Figure 8.2 we see that there is a substantial (in terms of the time commitment involved) shared role between KS2 and KS3. The activities are deliberately sequenced to build mutual understanding and some collaboration before any joint activity in the form of bridging units is launched. It is vital through all of this process that the secondary school staff understand how primary children learn and therefore how primary teachers teach. Throughout this book we have commented that we should not simply adopt secondary methodology in fashioning how we teach languages at primary level. This understanding needs to be at the core of transition activity or problems will be stored.

How can we address the strand that is missing from Figure 8.2 – the role of the children themselves in this process? There is some established practice through the use of the Junior European Language Portfolio and the Language Passport, both downloadable from CILT/NACELL: www.nacell.org.uk/resources/pub_cilt/portfolio.htm. The Junior Portfolio has been in existence longer of the two and is intended much more as a formative document based around 'I can' statements. The major pattern here is to colour in speech bubbles that express these competencies around each of the four skills as and when each pupil is ready to do so.

The Languages Passport (see example below) is badged by the Council of Europe and contains a proforma to record progress on the languages ladder scheme up to B1 (the first stage of intermediate level) and to note intercultural experiences. This proforma is intended to be used directly as a transfer document between schools and in that sense is a summative attainment document at the point of transfer.

Speaking and talking to someone

Tick when you can do these things. √

Breakthrough	
A1 COUNCIL OF EUROPE / CONSEIL DE L'EUROPE	
I can use simple phrases and sentences and I can also talk with someone in a simple way, asking and answering questions.	
Grade 1	I can say/repeat a few words and short simple phrases *e.g. what the weather is like; greeting someone; naming classroom objects …*	
Grade 2	I can answer simple questions and give basic information *e.g. about the weather; where I live; whether I have brothers or sisters, or a pet …*	
Grade 3	I can ask and answer simple questions and talk about my interests *e.g. taking part in an interview about my area and interests; a survey about pets or favourite foods; talking with a friend about what we like to do and wear …*	

Preliminary	
COUNCIL CONSEIL *A2* OF EUROPE DE L'EUROPE	
I can give a short prepared talk e.g. describe a picture or people, my school, my home, and take part in a simple conversation on familiar topics.	
Grade 4	I can take part in a simple conversation and I can express my opinions *e.g. discussing a picture with a partner, describing colours, shapes and saying whether I like it or not; asking for and giving directions; discussing houses, pets, food …*
Grade 5	I can give a short prepared talk, on a topic of my choice, including expressing my opinions *e.g. talking on a familiar subject; describing a picture or part of a story; making a presentation to the class …*

The vital importance of mixing peer- and self-evaluation and especially of success criteria, as demonstrated earlier in the chapter, is paramount here. If this Languages Passport is going to be a meaningful document which can also contribute to a better start at Y7, it needs to reflect true competence accurately. It also needs to be something that the children can talk about with confidence. This cannot be emphasised too much as the children can be their own ambassadors for change, as long as they have the written evidence and can support it with their use of language.

This brings together the two major strands of the chapter: the need for a range of monitoring and assessment strategies used by the teacher and the issues surrounding transition. If the Junior Portfolio or the Passport is used, there needs to be a portfolio of work and exemplars of the level of language the children are regularly meeting in Y6 supplied with it. This is a vital part of the information needed for communicating effectively with KS3 teachers. Equally, secondary colleagues need to look at this evidence carefully to start up the KS3 curriculum at an appropriate point. The inherent danger is that if they find that the transfer data is unreliable, secondary colleagues will cease to trust the judgement of primary colleagues. If that happens, the only losers will be the children.

Reflection point

How is transition organised in your current context? Do the measures currently taken fit into the table? Are there other activities not mentioned? How do the pupils currently see transition and what do they use to help them manage it?

 Chapter summary

This chapter has looked at a range of aspects relating to assessment including:

- the overarching rationale for approaches in general

- the issues around specific types of language use in the classroom and what sorts of assessment are demanded

- issues of correction and feedback

- where to find guidance

- issues of transition, especially the supply of reliable and purposeful information to colleagues in KS3.

It has attempted to locate ML assessment in the current overall assessment context and has suggested that the principles should be those adopted for other areas of the curriculum. It has especially drawn attention to the value of pupils understanding the assessment process and being empowered to self- and peer-assess themselves

Key and Further Reading 📖

The standard text on Assessment for Learning is Black, P. and Wiliam, D. (1998) 'Inside the Black Box: Raising Standards through Classroom Assessment' accessible at: http://ngfl. northumberland.gov.uk/keystage3ictstrategy/Assessment/blackbox.pdf.

A very full guide to the issues, but not aimed at the primary age range, is Genesee, F. and Upshur, J.A. (1996) *Classroom Evaluation in Second Language Learning*. Cambridge: Cambridge University Press.

The special issue of the journal *Language Testing,* vol. 17, April 2000, has a series of useful articles including two we quoted from in this chapter.

The CILT report on transition is available at www.cilt.org.uk/transition/transition_report.pdf.

What does research tell us about the integration of languages into the curriculum?

Introductory vignette

It's not very interesting and not very motivational because it's not person-alised to us and we learn words but we don't learn how to use them together. (Student at the beginning of Y9 speaking about her experience of language learning from being a Y7 beginner)

Comment

We have heard testimony from several secondary age learners in this book because, as we quoted in Chapter One from *14–19: Opportunity and Excellence* (DfES 2003), when 'students struggle with a subject in which they have little interest or aptitude' it is important to try to analyse why this has happened and what should be done to avoid repeating such apparent 'mistakes' in the primary phase. This chapter tries in a more theoretical way to describe some of the influences on what we might now call the 'traditional' foreign language methodology which is present in our secondary schools in a range of manifestations.

Chapter objectives

- **To outline the major elements of communicative language teaching and task-based language teaching and to relate these to a primary context.**

(Continued)

(Continued)

- **To offer a definition of CLIL (Content and Language Integrated Learning) and to show how research has evaluated it.**
- **To offer a framework for CLIL curriculum design, drawing on Coyle's 4Cs (2006) curriculum and categories of language and learning and on the Cummins matrix (1981).**

Relevant Q Standards: Q14, Q18, Q22

Initial reflection point

How do you best learn a language yourself? How did you learn at school? Do you learn any differently now? Try to think about the roles in this learning process – what did your teachers do at school and what does the 'tutor' (person or machine that you currently learn with) do now? What was and is your role in this learning process and did you feel comfortable with that role? What are the main barriers for you when you try to learn?

Response

The roles of teacher and learner are an important aspect of analysing learning. In a classroom situation, most of us (school students or adults) accept whatever structure we are given and work with it. Yet this structure has usually been chosen by the teacher or institution and works to suit their preferences. While classrooms cannot be personalised to suit all the different learning preferences of the pupils within it, it is important to plan to cater at least for a small range of different approaches. Above all we should certainly, as teachers, select a main approach that will set up a motivational and participatory basis for the majority of learners. This should be structured to allow them to engage with meaningful content, to see the purpose of the classroom activities and to gain as much as possible which is useable and transferable from the process.

Communicative language teaching

ML teachers in England have used the term 'communicative' to describe their practice for over 30 years and, after so long a period, in many ways this approach to teaching can almost be regarded now as 'traditional'. The change occurred during the 1970s when curriculum shapers, syllabus designers, examiners, publishers and teachers started to turn away from what had previously been felt to be a radical innovation: the audio-lingual approach, typified by resources such as the Nuffield language courses (*En Avant, Vorwärts, Adalante, ceneped*). This methodology itself grew with the 'direct method', which introduced major use of the target language for teaching for the first time and placed oral competence above grammatical capability. In audio-lingual approaches, despite the use of tape recordings and film-strips to enliven lessons, the shape of units was very fixed, the role of repetition and the order of using the skills was strictly prescribed. Drills were used to internalise both vocabulary and grammar and the units were still often grammar-led rather than centred on a topic.

The changes away from this method began with a focus on the syllabus content. There was a shift towards survival topics, inspired by the work on the Threshold Level (van Ek 1975, van Ek and Trim 1991), which was explored briefly in Chapter Two, and there was now a demand for authenticity of materials and tasks and for a lessening of focus on grammar. This led to the new GCSE syllabuses of 1988 which built on Mode 3 CSE work developed over the preceding five years. The new emphasis was on the communication of real or pseudo-real messages and so the term communicative was picked up from mainly English as a Foreign Language (EFL) writers of the time and quickly applied. The intention was certainly to personalise and develop real use of language.

Krashen's (1985) theory of second language acquisition consists of five main hypotheses:

- Acquisition-Learning: that we acquire language through a natural process of exposure to target language and learn grammar formally in classrooms.

- Monitor: that what we have 'learned' acts as an editor on what we have 'acquired' as we speak.

- Natural Order: that we tend to acquire and learn grammatical constructs in a set order.

- Input: that we need contextualised messages that carry clear meaning in order to acquire naturally.

- Affective Filter: that personal feelings such as confidence or anxiety as well as motivational level directly affect the extent to which we manage to learn language and communicate successfully.

Krashen's key work in the 1980s, as well as work since then, introduced terms such as those in the box above. An important term for classrooms and for the use of the target language was 'comprehensible input' (Krashen 1988) which describes the meaningful messages in context, used by teachers themselves or in the texts they choose. When learners are able to understand these messages, they 'intake' language and add it to their store. This is a relatively extreme view, but is vindicated through immersion contexts; that if the conditions are right (and they are not easy to set up) students can acquire language simply from being exposed to it. The principle of i+1 (Krashen 1988) stated that the language of the message should be just beyond current capability so that the learner has to work and think in order to process and intake. This is rooted in sound learning theory principles and Krashen's major message, though sometimes challenged, has tended to be amended and added to rather than overturned. It is the basis for structured 100 per cent target language use in classrooms now and certainly the notion that we should push the pupils to hear or read a little more than they already know is an important principle behind both learning and progression.

However, Krashen's (1988) distinction between acquisition and learning in the monitor model is perhaps more problematic. He sees learning as a process which is affected by error correction and form-focus whereas acquisition is a more natural process, which error correction cannot affect. What has been learned acts as a monitor of what is said during the output/productive process. But language competence is driven by the material that has been acquired. In the vast literature on acquisition through the use of communicative contexts and on what exactly is and is not acquired in this way, many researchers agree that there is a clear need for a focus on form as well as a focus on meaning if accurate language use is an aim of a learning programme. Swain and Lapkin's (1995) output hypothesis claimed that learners notice gaps in their competence as they produce language and that feedback at this point has an important role in learning. We noted the different effects of varieties of approach to error correction in Chapter Eight, citing Loewen (2007), and saw that giving feedback to learners about the accuracy of their utterances is necessary if they are to improve over time. Wesche and Skehan (2002) refer to strong and weak varieties of communicative language teaching and show that meaning-focused instruction (for example content-based courses) is the basis for stronger models. In this they agree with Krashen, but they also comment that the stronger models 'have ... increasingly sought ways to incorporate a focus on form and language awareness into classroom practice' (2002: 216) and go on to discuss about the need for microstrategies for specific purposes within a general teaching approach.

Taking into account these views about language learning through an essentially communicative model, if we now review practice since the 1980s how *communicative* have we really been? The quotation in the introductory vignette suggests that even in 2008 this is not always being achieved. The standard work, Littlewood's *Communicative Language Teaching: An Introduction* (1981), highlighted the difference between pre-communicative (practice) activities and communicative (production) activities. (We will focus on the so-called 3Ps of presentation, practice, production shortly.) Littlewood also stressed the difference between a focus on meaning and a focus on form (that is, syntax/ grammar) and explored in some detail communicative functions, such as how we use language to enquire, apologise, complain, and so on. He attempted in this way to show how the teaching and learning could progress from a necessary practising and fixing stage to something like real communication which truly prepared learners for language use in a target language setting.

In his concluding chapter, Littlewood defined the communicative activities as being where '[t]he learner is ... selecting suitable language forms from his total repertoire, and producing them fluently. The criterion for success is whether the meaning is conveyed effectively' (1981: 89). In contrast, pre-communicative activities:

> include the majority of the learning activities currently to be found in textbooks ... These aim above all to provide learners with a fluent command of the linguistic system, without actually requiring them to use this system for communicative purposes. Accordingly, the learners' main purpose is to produce language which is acceptable (i.e. sufficiently accurate or appropriate) rather than to communicate meanings effectively. (1981: 85)

We have chosen these quotations from Littlewood deliberately because many of the teaching and learning tasks that have been commonly used in language learning at any age over the last 30 years have been decidedly pre-communicative in their nature. The culmination of a pre-communicative phase, to lead to more authentic message-bearing communication, has often been absent, even though it appears on the surface to be part of the design. This is echoed by Legutke and Thomas (1991) where they make a distinction between language learning tasks, pre-communicative and communicative tasks, and between all three and an overall 'project' which should be the organising whole. Communicative tasks are intended to create discourse from genuine communicative needs and interaction and to go beyond a simple stage where learners merely begin to express their own opinions and meanings (which is still characterised as pre-communicative in Legutke and Thomas' system).

One way of exemplifying this is to examine a teaching and learning structure known as the 3Ps (Presentation, Practice, Production), which is still recommended by some teacher educators and consultants. In this format, the teacher first presents the material to be learned, often a topic-related vocabulary set, a structure, or perhaps a grammar point exemplified through a range of topic-related examples. Normally the teacher has chosen this material using a syllabus or course book or perhaps knowledge of what the learners may find useful and interesting. The teacher models the language, the learners imitate and give the language back in a cycle which generally involves simple repetition, then the choice of alternatives (offered by the teacher), then production of a word or phrase from a visual stimulus. Teachers are told that the best way to do this is to use the target language the entire time and use physical and visual prompt techniques to elicit the language. After this first phase learners are given tight practice tasks, based on substitution tables, guided role-plays, matching items to what is read or heard, or gap fill. Finally more open-ended tasks are given where learners have the opportunity to use language more fluently and independently (production activities).

In reality, much of the audio-lingual methodology seems to have survived in the presentation and practice phases of this approach and drilling is still in effect a vital part of these early stages. In our work on the PGCE secondary course in the 1990s, the team at the University of Nottingham moved away from the 3Ps structure because we felt it emphasised teacher control too much and because practice dominated production. Presentations and free role-plays which should have been production tasks too often seemed to revert to students reading out text with a very unnatural accent and intonation, and it appeared that lip-service was being paid to the independent phase, perhaps because of the earlier control by the teacher, the time-frame and the lack of thinking involved in the practice stage.

Our response to this, as we tried to link an alternative approach to the reality which we knew was still in schools, was to re-characterise the cycle as 3Ms (Meeting language, Manipulating language and Making language my own) which stressed at the beginning that learners should encounter language in a range of ways, including via free reading and listening. The difference here was that more often they were being asked to work out meanings from context clues rather than being presented with meanings by a teacher. The range of vocabulary and structures they met was also less controlled and defined, especially if they were more able students. We characterised the manipulation phase as one that should involve some thinking embedded in the tasks, and not just the use of a context for essentially a language drill. From a language only perspective the desirable nature of practice can be summarised as:

> When practice is defined as experience in using language for meaningful purposes, including opportunities for thoughtful retrieval of language features that ... have not become automatic, then practice is likely to be more predictive of long-term success. (Lightbown 2003: 6)

We challenged our students to ensure that the production task was scaffolded rather than scripted. In this way the learners had to know the language well before they moved to that stage or at least had to have strategies to 'keep talking' when they had forgotten an item. This was easier if they had become accustomed from the outset to using memorised language spontaneously, if need be with a prompt, but not to using a fully drafted piece of writing from which to 'speak'.

It seemed to us then, as it still does, that one of the biggest pitfalls of the 3Ps model is that teachers tend to 'measure out' what they think they can reasonably expect to get back in the production stage and then limit the input during presentation to precisely that. There is no language-rich classroom in which to meet and slowly acquire a range of language and when in a target language speaking context the normal language flow is too difficult for students to manage. In KS3 there is some resistance to the language-rich classroom from the consumers – they are by then much more concerned about not understanding every word and much more self-conscious if they feel they do not understand what is being said. Contrast this with the primary age-group who, as we have shown, accept much more naturally that they will interpret language as it comes, as long as the teacher is 'invisibly' conscious of managing what comes with a sensitive eye on the individual class context. As we have seen, much of what has already been explored in this book is aimed at developing that language-rich classroom and at using what are really communicative approaches at all points in the learning cycle.

Our conclusion from this review is that we have an opportunity to create much more communicative learning environments in our primary classrooms, but that an imitation of secondary coursebook approaches will probably not achieve this as well as we might wish.

 Reflection point

You want the children to experience getting their fruit in the target language. You could pre-teach the fruit vocabulary and practise in pairs asking for items with cards containing pictures, or you could simply offer choices of fruit with the frame: '*Möchtest du einen Apfel oder eine Banane?*' eliciting '*Eine Banane bitte*' or perhaps '*Ich möchte eine Banane*'. What is the difference between the processes that happen in the child's mind during these two variants?

Response

The first method emphasises the language-focus as a task and makes a game of using the cards. It remains a little abstract as no real items are used and no real purpose is activated. There is more intense practice because each item might be used several times between pairs but less able children might find the functional language of offering/accepting more difficult. The use of the cards works very much on a simple stimulus-response pattern which may internalise language but may also become mechanistic and be accomplished without thinking. So there are both gains and pitfalls with this approach.

In the second method there is a real choice to be made (that is, which fruit does the child really want) and a genuine politeness function (that is, of accepting, using please or thank you) which the teacher or teaching assistant could legitimately insist on for non-linguistic reasons. Although each child only says the item once, this occurs in a personalised dialogue with an adult and he or she is also aware of the language as the teacher asks different members of the class. There is a great deal of opportunity for repetition as this is a daily activity. The need to communicate a real message makes the point that language is a vehicle for authentic situations and this may give a better overall subconscious rationale for using the language.

The importance of task has emerged through this section looking at communicative teaching, both in terms of end-activities in a language learning cycle structure and in the reflection point above. We now explore aspects of task-based learning as another important variation of communicative language teaching.

Task-based learning

In the world of Teachers of English to Speakers of Other Languages (TESOL), there has been a move over the last 25 years from a broadly defined communicative language teaching to a range of more specific approaches. One of these is task-based learning which has been consistently explored and developed by a range of writers, for example Willis (1996) Willis and Willis (2007), Nunan (1989, 2004), Skehan (1998, 2003), Ellis (2003), Samuda and Bygate (2008). This range also reflects an array of different approaches to the methodology and, in fact, at one point Samuda and Bygate (2008: 195) offer six different interpretations of the term 'task-based'. Willis (1996) relates her view of task-based learning to the 3Ps structure with a pre-task, during and post-task series, where the learners' language focus follows actual task performance (for example, a whole role-play) so that learners can see what they are aiming for. Thus the use of the 3Ps is part of a more independent structure. Skehan (1998) also sees tasks as a means rather than an end. He visualises a three-stage process where material is encountered, fitted into the system and then added to total knowledge. Learners may be striving for any or all of the objectives of fluency, accuracy and complexity, depending on their needs and this may affect how they use the material given to complete the task. Thus, he views tasks in this language learning cycle as a positive way of offering a concrete context to bring these elements of the process together and to give an overall purpose in which to operate.

Samuda and Bygate (2008) present an overview of several different approaches and as part of this they include examples where task-based learning can be an end as well as a means. They note, for example, that 'Much first language learning occurs through holistic activities, and it seems likely that holistic activities can also play a significant role in second language learning, teaching and testing' (2008: 7). This view is closer to an approach that sees the task as an important factor that causes the learning rather than simply providing a way of implementing another theory. This was echoed in an interview with two girls at a Midlands language college at the start of their Y11. They had secured Grade A GCSE passes in French a year early, at the end of Y10. They were asked which period of their four years of French had been the most successful and enjoyable, and they replied that their two years of learning Geography through French in Y7 and Y8 had been the best. On being asked why, they replied that the outcomes they produced for each of those Geography topics (that is, the products of the overriding tasks set) constituted the work they were still most proud of more than two years later.

Linked to this is Breen's (1987) reference to the different phases of tasks. He makes the important point that task-as-workplan may differ from task-in-process. The underlying message of this is that teachers should design tasks to be stepped and progressive and in this sense maintain some directive control over learner activity, but that tasks should also be open-ended enough to allow the learners with particular abilities and needs to fulfil them in their own way and to learn from them what they can. Projects in any language always result in a range of different end-products – some more detailed, some more general, some more accurately presented, some more visually exciting – but what pupils should always feel is that they had an opportunity to learn new information and to show their knowledge in a way of which they feel proud.

In language learning there is often additional pride in the fact that the outcome has been produced in another language. Clearly task-based learning, when structured in this way, also meets most of the criteria for communicative teaching and learning.

This short summary of just a small set of facets of task-based learning is designed, therefore, to give a more concrete focus to what communicative language teaching could be and how to get there. We have spoken often throughout this book about the need for purposeful activities involving purposeful and natural use of language – real messages, language for enjoyment such as stories and songs, competitive and collaborative games, texts which teach something new or incorporate humorous use of language. We have argued that repetition should occur but as far as possible through sequences of questioning which have an exploratory purpose and are not just overt practice sessions. We have also recommended authentic materials and have highlighted continuously the need for these to reflect the real cultures of the target countries. In this way we have certainly advocated a form of true communicative teaching and some might maintain that we have been presenting a version of task-based learning.

What is CLIL and do we know if it can benefit learners?

Content and Language Integrated Learning (CLIL) has been both alluded to and directly referenced throughout this book. To reiterate, we are not holding up CLIL as the single way for primary languages to develop. This is not our 'preferred method'. Indeed it is not an overt method of language teaching at all. As we will see, CLIL is a way of organising a curriculum that leads to the *learning* of second or foreign languages, and is very close to EAL in the way it is theorised. As we mentioned in Chapter Two, it shows in a teacher's doorstep intentions what he or she is bringing to that class as a learning objective for that lesson. We hope that the next two sections will also shed some light on ways in which we might interpret communicative and task-based language teaching.

According to the CLIL Consortium website (www.clilconsortium.jyu.fi/): 'CLIL is a dual-focused educational approach in which an additional language is used for the learning and teaching of both content and language.' However, we maintain that the main focus in a CLIL approach is on the content to be taught and not primarily on the language. The key writer in this interpretation of CLIL is Coyle with the best brief summary of the approach to be found in Coyle (2006) and developed further in Coyle *et al.* (2009).

By content we mean either a subject such as Geography or Science or a cross-curricular topic, such as 'Water' or 'Our local environment' or 'The Second World War'. CLIL aims to teach content *via* the language by using methodologies associated with the content subjects rather than foreign language teaching methodology. We can demonstrate from research findings that the teaching of such content material through an *immersion* process is successful in terms both of the subject content and of the language.

In his overview of international research findings in school-based immersion programmes, Johnstone writes:

> Of the various main forms of immersion, research indicates that generally pupils develop a much higher level of proficiency in their IL [immersion language] than occurs when this language is simply taught as a school subject. They are not disadvantaged in their attainments in their L1 or in school subjects, e.g. mathematics, science, social studies. (2000: 2)

There are many examples that have contributed to this overview and which underpin its general findings. We can choose to look on a national scale and in a *second* rather than *foreign* language environment by examining the Canadian experience (for example, Cenoz and Genesee 1998, Day and Shapson 1996, Johnson and Swain 1997). Similarly, the USA bilingual education field identifies a broad range of research support for what is termed content-based instruction (Grabe and Stoller 1997). Or we can focus on a major regional foreign language experiment such as that in the Canton of Zurich (Stotz *et al.* 2005), where primary age children are successfully learning through English. We can also draw from examples of individual schools which immerse in French as a foreign language, for example Walker Road Primary in Aberdeen (Johnstone 2002, Johnstone and McKinstry 2008). Escola Vila Olímpica in Barcelona uses three working languages – Catalan, Spanish and English – and tries not to differentiate these as mother-tongue, second or foreign languages but rather uses each as a vehicle for learning parts of the curriculum. The list of research reports given above all agree that language learning is enhanced and that content subjects associated with CLIL do not suffer through the use of another language. Clearly different reports have varied focuses and produce different results, but there is a level of consistency about the findings from the different contexts that makes the case a serious one.

The Walker Road Primary Project
The most recent survey and the one single full evaluation which is UK-specific is The Walker Road (Early Primary Partial Immersion – EPPI) research (Johnstone and McKinstry 2008). We include here four sections in full from their conclusions because the case they make is so clear.

Attainments of EPPI pupils in English, Environmental Studies and Mathematics

84. The evidence of EPPI at primary school shows clearly that pupils have not been disadvantaged in English, Environmental Studies or Mathematics by receiving some of their education through the medium of French. Indeed, in English EPPI pupils demonstrated markedly greater fluency, range and confidence than their non-EPPI counterparts from the same year-group.

Progress of EPPI pupils in French

85. EPPI pupils have reached a level of proficiency in French which goes far beyond what can reasonably be expected of MLPS [Modern Languages in the Primary School]. This covers all four skills of listening, speaking, reading and writing. They have shown that they can use French in order to access with profit other areas of their curriculum. Their ability to cope with a fast flow of French input from their native-speaker teachers is particularly impressive.

Perceptions of EPPI by pupils, parents and native-speaker teachers

86. EPPI pupils hold positive perceptions of EPPI. In particular they clearly view it as an enjoyable experience and they would like to see it extended to other Scottish primary schools.

Factors linked to the success of EPPI

90. In the opinion of the evaluators, EPPI at Walker Road Primary School has been an outstanding success. It has brought something different and better into Scottish primary school education. In the era of Curriculum for Excellence it is preparing pupils very well for true international citizenship, not only through their outstanding proficiency in another major language but also in their confidence and international outlook. (2008: 13–14)

Does CLIL work without immersion?

These different contexts (Canadian immersion, Swiss immersion, partial immersion in Catalunya and in Scotland) share the fact that learners have had access to a partial or full immersion setting. Through this they have succeeded in mastering content taught through a foreign language and have made linguistic progress, often in advance of that made by students on more conventional language learning programmes. But many CLIL contexts are not partial or full immersion contexts. In Germany the tradition is to wait until language competence is well established. In Spain there is a tendency to innovate earlier and in smaller units of time. In France the secondary *sections européens* are slowly being supplemented by new projects in the primary age range.

In the UK any CLIL experiment has usually started in secondary schools, beginning with a very limited time-scale. But some of these trials have been successful. At Tile Hill Wood Language College, for example, they appeared to achieve noticeable progress in achievement in French and Geography and in attitudes towards language learning on an allocation of two hours per week of Geography through French supported by a further two hours of more conventional French teaching and a further one hour of Geography teaching in English (Woodfield and Neofitou 2006, also referred to in Coyle *et al.* 2009). The teachers involved acknowledged that their practice was influenced by the joint planning and resourcing of this programme – the teacher of French became more aware of the need for a deeper content in the language lessons and the teacher of Geography became more aware of the role of language in learning in her Geography teaching through English. At Hockerill Anglo-European Language College the German model was followed and CLIL was introduced after intensive language preparation. Again the model proved very successful. Clearly, although immersion will always produce more, a limited time allocation can still produce something.

How common are these approaches?

But these approaches are still rare, certainly in primary schools. In two important earlier reports produced for the Qualifications and Curriculum Authority (QCA) there were no instances of large-scale integration into the curriculum. Powell *et al.* found that 'There were only a few overt examples of links with other subjects in the teaching observed ... Links with Literacy were frequently mentioned but rather ill-defined' (2000: 64). Martin discussed the terms embedding and integration but noted: 'Both embedding and integration should not be confused with either total or partial immersion, and *do not imply* that the substance of the curricular areas should be taught through the medium of the foreign language' (2000: 35). Muir (1999) examines extensively the potential for embedding language into the curriculum but always speaks of it as reinforcement of content, also commenting that this is not subject teaching through the medium. He also quotes from Johnstone (1994: 8) who had warned about the possibility of a fragmented approach (that is, across several content subject areas) which could not easily be drawn together into a language system which could be used by the learners. This view is more important now that topic planning is again becoming common in primary schools. We have tried to show earlier in this book that there is a fully justified language curriculum around survival topics, as well as the embedded and integrated work we have also promoted, and that teachers do need to deal with language aspects such as grammar, spelling, syntax when appropriate to do so. We hope in this way that we have addressed Johnstone's (1994) reservations about topic planning.

Martin commented about the issues for teachers, citing Driscoll (1999): 'Even though generalist teachers have the opportunities to integrate the foreign language, they often have neither the personal linguistic resources nor materials to exploit these fully. The integrative approach is difficult to keep track of and to test' (2000: 35). But, conversely, she cites Kubanek-German (1996) and notes 'that in Germany, where the cross-curricular dimension is highlighted, there is unanimous agreement that foreign language work should be embedded in the pedagogical work of the primary school' (2000: 34). This is underpinned by Wode (1999) and, although in Blondin *et al.* (1998) curriculum integration does not emerge as a strong theme in previous research or in recommended action, there is now clear European Commission support (Marsh 2002).

At the time of writing, primary CLIL developments are visible on the Training Zone website where there are currently three video clips for CLIL teaching and one for CLIL planning which makes very many of the same points that we raise here, and a further eight for cross-curricular work. Teachers TV has just one clip which edges towards a CLIL context. In terms of published resources only *A La Française* (Tobutt and Roche 2007) is overtly CLIL-oriented.

How does CLIL work? Is there potential for confusion between languages?

With balanced bilingualism, that is, from birth (see summary in Baker 2006), there is no real evidence of children or young adults confusing languages, even if they occasionally mix them. The code-switching (moving between languages even within a sentence) that occurs with bilinguals can often be one-way, into the more frequently spoken language, and a change of location can strip out such code-switching very quickly. Similarly we have no evidence of language confusion caused by CLIL. Some people find it odd that children might know about a topic better in French, German or Spanish than in English (in terms of specialist vocabulary for example) but there is nothing inherently wrong with this and if they need to talk about it in English they can very quickly look for translations of the words they need. This is also a feature of linguistic competence which in the UK is seen as rare but elsewhere is much more accepted as the norm.

The functioning of the bilingual process (and therefore by analogy with well-developed CLIL schemes where there is a reasonable time allocation for the work) may be explained by the concept of the common underlying proficiency (Cummins 1991), which suggests that cognitive functioning and information processing skills may be developed and channelled through two languages as well as through one language. Thus, the thoughts that accompany talking, reading, writing and listening come from the same central processor. Knowledge gained through using one language will be available to the other language. In one representation (Cummins 1984) this is described as an iceberg which has two peaks showing above the surface of the sea but which is joined below water. Baker (2006) is at pains to be even-handed in his review of evidence on bilinguals but still concludes that there are clear cognitive gains at different intelligence levels from a bilingual experience. These may or may not be directly linked to having two languages and may also include cultural elements as major influences, but we can be sure that there is little negativity associated with 'natural' bilingualism.

There is a need of course for teachers to monitor the success of a programme as it develops and to do this rigorously. It often requires some professional development to be offered and it clearly works best when teachers plan and even teach collaboratively. A CLIL approach, then, can bring benefits but does demand a flexible attitude:

> Research on second language acquisition at various ages indicates the ultimate strength of learning that is pointed toward practical non-language goals ... Content-based teaching presents some challenges to language teachers. Allowing the subject matter to control the selection and sequencing of language items means that you have to view your teaching from an entirely different perspective. (Brown 1994: 220)

We will next look at how that doorstep intention we referred to earlier in the book is theorised within a recognised CLIL framework and how it can then be applied to real curricula and schemes of work.

Designing a CLIL curriculum and planning CLIL lessons: the theoretical perspective

In work located in research, teaching, teacher education and continuing professional development at the University of Nottingham over the last 15 years, a CLIL framework has evolved which can be most easily accessed through two main publications: Coyle (2006) and Coyle et al. (2009). This is a summary of the principles involved seen through a planning process which is intended to make theory overt and practice directed. Imagine you are embarking on an art topic in lower KS2 along the lines of the QCA Scheme: 'Unit 3a Portraying relationships'. You will want to decide as you populate your medium term plan, with your art teaching hat on, which elements of content from the unit plan you would select (and what you might add), how this would build on prior knowledge and what activities you would choose to engage learners and also to challenge them. In your language teacher 'hat' you would be looking for opportunities for the children to hear and speak the target language and to read and write to an appropriate extent. You will identify certain linguistic items which they

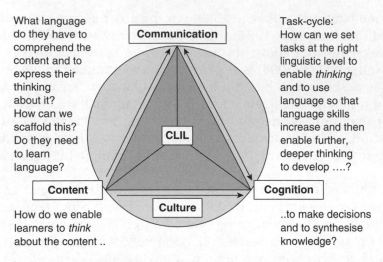

Figure 9.1   CLIL Pyramid (adapted from Coyle 2006)

will have the opportunity to learn through this work and which items they already need in place in order to achieve this. You will be actively seeking ways to include intercultural elements.

The 4Cs approach

Coyle's 4Cs structure (1999, 2006) not only formalises this planning into four separate but interlinked areas – content, cognition, communication and culture – but also offers a framework for how the four areas interact. We will first look at this from a theoretical standpoint.

The pyramid diagram in Figure 9.1, adapted from Coyle (2006), is used by the University of Nottingham to show the four key components of a CLIL curriculum. These can also be present in individual lesson plans, depending on the subject, topic and learners. Starting at the bottom of this diagram, we find a dynamic highlighted between content and cognition. The questions posed around the pyramid deliberately ground the planning into a series of processes. First the teacher decides how the content he or she is including in the plan can be made into tasks, which both explain the material and ask the learners to process and manipulate it. This is the initial planning step by every good teacher in every context, of course. Learning occurs through a whole range of interactions both in the brain and externally with a teacher or other learners. So we work out how to get our pupils *thinking* about the concepts or experiences they are encountering, making decisions (the simplest way of describing a problem-solving process by which input is filtered through a task to become output) and synthesising through an assimilation or accommodation process (Piaget 1955) into new total knowledge. By foregrounding this part of the planning we ensure that the content remains the main objective and that the science, art, or PE gets taught.

In mother tongue, the element of language in this process is often forgotten, although good primary teachers have a sense of 'language pitch' that allows them to consider it intuitively. Two processes are involved: receptive processing of information or concepts and the spoken or written expression of understanding resulting from participation in a task. In a CLIL context, language scaffolding becomes paramount. But we should remember that in 'scaffolding the language' we are actually scaffolding the thinking – there is no point in offering language structures for the sake of it. To put it another way, we are firstly considering which vocabulary and structures will best allow pupils to make sense of the stimulus we have offered. Next we are considering which vocabulary and structures will allow pupils to move towards a response. Finally we decide how to use the language that we have decided is at an appropriate level to facilitate that response. For example, a particular question sometimes suggests a particular answer format and so allows the thinking to be expressed with language as a facilitator rather than as a barrier. We can find many arguments on both sides of the contention that you can or cannot have thought without language, but we can be sure that if someone is presented with two tables of parallel data (for example, facts about two countries) they will instinctively make comparisons and be ready (language permitting) to express conclusions from those comparisons. In other words the thinking can be relatively language free, but the expression of that thinking is of course not, unless we include pictorial representation as a means of communicating ideas.

Here we are getting to grips with the two other sides of the pyramid base – the dynamics of content/language and language/cognition. The questions therefore ask us to consider how language can facilitate our intentions stemming from a content-cognition interaction. Can we find the form of language to use to achieve our objective? Will we stray into using language that will cloud comprehension, thinking and expression? Do learners need to learn some language in order to do this or can we structure the task so they learn the language they need while doing it? Will we find the route through words, symbols, diagrams and images to input our content and then allow the learners to express the thinking we have engendered through a parallel set of 'outcome facilitator devices'?

The 4Cs in practice

We hope that by focusing now on the following example we can make our description of the pyramid more concrete. Imagine we are planning the art unit and we want to look specifically at portraits showing more than one person, so we can begin to discuss relationships and how they might be shown in an image. A Google image search on family portraits in the target language (for example, *portraits famille*) will bring up a range of mostly modern images that could be used to start a discussion (as shown below). We could also use a published source where available (Salgado's, 2003 *Children* collection, for example) or even our own family and friends' portraits if we do not mind exposing part of our real lives to the children! We might want to link this further with another curriculum area and could therefore choose a small set of portraits from the past to compare with the set we have assembled from the present. The National Portrait Gallery website is one source where you can be sure that you will get some detail about who is who and when the work was created. From there you can do a search, for example, around a certain group from a historical period: for example 'sitters from the Pre-Raphaelite group' brings up a large selection of Victorian portraits from which five or six could easily be chosen.

If we take either set of portraits and brainstorm views of them in English, we could almost certainly quickly establish a number of ways to look at the pictures. This might include relationships (family, friends, colleagues), positions (sitting, standing, lying), attitudes to the camera or others involved (posed, natural, facing camera, engaged with someone else), dress, 'props' included and why. But we do not need to do this in English! With a target language focus, a teacher preparing the unit can immediately divide the language into three categories: language which is already known by the class, new language which we want to highlight because it is central and language which we might want to have in reserve if children themselves raise it. By using the images in a PowerPoint presentation format we can show them to the class on a large scale, evoking interest and allowing the children to see detail. We can also control any foreign language words they actually see and when.

It is at this point that we discover whether we are using a CLIL approach. If we are, we will want the children to access language while they think and perform another task. Our questioning while showing the prints might be along the lines discussed in Chapter Six. We would start by asking simple decision questions: Are they sitting or standing? Do they look happy or serious or sad? Are they quiet or speaking? Are they looking at the camera, at each other, at nothing? Many of these questions can legitimately be asked to more than one person because there can be different answers, at least to some, so we have an example of natural repetition rather than parroting. As we ask questions, we can use mime, supplementary images or notes to clarify what the choice is. As we gather in the responses, the children start to use words which may be half-familiar or unknown, and we can easily find ways of echoing in a natural manner so the exposure to this language continues to be very high. Some portraits readily lend themselves to deeper questioning. The subjects may be looking quizzically at something which is not visible for example, in which case you can ask if they look interested, bored, frightened or puzzled and then follow by asking what they are looking at. The question *why* might also be raised as children are asked to explain a mood. In these deeper questions it helps to have possible simple answers ready but not to offer them too quickly. Let the children think first and then start to suggest, again through choices so that they still have to process, make a decision and then respond.

When sufficient discussion has taken place, the language can be gathered onto the whiteboard around an image so it is still contextualised and children can be asked to start to think about describing one of the pictures to each other in very simple terms. You may want to do this as a competitive guessing game (which picture am I describing?) or a positive or negative preference to swap with a partner (my favourite or my least favourite) or a simple description of a portrait imagined by one partner to generate a simple drawing by the other partner or a small group.

We have achieved here the two sides of the pyramid which have communication and language at their centre. We have prioritised language that is needed and have given the learners access to it while still allowing them to ask for other items which they decide within the process that they want to use to express their thoughts. The language is consistently angled towards allowing them to think and to express what they really want to say.

The language which we decide is key to the topic is described by Coyle (2006) as the language *of* learning. The language that we need for that discussion – in this example it is the positional language for description and the language of agreement or disagreement and of opinions – is identified as the language *for* learning. Any language that appears while the learning is in process is the language *through* learning. If these distinctions are made at the planning stage it helps us to conceptualise what we both expect from the children and what we will give to them.

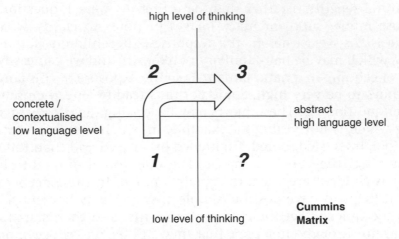

How ? – the role of context and levels of thinking

high level of thinking

2   **3**

concrete /
contextualised   abstract
low language level   high language level

1   **?**

low level of thinking   **Cummins
                                            Matrix**

Figure 9.2   The Cummins Matrix (adapted from Cummins 1981 by Coyle 2006)

Progression in questioning

The Cummins matrix (Cummins 1981), shown in Figure 9.2, is intended
to help with conceptualising the levels of questioning we use during a
CLIL process, as we described above. It explores the relationship
between low and high cognitive demands and concrete/contextual as
against abstract social/educational contexts for learning. Cummins
devised the categories of languages' demand and nature called BICS
(basic interpersonal communicative skills) and CALP (cognitive academic language proficiency), showing that learners could reach apparent oral fluency in interactional contexts comparatively quickly but
would take much longer to reach academic proficiency in the second
language. He wanted teachers to focus on the different contexts learners
of any age might find themselves in and to see what demands might be
made on them in those contexts. Cummins uses a different layout and
numbering system from Coyle's (2006) version of the matrix given in
Figure 9.2 and explains his thinking on the matrix very fully in an article
accessible on his personal website: www.iteachilearn.com/cummins/
converacademlangdisti.html.

Coyle's adaptation of the matrix, including the extra elements of low
and high language level, was made to theorise a need in CLIL planning
for the thinking to be seen as independent of the language levels and
to indicate the need for focus on concrete contextualised input and task
materials. The questions in our portraits topic will fall mainly into our
quadrants 1 and 2 because realistically, with primary age learners using
another language, the more abstract context signalled by quadrant 3 is

unlikely to be reached. When we ask questions which demand less thinking, such as those where we effectively offer the children a multiple choice framework for response, we are using quadrant 1, but still asking for some thinking and not just imitation or repetition. But as we start to ask the question 'why', or to ask for reasons or elaborations, we move into quadrant 2. The important point is that the language and content are still both fully contextualised. In addition the language level has been structured to be accessible, with any new material very clearly guessable from the context.

In a way we are using Krashen's (1988) idea of comprehensible input, where the current level of language known plus a small amount of new material (described by Krashen as 'i+1') is utilised for input in a context that will be meaningful and purposeful and therefore comprehensible. He felt that language learners experiencing this process would be more likely to acquire the language naturally.

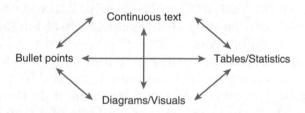

Figure 9.3 Text support and modification

Types and difficulty of text

Figure 9.3 considers the different types of text a language teacher might use during a unit, especially one that has a content base. 'Diagrams/ visuals' can also include artefacts and other realia. In terms of comprehension the diagram shows the more difficult text types at the top and the more accessible at the bottom. This is generally likely to be true although of course some objects or pictures can be culturally more obscure. But as primary age learners gain in age, experience and language knowledge and competence, they can be offered more complex text types to manage. The downward arrows therefore show how a teacher may like to evaluate a text and seek something easier if it seems too difficult, or to modify it into an easier version if that is possible. A continuous text can often be turned quite quickly into simple bullet points or even a table, for example. The upward facing arrows are more likely to be used to extend more able children when they are creating a piece of work in written or spoken language. A diagram or a photo (or even a table) might be the source for a few very simple sentences. A small set of visuals might generate a summary table. So, a body of descriptive text around a portrait might be far too complex to use with primary learners, but modified into a series of short bulleted sentences, and mixed in with others which describe other portraits, it becomes a resource which can be used to help gather thoughts and learn language through a simple matching to target process. In another topic, a table of statistics about health factors in different countries can be used to stimulate true/false judgements on sentences which make comparisons. When this approach was used in a primary classroom (Jones 2004) children learned the comparative form in French through working on the task. The statistics table acted as a language-free stimulus to thinking, which then facilitated language learning.

Summary – why should a CLIL approach be part of our methodology?

This section has been intended to de-mystify CLIL and present it as an approach which can be used at different levels of language, content complexity and teacher competence. If you return to Chapters Three and Four you will find that in the activities suggested for EYFS contexts there is a strong parallel between what children do regularly through English and what we suggest they might do through the target language. Similarly in our starter contexts of Y1 and Y3 we saw that there were links into classroom routines, into very simple work with Art and Mathematics and that even more conventional language topics had an element of learning beyond just language. CLIL is not an approach you progress towards when you have enough language (as either teacher or pupils) but one that can grow from the beginning. It can organise your entire teaching approach, but does not have to. Children respond well when it forms part of their language learning programme because it brings fresh topics into the classroom, links with things they are learning elsewhere in the week and takes the pressure off performing with the language and puts it onto using the language more naturally.

Clearly there is an issue in all of this about finding sufficient numbers of teaching personnel to deliver KS2 foreign language learning. This needs further funding and government research but the path chosen by those who are in place now, teaching children, is crucial.

We have seen a decline in motivation in learners aged 14, resulting in a dramatic fall in uptake in KS4 since compulsory foreign language study was abolished. We cannot afford to engender the same decline in motivation at the age of 11. Where language learning is being located in KS1 or even in Foundation Stage, teachers are reporting that it appears to be entirely natural to a great number of children. This is where language is most often embedded through songs, stories and activities based, for example, around classroom role-play areas. The topics chosen for inclusion in lessons are nearly always based on the current scheme of work and the ML input offers another perspective on that learning. The language children hear is rich and authentic, always forming complete sentences and chunks of meaning, not pared down to a few isolated words that are measured out and measured back in again through consolidation tasks. This is the approach that can inform the beginning of KS2 and which can make links across to other learning that is happening at the same time. The language curriculum is therefore the existing curriculum because language is about what people sense to be all around them.

With some linking in place from the start, so that this is quickly established as a normal aspect of language learning, the extent to which another subject area can be covered can grow steadily. In the way that the CILT CLIP project proved that Y7 language-learning beginners can adapt quickly to integrated work, for example in Geography, clearly children in Y5 or Y6 after two to three years of language learning will be able manage curricular topics in the foreign language. In following a Science, History or Geography unit entirely in the foreign language and not, as we saw earlier, simply taking quite trivial aspects of the cognition offered by a unit, they will have a richer experience which will also offer curriculum efficiency in the foundation subjects to an overcrowded timetable. From there they will be able to embark on KS3 learning as natural language 'users' rather than only as word-level learners tied to a diet of survival topics. Their view of the ML will be able to move beyond descriptors such as 'fun' and into those associated with other subjects, such as 'challenging', 'satisfying' and 'motivating'. This is a real opportunity for primary teachers to make language learning different and, most importantly, sustainably successful for a majority rather than a minority of learners.

Chapter summary

This chapter has attempted to rationalise what has been discussed earlier in the book. We have shown that communicative and task-based learning have real relevance for primary ML but to an even greater extent if these approaches are interpreted in the way that stresses real and authentic use of language. We have explored CLIL as a way of integrating ML into the wider curriculum and the wider curriculum into ML.

Key and Further Reading 📖

Although difficult to obtain, this is a short and concise overview of a recognised CLIL methodology: Coyle, D. (2006) *Monograph 6 Developing CLIL: Towards a Theory of Practice*. Barcelona: APAC (Associació de Professors d'Anglès de Catalunya).

This book offers both a theoretical and a more practical overview: Coyle, D., Marsh, D. and Hood, P. (2009) *Content and Language Integrated Learning*. Cambridge: Cambridge University Press.

For insights into language teaching and learning methodology in general, you are recommended to read Richards, J. and Rodgers, T. (2001) *Approaches and Methods in Language Teaching*. Cambridge: Cambridge University Press.

A highly respected book on language learning, now in its third edition, is Lightbown, P. and Spada, N. (2006) *How Languages Are Learned*. Oxford: Oxford University Press. This work summarises the classroom impact of second language acquisition theories.

10

Where can I find good materials and information?

This short final chapter is different from the others in that it aims to give you an overview of some of the important contacts (mainly internet websites) for both resources and useful information. The materials mentioned here are those more commonly used in schools, but the list is not at all exhaustive and inclusion of material is not intended to be any kind of endorsement. We have chosen to present the information in certain sections, but we do not imply any sort of hierarchy within or between each of these.

'Super websites' – a range of information and many important links

The Training Zone www.primarylanguages.org.uk/ is the first stop for support for ideas and links to other provision such as language enhancement, the NACELL site and video material which exemplifies current good practice. The site has considerable depth and includes background to the material featured in the short video clips.

The Framework and schemes A downloadable version of the Framework is at www.standards.dfes.gov.uk/primary/publications/languages/framework/.

The new QCA Schemes of work for KS2 are at www.standards.dfes.gov.uk/schemes3/subjects/primary_mff/?view=get (French), www.standards.dfes.gov.uk/schemes3/subjects/primary_mfg_new/?view=get (German) and www.standards.dfes.gov.uk/schemes3/subjects/primary_mfs_new/?view=get (Spanish).

CILT (Centre for Information on Language Teaching and Research) www.cilt.org.uk. The CILT Library in London has a stock of books and other materials for viewing. The website offers an online searchable catalogue which can be used to locate books and so on for further investigation.

A search using 'primary French' brings up 354 results, 'primary German' 140 and 'primary Spanish' 145. 'Primary Italian' produces 63 results and 'primary community languages' 25. This gives an indication of the sheer number of items which are becoming available and which are being added to.

CILT also publish curriculum guides and teaching guides in the form of short books called *Young Pathfinders*. The full set available can be viewed at www.cilt.org.uk/books/primary.htm

At the time of writing there are regional CILT (Comenius) support centres, but these are likely to close in 2009 and be replaced by another format of regional support. Each region has also had a resource library and these may continue under LA control. Information on this should be obtainable from CILT.

ALL (Association for Language Learning) www.all-languages.org.uk/default.asp. This is the main teaching association for language teachers and it runs conferences and workshops, and publishes journals and reports. The website does not at present have a separate primary languages section but some of the network groups focus on both sectors.

Other sources www.scilt.stir.ac.uk/ and www.ciltcymru.org.uk/english/home.htm are the CILT sites respectively for Scotland and Wales. They each offer different perspectives on primary languages and are worth including in searches for information, views on practice or resources.

www.ltscotland.org.uk/mfle/primaryzone/index.asp is the MFL Environment (primary section) from Learning and Teaching Scotland.

Choosing resources There is advice about how to choose resources from NACELL, which is a branch of CILT at www.nacell.org.uk/resources/teaching_materials.htm

There are also, for the four major languages, individual primary-oriented downloadable resource sheets from CILT/NACELL at www.nacell.org.uk/resources/info_sheets.htm

Another NACELL page gives you access to a whole range of online resources in a range of languages: www.nacell.org.uk/resources/online_resources.htm

Online bookstores A good commercial source of books of all types is the European Bookshop website. For French books you can access www.europeanbookshop.com/languagebooks/subject/FRE and check the menu for particular resource types and ages. The booklists for the other three languages are also available by substituting 'GER', 'SPA', 'ITA' for 'FRE' at the end of this address.

Amazon sites exist in France and Germany and these are linked to Amazon UK in terms of personal account details, but all countries also have their own online booksellers.

Specific and commercial websites

A sample set of teaching resources An appropriate place to start to look for resources would be the supplier Little Linguist: www.little-linguist.co.uk/.While not all materials are available through this outlet, they do have a fairly comprehensive catalogue and they feature a very wide range of languages (33 at the time of writing). The catalogue is divided clearly into sections for books, DVDs, games, posters, CD ROMs, and so on. The material is not exclusively for primary learners but does include a great deal for the age range nevertheless.

Major self-standing courses These are available from the separate publishers. At the time of writing these are limited to French in terms of material targeted for the UK context. The European Bookshop address given above may be useful for looking at material originating abroad. Only Early Start and Pilote have parallel versions so far.

'Early Start' is available at different levels in French, German and Spanish. It contains authentic video material. The company also sell the talking books and other linked resources. www.earlystart.co.uk/index.html

'Pilote' (French) and 'Pilote' (Spanish) as well as '3-2-1 Los!' (German) are available from www.ketv.co.uk/products.htm. These were developed from the ML initiative in Kent which was one of the earlier projects in England during the 1990s. They contain authentic age appropriate video material.

Babelzone run by LCF Clubs and offering French and Spanish requires a subscription and can be accessed at www.lcfclubs.com/babelzoneNEW/index.asp

La Jolie Ronde was an extra-curricular provider of French and Spanish and now also publishes materials which are used in some schools – these can be seen at www.lajolieronde.co.uk/online-shop.asp

French only 'Tout le monde' (Heinemann), is an electronic, web-based resource. It contains stories, games and songs for interactive whiteboards and some video material.

'Comète' (Oxford University Press) is a course designed for Y5 and Y6 which links more to a secondary model in some respects (it contains a set of flashcards). There are integrated songs and stories.

'Rigolo' (Nelson Thornes) contains electronic resources and also big books and a puppet.

Curriculum-linked materials 'A La Française' (Authentik) French cross-curricular resources consist of taster lessons for most subjects with lesson plans, a CD with audio recordings of the language used in the lessons to support non-specialist teachers, and PowerPoints to present the topics. They also include photocopiable worksheets. They are aimed mainly at Upper KS2, but some lessons may be used also with Y3 and Y4.

Other language learning websites The BBC website includes sections for Primary Spanish and French at www.bbc.co.uk/schools/primary spanish and www.bbc.co.uk/schools/primaryfrench/. These are beginner pages with basic vocabulary to hear and repeat, online games and worksheets.

The generalist Primary Resources website has some languages resources such as PowerPoint presentations and worksheets at www.primary resources.co.uk/mfl/mfl.htm

Some language colleges have resources online. These three examples from Essex, North Tyneside and Surrey have a variety of different approaches, which include resources and advice and support for teachers: www.anglo european.essex.sch.uk/resources/primary_resource.htm,www.monkseaton. org.uk/languages/Pages/Home.aspx and www.ashcombe. surrey.sch.uk/ Curriculum/modlang/index_primary.htm

As mentioned earlier in the book, one very wide-ranging French site aimed at French children but containing an enormous amount of potentially useful material is www.momes.net. Because this has a general and an education section it offers material of different types. There are traditional songs some of which have sound files so you can hear the tune alongside the lyrics. There are also many pages devoted more to children's spare time interests such as film and television. Some links go out to other sites so are less predictable, and the penfriend requests might need to be monitored before being used, depending on your choice of themes. But, in general, it offers a good starting point for teachers and an interesting limited surf opportunity for older pupils.

Songs There are great numbers of sites, some selling recordings or downloads and some offering online songs, which can be watched or heard for free. The best way to access this is to run a basic Google search on children's songs in Spanish, French, German or Italian. This will bring up sites like the two below and many others: www.hello-world.com/ has songs in several languages, some with animations. www.songs forteaching.com/ has songs in French, German and Spanish which can be heard with lyrics on the site and bought as downloads or on CD.

Two sites have specifically Spanish songs and other resources: www.elhuev odechocolate.com/cancion1.htm and www.pequenet.com/cantar.asp

The site www.kindergarten-workshop.de/, although set up for pre-school children in Germany, does have some songs (and other material) suitable for KS1 and lower KS2.

Our favourite (though very specific) song site is a Christmas site from Canada in French: www.csdraveurs.qc.ca/musique/noel/calendrier 2007d. html. This has an animated song (sung by children) for each day of the advent calendar, with a link to lyrics. Some are traditional and some less so – try noël-jazz (December 4th) with the whole of KS2 in assembly!

Discussion forums for CPD and good practice ELL forum: www. mailtalk.ac.uk/cgi-bin/webadmin?A0=ELL-FORUM. From this page you can subscribe to the e-mail discussion forum which will bring on average about two or three messages per day. The archives are available to search as well and you can put in a term such as 'Spanish songs' and get all relevant messages from the last eight years (50 items in that case).

There are enormous numbers of blogs. Here are three samples. Talkabout Primary MFL is one of the largest we have seen and encompasses many features, many members and all main languages: http://primarymfl.ning. com/profiles/blog/list. There is also one from the North Kent LA in England: http://nks-pfml.blogspot.com/ and one from a USA-based French teacher: http://foreignlanguagefun.com/

References

Allford, D. (2000) 'Pictorial Images, Lexical Phrases and Culture'. *Language Learning Journal.* 22(1): 45–51.

Ames, C. and Ames, R. (1984) 'Systems of Student and Teacher Motivation: Toward a Qualitative Definition'. *Journal of Educational Psychology.* 76(4): 535–56.

Arnold, J. (2007) 'Self Concept and the Affective Domain in Language Learning' in F. Rubio (ed.) *Self-Esteem and Foreign Language Learning.* Cambridge: Cambridge Scholars Publishing.

Baker, C. (2006) *Foundations of Bilingual Education & Bilingualism.* Clevedon, UK: Multilingual Matters.

Barnett, M. (1991) *More Than Meets the Eye – Foreign Language Reading: Theory and Practice.* Washington: Center for Applied Linguistics.

Bauer, J. (2003) *Opas Engel.* Hamburg: Carlsen.

Bell N. (2005) 'Exploring L2 Language Play as an Aid to SLL: A Case Study of Humour in NS–NNS Interaction'. *Applied Linguistics.* 26: 192–218.

Birdsong, D. (ed.) (1999) *Second Language Acquisition and the Critical Period Hypothesis.* Mahwah, NJ: Erlbaum.

Black, P. and Wiliam, D. 'Inside the Black Box: Raising Standards Through Classroom Assessment'. www.pdkintl.org/kappan/kbla9810.htm

Blanpain, J-P. (2001) *Mon cochon.* Arles: Actes-Sud.

Blondin, C., Candelier, M., Edelenbos, P., Johnstone, R., Kubanek-German, A. and Taeschner, T. (1998) *Foreign Language in Primary and Pre-School Education.* London: CILT.

Bloom, B.S. (1968) *Learning for Mastery. Evaluation Comment.* Los Angeles: University of California.

Breen, M.P. (1987) 'Learner Contributions to Task Design' in C.N. Candlin and D.F. Murphy (eds) *Language Learning Tasks.* Englewood Cliffs, NJ: Prentice-Hall.

Brown, H.D. (1994) *Teaching by Principles.* Englewood Cliffs, NJ: Prentice-Hall.

Brown, R. (1992) *A Dark Dark Tale,* London: Red Fox.

Brown, R. (2001) *Une histoire sombre, très sombre.* Paris: Gallimard Jeunesse.

Browne, E. (1994) *Handa's Surprise.* London: Mantra.

Brussels, *Action Plan for Promoting Language Learning and Linguistic Diversity 2004–6.* 24.07.2003 C.M. (2003) 449 final.

Burstall, C., Jamieson, M., Cohen, S. and Hargreaves, M. (1974) *Primary French in the Balance.* Slough: NFELR Publishing Co.

Byram M.S. (1997) *Teaching and Assessing Intercultural Communicative Competence.* Clevedon, UK: Multilingual Matters Ltd.

Byram, M. and Zarate, C. (1994) *Definitions, objectifs et évaluation de la competence socio-culturelle.* Strasbourg: Council of Europe.

Byram, M., Nichols, A. and Stevens, D. (2001) *Developing Intercultural Competence in Practice.* Clevedon, UK: Multilingual Matters.

Cameron, L. (2001) *Teaching Languages to Young Learners.* Cambridge: Cambridge University Press,

Carle, E. (1979) *Do You Want to Be My Friend?* London: Puffin Books.

Carle, E. (1995) *The Very Hungry Caterpillar.* London: Puffin Books.

Carle, E. (2006) *Panda Bear, Panda Bear, What Do You See?* London: Holt.

Cenoz, J. and Genesee, F. (eds) (1998) *Beyond Bilingualism: Multilinguism and Multilingual Education.* Clevedon, UK: Multilingual Matters.

Cheater, C. (2006) *The Catherine Cheater Scheme of Work.* Wakefield: Teaching and Learning Publications.

Clarke, S. (1998) *Targeting Assessment in the Primary School: Strategies for Planning, Assessment, Pupil Feedback and Target Setting.* London: Hodder & Stoughton.

Clarke, S. (2001) *Unlocking Formative Assessment: Practical Strategies for Enhancing Pupils' Learning in the Primary Classroom.* London: Hodder & Stoughton.

Clarke, S. (2003) *Enriching Feedback: Oral and Written Feedback from Teachers and Children.* London: Hodder & Stoughton.

Clarke, S. (2005) *Formative Assessment in Action: Weaving the Elements Together.* London: Hodder Education.

Coffield, F., Moseley, D., Hall, E. and Ecclestone, K. (2004) *Should We Be Using Learning Styles? What Research Has to Say to Practice.* London: Learning and Skills Research Centre. www.lsneducation.org.uk/user/order.aspx?code=041540&src=xoweb

Cohen, A. (1994) *Assessing Language Ability in the Classroom* (2nd edition). Boston: Newbury House/Heinle & Heinle.

Commission of the European Communities (2003) *Action Plan for Promoting Language Learning and Linguistic Diversity 2004–2006.* 24.07.2003 COM (2003) 449 final. Brussels: Commission of the European Communities. http://ec.europa.eu/education/doc/official/keydoc/actlang/act_lang_en.pdf

Cook, G. (1997) 'Language Play, Language Learning'. *ELT Journal.* 51(3): 224–31.

Council of Europe (2001) *The Common European Framework of Reference for Languages: Learning, Teaching and Assessment.* Cambridge: Cambridge University Press.

Coyle, D. (1999) 'Theory and Planning for Effective Classrooms: Supporting Students in Content and Language Integrated Learning Contexts: Planning for Effective Classrooms' in *Learning through a Foreign Language: Models, Methods and Outcomes.* London: Centre for Information on Language Teaching & Research. pp. 46–62.

Coyle, D. (2006) *Monograph 6 Developing CLIL: Towards a Theory of Practice.* Barcelona: APAC (Associació de Professors d'Anglès de Catalunya).

Coyle, D., Marsh, D. and Hood, P. (2009) *Content and Language Integrated Learning.* Cambridge: Cambridge University Press.

Crandall, J.A. (1999) 'Cooperative Language Learning and Affective Factors' in J. Arnold (ed.) *Affective Factors in Language Learning.* Cambridge: Cambridge University Press.

Csizér, K. and Dörnyei, Z. (2005) 'The Internal Structure of Language Learning Motivation and its Relationship with Language Choice and Learning Effort'. *Modern Language Journal.* 89(1): 19–36.

Cummins, J. (1981) 'Empirical and Theoretical Underpinnings of Bilingual Education'. *Journal of Education.* 163: 16–29.

Cummins, J. (1981) 'The Role of Primary Language Development in Promoting Educational Success for Language Minority Students' in California State Department of Education (ed.) *Schooling and Language Minority Students: A Theoretical Framework.* Los Angeles: National Dissemination and Assessment Center. pp. 3–49.

Cummins, J. (1984) 'Language Proficiency and Academic Achievement Revisited: A Response' in C. Rivera (ed.) *Language Proficiency and Academic Achievement.* Clevedon, Avon: Multilingual Matters. pp. 71–6.

Cummins, J. (1991) 'Language Development and Academic Learning' in L. Malavé and G. Duquette (eds) *Language, Culture and Cognition.* Clevedon, UK: Multilingual Matters. pp. 161–75.

Cury, F., Elliot, A., Da Fonseca, D. and Moller, A.C. (2006)'The Social Cognitive Model of Achievement Motivation and the 2×2 Achievement Goal Framework'. *Journal of Personality and Social Psychology.* 90: 666–79.

David, T. (2003) *What Do We Know about Teaching Young Children?* London: DfES. www.standards.dfes.gov.uk/eyfs/resources/downloads/eyyrsp1.pdf

Davies, M. (2000) 'Learning ... The Beat Goes On'. *Childhood Education.* 76(3): 148–53.

Day, E. and Shapson, S. (1996) 'A National Survey: French Immersion Teachers' Preparation and their Professional Development Needs'. *The Canadian Modern Language Review.* 52(2): 248–70.

DCSF (2007) *Letters and Sounds: Principles and Practice of High Quality Phonics.* London: DCSF.

DCSF (2008) *Practice Guidance for the Early Years Foundation Stage.* London: DCSF.

de Andres, V. (1999) 'Self-Esteem in the Classroom or the Metamorphosis of Butterflies' in J. Arnold (ed.) *Affect in Language Learning.* Cambridge: Cambridge University Press. pp. 87–102.

Demetriou, H., Goalen, P. and Rudduck, J. (2000) 'Academic Performance, Transfer, Transition and Friendship: Listening to the Student Voice'. *International Journal of Educational Research.* 33: 425–41.

DES (1990) *Starting with Quality: The Rumbold Report of the Committee of Inquiry into the Quality of Educational Experience Offered to 3 and 4 year olds.* London: HMSO.

DfES (2002) *Languages for All, Languages for Life.* London: DfES. http://publications.teachernet.gov.uk/eOrderingDownload/DfESLanguagesStrategy.pdf

DfES (2003) *14–19: Opportunity and Excellence* 0744/2002. London: DfES. http://publications.teachernet.gov.uk/eOrderingDownload/DfES-0744-2002Main.pdf

DfES (2005) *The KS2 Framework for Languages.* London: DfES. www.standards.dfes. gov.uk/primary/publications/languages/framework/

DfES (2006) *Grouping Pupils for Success* 03945-2006 DWO-EN. London: DfES.

DfES (2007) *Languages Review* (The Dearing Review) 00212-2007DOM-EN. London: DfES. www.teachernet.gov.uk/_doc/11124/LanguageReview.pdf

DfES (2007) *Letters and Sounds* 00282-2007 BKT-EN. London: DfES. www.standards. dcsf.gov.uk/local/clld/resources/letters_and_sounds/00282_2007BKT_EN.pdf

DfES (2008) *The Early Years Foundation Stage Statutory Framework.* London: DfES. www. standards.dfes.gov.uk/eyfs/site/resource/pdfs.htm

DfES (2008) *Practice Guidance.* London: DfES. www.standards.dfes.gov.uk/eyfs/site/resource/pdfs.htm

Dillenbourg, P. (1999) 'What Do You Mean by Collaborative Learning?' in P. Dillenbourg (ed.) *Collaborative-learning: Cognitive and Computational Approaches.* Oxford: Elsevier. pp. 1–19.

Dörnyei, Z. (2006) 'Individual Differences in Second Language Acquisition'. *AILA Review.* 19: 42–68.

Dörnyei, Z. and Csizér, K. (2002) 'Some Dynamics of Language Attitudes and Motivation: Results of a Longitudinal Nationwide Survey'. *Applied Linguistics.* 23: 421–62.

Driscoll, P. (1999) 'Modern Foreign Languages in the Primary School: A Fresh Start' in P. Driscoll and D. Frost *The Teaching of Modern Foreign Languages in the Primary School.* London: Routledge.

Driscoll, P. and Frost, D. (1999) *The Teaching of Modern Foreign Languages in the Primary School.* London: Routledge.

Dweck, C.S. (1986) 'Motivational Processes Affecting Learning'. *American Psychologist.* 41: 1040–48.

Dweck, C.S. (2000) *Self Theories: Their Role in Motivation, Personality and Development.* Philadelphia: Psychology Press.

Edgington, M. (2004) *The Foundation Stage Teacher in Action.* London: Paul Chapman Publishing.

Ellis, R. (2003) *Task-Based Language Learning and Teaching.* Oxford: Oxford University Press.

Ellis, G. and Brewster, J. with Girard, D. (2002) *The Primary English Teacher's Guide.* London: Pearson Education.

Elvin, P., Maagerø, E. and Simonsen, B. (2007) 'How Do the Dinosaurs Speak in England? English in Kindergarten'. *European Early Childhood Education Research Journal.* 15(1): 71–86.

Fisher, R. (2002) *Inside the Literacy Hour: Learning from Classroom Experience.* London: Routledge.

Galton, M., Gray, J. and Rudduck, J. (1999) *The Impact of School Transitions and Transfers on Pupil Progress and Attainment.* Research Report 131. London: DfES.

Gardner, H. (1999) *Intelligence Reframed: Multiple Intelligences for the 21st century.* New York: Basic Books.

Gardner, H. and Hatch, T. (1989) 'Multiple Intelligences Go to School: Educational Implications of the Theory of Multiple Intelligences'. *Educational Researcher.* 18(8): 4–9.

Gardner, R.C. (1985) *Social Psychology and Second Language Learning: The Role of Attitudes and Motivation.* London: Edward Arnold.

Gattullo, F. (2000) 'Formative Assessment in ELT Primary (Elementary) Classrooms: An Italian Case Study'. *Language Testing.* 17: 278–88.

Genesee, F. and Upshur, J.A. (1996) *Classroom Evaluation in Second Language Learning.* Cambridge: Cambridge University Press.

Gibbons, S. and Telhaj, S. (2006) *Peer Effects and Pupil Attainment: Evidence from Secondary School Transition.* London: Centre for the Economics of Education, London School of Economics.

Giddens, A. (1991) *Modernity and Self-Identity: Self and Society in the Late Modern Age.* Cambridge: Polity.

Grabe, W. and Stoller, F.L. (1997) 'Content-based Instruction: Research Foundations' in M.A. Snow and D.M. Brinton (eds) *The Content-based Classroom: Perspectives on Integrating Language and Content.* New York: Longman. pp. 5–21.

Grabe, W. and Stoller, F. (2002) *Teaching and Researching Reading: Applied Linguistics in Action.* New York: Longman.

Guilloteaux, M.J. and Dörnyei, Z. (2008) 'Motivating Language Learners: A Classroom-oriented Investigation of the Effects of Motivational Strategies on Student Motivation'. *TESOL Quarterly.* 42(1): 55–77.

Hood, P. (unpublished) 'Children's Voices: *I like French and I always sing it when I walk home*'. Keynote speech at Primary Languages Show, 16 March 2007.

Hood, P. (1994) 'Primary Foreign Languages – The Integration Model: Some Parameters for Research'. *Curriculum Journal.* 5(2): 235–47.

Hood, P. (2000) 'Reading the Discourse of Reading: A Window on the Meaning Construction Processes of their Year as Third Year Learners of French'. Unpublished thesis. Nottingham: University of Nottingham.

Hood, P. (2006) 'Can Early Foreign Language Learning Contribute to the Shared Emotional and Motivational Landscape of a Primary School?' *Pastoral Care in Education.* 24(4): 4–12.

Horwitz, E.K. (2001) 'Language Anxiety and Achievement'. *Annual Review of Applied Linguistics.* 21: 112–26.

Ireson, J. and Hallam, S. (1999) 'Raising Standards: Is Ability Grouping the Answer?' *Oxford Review of Education.* 25(3): 343–58.

Johnson, R.K. and Swain, M. (1997) *Immersion Education: International Perspectives.* Cambridge, UK: Cambridge University Press.

Johnstone, R.M. (1994) *The Impact of Current Developments to Support the Gaelic Language: Review of Research.* Stirling: Scottish CILT.

Johnstone, R.M. (2000) *Immersion in a Second Language at School: Evidence from International Research.* Stirling: Scottish CILT.

Johnstone, R.M. (2002) 'Context-sensitive Assessment of Children Learning Modern Languages at Primary School'. *Language Testing.* 17: 123–43.

Johnstone, R.M. and McKinstry, R. (2008) *Evaluation of Early Primary Partial Immersion in French.* Stirling: Scottish CILT. www.scilt.stir.ac.uk/projects/evaluationwr/documents/EPPI_BOOK.pdf

Jones, N. (2004) Unpublished data. Elliott School and Language College. www.elliott-school.org.uk/langcol/Langcol/Langcolprimary.html

Jones, B., Halliwell, S. and Holmes, B. (2002) *You Speak, They Speak.* London: CILT.

Koda, K. (2005) *Insights into Second Language Reading.* Cambridge: Cambridge University Press.

Kormos, J. and Dörnyei, Z. (2004) 'The Interaction of Linguistic and Motivational Variables in Second Language Task Performance'. *Zeitschrift für Interkulturellen Fremdsprachenunterricht.* 9(2). www.ualberta.ca/~german/ejournal/kormos2.htm

Kramsch, C. (1996) 'The Cultural Component of Language Teaching'. *Zeitschrift fürinterkulturellen Fremdsprachenunterricht.* 1(2). www.ualberta.ca/~german/ejournal/archive/krams ch2.htm

Krashen, S. (1985) *Language Acquisition and Language Education.* Haywood, CA: Alemany Press.

Krashen, S. (1988) *Second Language Acquisition and Second Language Learning.* Upper Saddle River, NJ: Prentice Hall.

Krashen, S.D. and Terrell, T.D. (1983) *The Natural Approach: Language Acquisition in the Classroom.* London: Prentice Hall Europe.

Kress, G. and van Leeuwen, T. (2006) *Reading Images: The Grammar of Visual Design.* London: Routledge.

Kubanek-German, A. (1996) 'Research into Primary Foreign-language Learning in Germany: A Trend towards Qualitative Studies' in P. Edelenbos and R. Johnston (eds) *Researching Languages at Primary School: Some European Perspectives.* London: CILT. pp. 3–15.

Le Notre, P. (1999) *Mon âne.* DVD. Wakefield: Teaching and Learning Publications.

Legutke, M. and Thomas, H. (1991) *Process and Experience in the Language Classroom.* Harlow: Longman.

Lenneberg, E. (1967) *Biological Foundations of Language.* New York: Wiley.

Lepine, J.A., Lepine, M.A. and Jackson, C.L. (2004) 'Challenge and Hindrance Stress: Relationships with Exhaustion, Motivation to Learn, and Learning Performance'. *Journal of Applied Psychology.* 89(5): 883–91.

Lewis, J. (1999) *The Enormous Turnip.* London: Ladybird Books.

Lightbown, P. (2003) 'SLA research in the Classroom'. *Language Learning Journal.* 28: 4–13.

Lightbown, P. and Spada, N. (2006*) How Languages are Learned.* Oxford: Oxford University Press.

Littlewood, W.A. (1981) *Communicative Language Teaching: An Introduction.* Cambridge: Cambridge University Press.

Loewen, S. (2007) 'Error Correction in the Second Language Classroom'. *CLEAR News.* 11(2): 1–5. http://clear.msu.edu/clear/newsletter/files/fall2007.pdf

Lucey, H. and Reay, D. (2000) 'Identities in Transition: Anxiety and Excitement in the Move to Secondary School'. *Oxford Review of Education.* 26(2): 191–205.

Lyster, R. (1998) 'Negotiation of Form, Recasts, and Explicit Correction in Relation to Error Types and Learner Repair in Immersion Classrooms'. *Language Learning.* 48(2): 183–218.

Marsh, D. (2002) 'Content and Language Integrated Learning: The European Dimension – Actions, Trends and Foresight Potential'. Jyväskyla: University of Jyväskyla. http://europa.eu.int/comm/education/languages/index.html

Martin, C. (2000) 'An Analysis of National and International Research on the Provision of Modern Foreign Languages in Primary Schools. A Report Prepared for the Qualifications and Curriculum Authority'. London: QCA. www.qca.org.uk/downloads/3809_cmartin_rpt_mfl_primaryschools.pdf

Mayer, M. (1988) *There's an Alligator under My Bed.* London: Macmillan.

Mayer, M. (1992) *There's a Nightmare in My Wardrobe.* London: Picture Puffin.

Menken, K. (2006) 'Teaching to the Test: How No Child Left Behind Impacts Language Policy, Curriculum, and Instruction for English Language Learners'. *Bilingual Research Journal.* 30(2): 521–46.

Mercer, N. (1995) *The Guided Construction of Knowledge.* Clevedon: Multilingual Matters.

Moyles, J. (2007) *Early Years Foundations: Meeting the Challenge.* Maidenhead: McGraw-Hill/Open University Press.

Muijs, D., Barnes, A., Hunt, M., Powell, B., Martin, C. and Arweck, E. (2005) *Evaluation of the Key Stage 2 Language Learning Pathfinders.* London DfES.

Muir, J. (1999) 'Classroom Connections' in P. Driscoll and D. Frost (eds) *The Teaching of Modern Foreign Languages in the Primary School.* London: Routledge.

Nuffield Foundation (2000) *Languages: The Next Generation.* London: Nuffield Foundation. http://languages.nuffieldfoundation.org/filelibrary/pdf/languages_finalreport.pdf

Nunan, D. (1989) *Designing Tasks for the Communicative Classroom.* Cambridge: Cambridge University Press.

Nunan, D. (2004). *Task-based Language Teaching.* Cambridge: Cambridge University Press.

O'Hagan, C. (2007) *The CILT 7–14 Project.* London: CILT. www.cilt.org.uk/transition/transition_report.pdf

Ortega, A.M. (2007) 'Anxiety and Self-Esteem' in F. Rubio (ed.) *Self-Esteem and Foreign Language Learning.* Cambridge: Cambridge Scholars Publishing.

Oxford, R.L. (1997) 'Cooperative Learning, Collaborative Learning, and Interaction: Three Communicative Strands in the Language Classroom'. *Modern Language Journal.* 81(4): 443–56.

Oxford, R.L. (1999) 'Anxiety and the Language Learner: New Insights' in J. Arnold (ed.) *Affect in Language Learning.* Cambridge: Cambridge University Press.

Parliament, House of Lords (1990) 'European Schools and Language Learning: ECC Report'. HL Deb 13 July 1990, vol. 521 cc554–95.

Piaget, J. (1955) *The Construction of Reality in the Child* (trans. Margaret Cook). London: Routledge.

Pollard, A. and Triggs, P. (2000) *What Pupils Say: Changing Policy and Practice in Primary Education.* London: Continuum.

Powell, B., Wray, D., Rixon, S., Medwell, J., Barnes, A. and Hunt, M. (2000) *QCA Project to Study the Feasibility of Introducing the Teaching of a Modern Foreign Language into the Statutory Curriculum at Key Stage 2.* London: QCA. www.qca.org.uk/downloads/3807_mfl_feas_ks2.pdf

QCA (2007) *A Scheme of Work for KS2 French.* QCA/07/3087. London: QCA. www.qca.org.uk/qca_11752.aspx

Reasoner, R. (1982) *Building Self-Esteem in Secondary Schools.* Palo Alto: Consulting Psychologists Press Inc.

Richards, J.C. and Rodgers, T.S. (2001) *Approaches and Methods in Language Teaching.* Cambridge: Cambridge University Press.

Riding, R. and Rayner, S. (1998) *Cognitive Styles and Learning Strategies.* London: David Fulton.

Riley, J. (ed.) (2007) *Learning in the Early Years.* London: Sage.

Robinson, P. (ed.) (2002) *Individual Differences and Instructed Language Learning.* Amsterdam: John Benjamins.

Rose, J. (2006) *Independent Review of the Teaching of Early Reading.* London: DfES. www.standards.dfes.gov.uk/phonics/report.pdf

Rowe, J. (2008a) 'Transition KS2-KS3'. Conference presentation, 12 September 2008, Loughborough.

Rowe, J. (2008b) 'Statements on Transition KS2-KS3'. Unpublished materials.

Rumney, G. (1990) *Pilote.* Dover: KETV.

Sadler, D.R. (1989) 'Formative Assessment and the Design of Instructional Systems'. *Instructional Science.* 18: 119–44.

Salgado, S. (2003) *The Children.* New York: Aperture.

Samuda, V. and Bygate, M. (2008) *Tasks in Second Language Learning.* Basingstoke: Palgrave Macmillan.

Scarino, A., Liddicoat, T., Carr, J., Crichton, J., Crozet, C., Dellit, J., Kohler, M., Loachel, K., Mercurio, N., Morgan, A., Papademetre, L. and Scrimgeour, A. (2007) *Intercultural Language Teaching and Learning in Practice: Professional Learning Programme Resource for Participants* (ILTLP). Adelaide: Research Centre for Languages and Cultures Education, University of South Australia.

Scriven, M. (1967) 'The Methodology of Evaluation' in R.E. Stake (ed.) *Curriculum Evaluation.* American Educational Research Association Monograph Series on Evaluation, no. 1. Chicago: Rand McNally.

Sharp, K. (2001) *Modern Languages in the Primary School.* London: Routledge.

Singleton, D. (2003) 'Le facteur de l'âge dans l'acquisition d'une L2: remarques préliminaires'. *Acquisition et Interaction en Langue Étrangère.* 18: 1–15.

Skehan, P. (1998) *A Cognitive Approach to Language Learning.* Oxford: Oxford Applied Linguistics.

Skehan, P. (2002) 'Theorising and Updating Aptitude' in P. Robinson (ed.) *Individual Differences and Instructed Language Learning.* Amsterdam: John Benjamins. pp. 69–93.

Skehan, P. (2003) 'Task-based Instruction'. *Language Learning.* 36: 1–14.

Smith, A. and Call, N. (1999) *The ALPS Approach, Accelerated Learning in Primary Schools.* London: Network Educational Press.

Sternberg, R.J. (1997) *Thinking Styles.* New York: Cambridge University Press.

Stewart, J.H. (2005) 'Foreign Language Study in Elementary Schools: Benefits and Implications for Achievement in Reading and Math'. *Early Childhood Journal.* 33(1): 11–16.

Stotz, D., Bossart, M. and Fischli, P. (2005) 'Bilingual Secondary Students and Foreign Language Learning: Positionings and Investments'. Zürich: University of Zürich. www.phzh.ch/webautor-data/775/d_stotz.pdf

Swain, M. and Lapkin, S. (1995) 'Problems in Output and the Cognitive Processes They Generate: A Step Towards Second Language Learning'. *Applied Linguistics.* 16(3): 371–91.

Tarone, E. (2000) 'Getting Serious about Language Play: Language Play, Interlanguage Variation and Second Language Acquisition' in B. Swierzbin, F. Morris, M. Anderson, C. Klee and E. Tarone (eds) *Social and Cognitive Factors in SLA: Proceedings of the 1999 Second Language Research Forum.* Somerville: Cascadilla Press.

Tobutt, K. and Roche, C. (2007) *A La Française: A Cross-Curricular Approach to Teaching French.* Dublin: Authentik.

Tremblay, P.F., Gardner, R.C. and Heipel, G. (2000) 'A Model of the Relationships Among Measures of Affect, Aptitude, and Performance in Introductory Statistics'. *Canadian Journal of Behavioural Science.* 32(1): 40–8.

van Ek, J.A. (1975) *The Threshold Level for Modern Language Learning in Schools.* Strasbourg: Council of Europe.

van Ek, J.A. and Trim, J. (1991) *Waystage 1990.* Cambridge: Cambridge University Press.

Volante, L. (2004) 'Teaching to the Test: What Every Educator and Policy-maker Should Know'. *Canadian Journal of Educational Administration and Policy.* 35: unpaginated. www.umanitoba.ca/publications/cjeap/

Vygotsky, L.S. (1978) *Mind in Society: The Development of Higher Psychological Processes.* Cambridge, MA: Harvard University Press.

Weare, K. (2004) *Developing the Emotionally Literate School.* London: Paul Chapman Publishing.

Wells, G. (1999) *Dialogic Inquiry: Towards a Sociocultural Practice and Theory of Education.* Cambridge: Cambridge University Press.

Wesche, M.B. and Skehan, P. (2002) 'Communicative, Task-based, and Content-based Language Instruction' in R.B. Kaplan (ed.) *The Oxford Handbook of Applied Linguistics.* Oxford: Oxford University Press.

West Sussex Grid for Learning (2006) *Le Départ – Children in Wartime.* Chichester: West Sussex Local Authority.

West Sussex Grid for Learning (2008) *Storms and Shipwrecks.* Chichester: West Sussex Local Authority.

Willis, J. (1996) *Challenge and Change in Language Teaching.* London: Macmillan.

Willis, D. and Willis, J. (2007) *Doing Task-Based Teaching.* Oxford: Oxford University Press.

Wode, H. (1999) 'Incidental Vocabulary Acquisition in the Foreign Language Classroom'. *Studies in Second Language Acquisition.* 21: 243–58.

Woodfield and Neofitou (2006) 'Evaluating a CLIL Project'. Unpublished data.

Zangl, R. (2000) 'Monitoring Language Skills in Austrian Primary (Elementary) Schools: A Case Study'. *Language Testing.* 17: 250–60.

Index